Lecture Notes in Computer Science 6569

Commenced Publication in 1973
Founding and Former Series Editors:
Gerhard Goos, Juris Hartmanis, and Jan van Leeuwen

W0193067

Services Science

Subline of Lectures Notes in Computer Science

Michel Cezon   Yaron Wolfsthal (Eds.)

Towards a Service-Based Internet

ServiceWave 2010 Workshops

International Workshops
OCS, EMSOA, SMART, and EDBPM 2010
Ghent, Belgium, December 13-15, 2010
Revised Selected Papers

 Springer

Volume Editors

Michel Cezon
INRIA
655, Avenue de l'Europe, Montbonnot
38334 Saint Ismier Cedex, France
E-mail: michel.cezon@inria.fr

Yaron Wolfsthal
IBM Haifa Research Laboratory
Haifa University
Mount Carmel, Haifa 31905, Israel
E-mail: wolfstal@il.ibm.com

ISSN 0302-9743   e-ISSN 1611-3349
ISBN 978-3-642-22759-2   ISBN 978-3-642-22760-8 (eBook)
DOI 10.1007/978-3-642-22760-8
Springer Heidelberg Dordrecht London New York

Library of Congress Control Number: 2011936780

CR Subject Classification (1998): D.2, J.1, C.2, H.4, H.3, I.2, H.5

LNCS Sublibrary: SL 2 – Programming and Software Engineering

Typesetting: Camera-ready by author, data conversion by Scientific Publishing Services, Chennai, India

Printed on acid-free paper

Springer is part of Springer Science+Business Media (www.springer.com)

Preface

This volume contains the proceedings of the workshops that were held in conjunction with the 2010 International Conference ServiceWave, held during December 13–15, 2010 in Ghent, Belgium. As in previous years, this satellite event attracted a strong interest that elicited as many as eight different workshop session proposals, which were of particularly high quality and addressed various challenging research issues within the domain of the conference. Following a thorough and competitive review process, the Selection Committee eventually selected the following four workshops:

Workshop 1: OCS 2010
First Workshop on Optimizing Cloud Services

Workshop 2: EMSOA 2010
International Workshop on Emergency Management Through Service-Oriented Architectures

Workshop 3: SMART 2010
First International Workshop on Service Modelling and Representation Techniques

Workshop 4: EDBPM 2010
From Event-Driven Business Process Management to Ubiquitous Complex Event Processing

The specific scope of each of the workshops is described on the following pages. Altogether, these workshops represent diverse aspects of the theory and practice of service computing, ranging from service engineering to service infrastructures.

Given the success of these workshop sessions and the high quality of the papers, we believe the choice of the workshops has proven adequate to meet the expectation of the conference attendees. We would like to thank all authors for their great contributions and hope that readers will enjoy the material provided herein. It has been a great honor and pleasure to chair these workshop sessions and we are sure that ServiceWave 2011 will continue to provide valuable input to the ICT community toward the Future of Internet technologies and its related trends.

January 2011

Michel Cezon
Yaron Wolfsthal
Workshops Chairs
ServiceWave 2010

OCS 2010 Workshop Organizers' Message

As clouds are on the way to replacing traditional IT infrastructures for providing and consuming services in research and commercial environments, mechanisms are needed to allow optimization of such cloud environments in multiple dimensions, e.g., in terms of the infrastructure, management of trust, security and risk, service deployment and provisioning, guarantees for the QoS, federation of clouds and appropriate selection mechanisms for bursting into the cloud. There is already research in several areas as well as a number of ongoing national, international and European projects. However, until now there was no forum where optimization of cloud infrastructures was in the focus. In contrast, contributions to this topic have been scattered across different cloud conferences as, for instance, the IEEE Cloudcom.

In June 2010 the European integrated project OPTIMIS (Optimising Cloud Infrastructure Services) started with the objective to deliver the tools required by both service providers and infrastructure providers to optimize cloud resources and placement of services onto cloud resources. Hence, OPTIMIS decided to organize the First Workshop on Optimizing Cloud Infrastructures (OCS 2010) as a workshop of the ServiceWave conference. OCS 2010 aimed at bringing together researchers and practitioners from academia and industry to exchange research results and experience achieved in the field of optimizing cloud infrastructures. Topics of interest for the Optimizing Cloud Services Workshop workshop included:

- Trust and security
- Risks, risk assessment and risk management
- QoS and service configuration
- Service deployment and service configuration
- Cloud monitoring and run-time optimization
- License service for commercial applications
- Cloud programming models
- Cloud service level agreements

The workshop received seven contributions out of which four were accepted after peer reviewing. Each paper was reviewed by at least three reviewers. The selected workshop contributions cover research and development done in two European projects, and research done in the context of a project of the South-East European Research Centre in Greece, the fourth contribution presents research done at SAP.

The workshop would not have been possible without the help from many people and organizations. Firstly, we would like to thank the Program Committee members for evaluating the submissions in a prompt and professional manner. Finally, we thank all authors and participants of the workshop for their con-

tributions, camera-ready versions, and presentations at the Optimizing Cloud
Services Workshop in Ghent.

We believe that the first OCS Workshop provided an exciting platform for
exchanging interesting ideas and insights on novel research problems related to
cloud services. We trust that the workshop will become a traditional annual
meeting opportunity for researchers on cloud service optimization.

January 2011   Rosa M. Badia
                                                            Wolfgang Ziegler

OCS 2010 Workshop Organization

Workshop Co-chairs

Rosa Badia   Barcelona Supercomputing Center, Spain
Wolfgang Ziegler   Fraunhofer Institute SCAI, Germany

Program Committee

Oliver Wäldrich   Fraunhofer Institute SCAI, Germany
Thomas Weuffel   Fraunhofer Institute SCAI, Germany
Ramin Yahyapour   Dortmund University of Technology, Germany
Igor Rosenberg   ATOS Origin, Spain
Wolfgang Gentzsch   DEISA, Germany
Daniel Veit   University of Mannheim, Germany
Bastian Koller   HLRS, Germany
Gregor von Laszewski   Indiana University, USA
Afnan Ullah Khan   BT, UK
Ana Juan   Atos Origin, Spain
Andrea Zisman   City University, UK
Benoit Hudzia   SAP, France
Craig Sheridan   Flexiant Limited, UK
Csilla Zsigri   The 451 Group, UK
Erik Elmroth   Umeå University, Sweden
George Kousiouris   NTUA, Greece
Jordi Guitart   BSC, Spain
Karim Djemame   University of Leeds, UK
Marcelo Corrales   Leibniz University Hannover, Germany
Raül Sirvent   Barcelona Supercomputing Center, Spain
Srijith K. Nair   BT, UK
Johan Tordsson   Umea University, Sweden

EMSOA 2010 Workshop Organizers' Message

Emergency management information systems (EMISs), usually employed in emergency operation centers (EOCs), provide a set of ICT tools for supporting the emergency management process during its entire life-cycle: mitigation, preparedness, response, and recovery phases. More specifically, during the pre-event phases, emergency operators can take advantage of an EMIS to design a contingency scenario and derive the related contingency plan. Likewise, during an emergency, information systems guide the involved EOC operators through the execution of the contingency plan workflows. At the current stage, the presence of diverse EMISs accessible to heterogeneous users and stakeholders both in expertise and in specializations generates in a non-crisis time the collection of a huge amount of disaggregated data and misaligned procedures that may cause, in an emergency context, failing results. In addition, in multi-hazard and multi-risk scenarios, the collection of disaster agent-generated requests changes as time passes from the time of impact: requests associated with initial impact may decline while new demands arise from secondary threats. These changes occurring over time may be associated to information and/or operation management needs. Moreover, the coordination of actors on the field requires flexible approaches based on collaborative tools supporting processes/workflows and access to services. ICT solutions for emergency management need to cope with these dynamic scenarios by proposing methods and tools for integrating heterogeneous systems. In this scenario, service orientation is considered as the most promising paradigm to make the integration possible.

The goal of EMSOA 2010 - International Workshop on Emergency Management Through Service-Oriented Architectures, co-located with the ServiceWave 2010 Conference, was to bring together researchers and practitioners in the area of emergency management in order to improve these current approaches. In particular, crisis and risk management requires a flexible EMIS architecture, easily customizable, to support people on the field by considering the actual characteristics of the disruptive event that has occurred. This architecture needs to involve the adoption of emergent technologies, such as lightweight and highly configurable multi-agent systems, service-oriented solutions in mobile environments, or ad-hoc sensor networks. In addition, it is fundamental to have an enriched information management that allows the collection, the classification and the extraction of data throughout the overall amount of information flowing into the process. Such information regards data not only coming from sensor networks and connected EMIS, but also gathered from external and non-supervised data sources such as websites and social networks.

After receiving an interesting number of submissions from several European countries, the EMSOA 2010 Program Committee selected five papers, collected in these proceedings based on comments and feedbacks received during the workshop.

The EMSOA Chairs are grateful to the Program Committee for helping in the reviewing process and to the ServiceWave 2010 Organization for supporting the workshop. We are also grateful to Massimiliano de Leoni for accepting our invitation to give a keynote talk on the latest developments in the use of process-aware information systems (PAISs), currently widely used in many business scenarios, e.g., by government agencies, by insurance companies, and by banks, in the case of emergency management.

December 2010   Massimo Mecella
                                                                 Pierluigi Plebani

EMSOA 2010 Workshop Organization

Workshop Co-chairs

Massimo Mecella   Università di Roma "La Sapienza", Italy
Pierluigi Plebani   Politecnico di Milano, Italy

Program Committee

Massimiliano De Leoni   Eindhoven University of Technology
Alessandro Faraotti   IBM Italy
John Krogstie   NTNU, Norway
Guido Vetere   IBM Italy
Ouejdane Mejri   Politecnico di Milano, Italy

First International Workshop on Service Modelling and Representation Techniques (SMART 2010)

At the heart of virtually any endeavor in the area of service science, management and engineering (SSME) is the fundamental necessity to reduce complexity and represent the universe of discourse by means of models in order to better understand, communicate, analyze, plan, control, monitor and evaluate the procedure. Modelling, despite being well established in many areas, is a challenge in SSME. Services require multi-disciplinary perspectives including economic, legal, social and technical aspects. Furthermore, services exhibit generic as well as domain-specific characteristics.

Creating and utilizing expressive yet manageable models of sophisticated service systems requires specific approaches for modelling languages, techniques, tools and methodologies. Service modelling techniques need to address the diverse aspects of service systems while also embracing the wealth of existing modelling approaches from associated disciplines and application domains.

Although promising research has begun in various related areas, service modelling techniques along the life cycle of service systems, starting from planning and analysis, down to design, development, testing, deployment, monitoring and management are still in their infancy. The separation of ongoing efforts into highly specific domains and research areas as well as between academia and industry contribute to the challenges faced in this area.

The SMART workshop was held in conjunction with the ServiceWave conference in Ghent, on December 13, 2010, and addressed issues related to modelling holistic service systems. Going beyond Web services or SOA, SMART aimed to contribute to a holistic approach of designing, building and managing IT-enabled real-world services.

The SMART workshop major focus was on service-specific aspects such as co-creation mechanics, service network structure and dynamics, service value exchange, service interaction processes as well as service flexibility, variation and customization.

SMART 2010 included the following presentations:

- Arne Berre : Keynote Speech (not included in this volume)
- Konstadinos Kutsikos and Gregoris Mentzas: A Service Portfolio Model for Value Creation in Networked Enterprise Systems
- Erik Wittern and Christian Zirpins: On the Use of Feature Models for Service Design: The Case of Value Representation
- Yan Wang and Willem-Jan van den Heuvel: Towards A Hybrid Simulation Modelling Framework for Service Networks

- Yehia Taher, Willem-Jan Van Den Heuvel and Sotirios Koussouris: Empowering Citizens in Public Service Design and Delivery: A Reference Model and Methodology
- Yannis Charalabidis and Fenareti Lampathaki: A Description Framework for Digital Public Services
- Aditya Ghose: The Business Service Representation Language: A Preliminary Report
- Susan Stucky, Melissa Cefkin, Yolanda Rankin and Ben Shaw: Modeling the Co-creation of Value in Complex IT Service Engagements (not included in this volume)

In the discussion that followed, several issues were analyzed, relating to a unified modelling method for services of any kind, service collaboration patterns and service value modelling and simulation.

January 2011   Alan Hartman

SMART 2010 Workshop Organization

Organizing Committee

Yannis Charalabidis	NTUA, Athens, Greece
Christos Georgousopoulos	INTRASOFT International S.A., Athens, Greece
Alan Hartman	IBM, Bangalore, India
Willem-Jan van den Heuvel	Tilburg University, Tilburg, The Netherlands
Anshu N Jain	IBM, Bangalore, India
Antonis Ramfos	INTRASOFT International S.A., Athens, Greece
Christian Zirpins	KIT, Karlsruhe, Germay

Program Committee

Dimitris Askounis	NTUA, Athens, Greece
Kamal Bhattacharya	IBM, Bangalore, India
Yannis Charalabidis	NTUA, Athens, Greece
Joseph Davis	University of Sydney, Sydney, Australia
Nirmit Desai	IBM, Bangalore, India
Brian Elvesæter	SINTEF, Oslo, Norway
Christos Georgousopoulos	INTRASOFT International S.A., Athens, Greece
Aditya Ghose	University of Wollongong, Wollongong, Australia
Ricardo Goncalves	Universidade Nova, Lisbon, Portugal
Sudip Gupta	ISB, Hyderabad, India
Alan Hartman	IBM, Bangalore, India
Anshu N Jain	IBM, Bangalore, India
Marijn Janssen	TU Delft, Delft, The Netherlands
Atreyi Kankahalli	NUS, Singapore
Holger Kett	Fraunhofer IAO, Stuttgart, Germany
Roger Kilian-Kehr	SAP, Mannheim, Germany
Evripidis Loukis	University of the Aegean, Samos, Greece
Michiel Malotaux	Gartner Group
Parastoo Mohaghegi	SINTEF, Oslo, Norway
Rajiv Narvekar	Infosys, Bangalore, India
Richard Paige	York University, York, UK
Mike Papazoglou	Tilburg University, Tilburg, The Netherlands
Antonis Ramfos	INTRASOFT International S.A., Athens, Greece
Omer F. Rana	University of Wales, Cardiff, UK
Gerd Schuermann	Fraunhofer FOKUS, Berlin, Germany
Siddhartha Sengupta	TCS, Mumbai, India
Willem-Jan van den Heuvel	Tilburg University, Tilburg, The Netherlands
Christian Zirpins	KIT, Karlsruhe, Germany

From Event-Driven Business Process Management to Ubiquitous Complex Event Processing (EDBPM 2010)

Rainer von Ammon

Abstract. This workshop focuses on the topics of connecting the Internet of Services and Things as event sources of a global "smart dust" with the management of business processes and the Future and Emerging Technologies as addressed by the European FET-F 2020 and Beyond Initiative. Such FET challenges are no longer limited to business processes, but focus on new ideas in order to connect processes on the basis of CEP with disciplines of cell biology, epigenetics, brain research, robotics, emergency management, sociogeonomics, bio- and quantum computing - summarized under the concept of U-CEP. This workshop extends edBPM as "commodity" from the perspective of the scientific state of the art, although there are no real adopters so far and we are far from standards. This workshop extends edBPM as ed(B)PM (not all processes must be "business" processes) to U-CEP (new application domains, new services from the "Universe"). In continuation with the edBPM workshops at the First ServiceWave in 2008 in Madrid and the Second ServiceWave in 2009 in Stockholm, this third workshop is a thematical enhancement considering the grand challenges defined by the Future Internet Initiative and FET-F. The workshop positions U-CEP as an appropriate umbrella for the new medium-term Future Internet- and long-term FET-F technologies, products and ideas.

The Idea and Background - From edBPM to U-CEP

This workshop focuses on the topics of connecting the Internet of Services and Things with the management of business processes and the Future and Emerging Technologies as addressed by the ISTAG Recommendations of the European FET-F 2020 and Beyond Initiative [1]. Such FET challenges are no longer limited to business processes, but focus on new ideas in order to connect processes on the basis of CEP with disciplines of cell biology, epigenetics, brain research, robotics, emergency management, sociogeonomics, bio- and quantum computing - summarized under the concept of U-CEP [2].

In continuation from the edBPM workshops at the First ServiceWave in 2008 in Madrid and the Second ServiceWave in 2009 in Stockholm, this third workshop was a thematical enhancement considering the grand challenges defined by FET-F. The FET-F initiative looks for radically new ideas, products and outcomes and U-CEP is a contribution in order to bring together the relevant Future and Emerging Technologies under one umbrella.

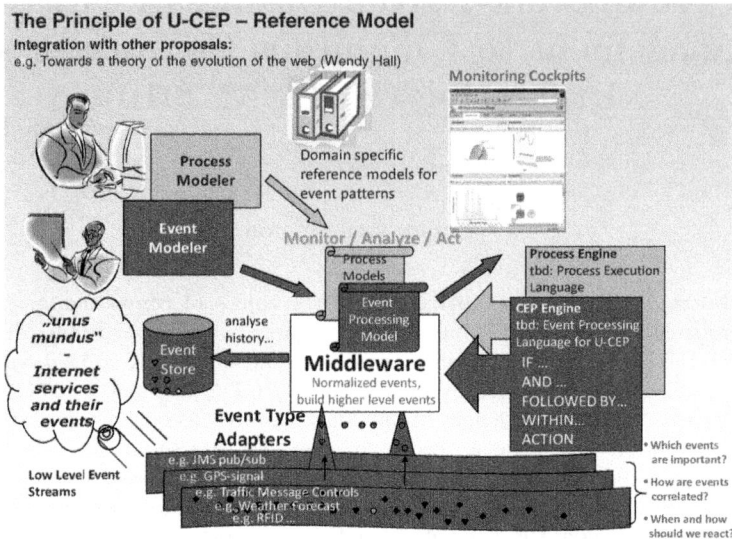

Fig. 1. The reference model of U-CEP consists of two ICT platforms which run in parallel [3]. The processes are modeled by process modelers with special skills in an application domain. The models are executed by a process engine. The other, corresponding platform monitors and processes complex events from different event types which are modeled as event patterns by event modelers with special skills in event modeling.

The term "event-driven business process management" (edBPM) was coined after the First CEP Symposion in Hawthorne/NY in March 2006 with its first BPM/CEP panel. edBPM today is an enhancement of BPM by new concepts of service-oriented architecture, event-driven architecture, software as a service, business activity monitoring and complex event processing. In this context BPM means a software platform which gives companies the ability to model, manage, and optimize these processes for significant gain. As an independent system, complex event processing (CEP) is a parallel running platform that analyzes and processes events. The BPM and the CEP platform correspond via events which are produced by the BPM workflow engine and by the - if distributed so - IT services which are associated with the business process steps. Events coming from different event sources in different forms can also trigger a business process or influence the execution of the process or a service, which can result in another event. Even more, the correlation of these events in a particular context can be treated as a complex, business level event, relevant for the execution of other business processes or services. A business process - arbitrarily fine or coarse grained - can be seen as a service again and can be "choreographed" with other business processes or services, even between different enterprises and organizations.

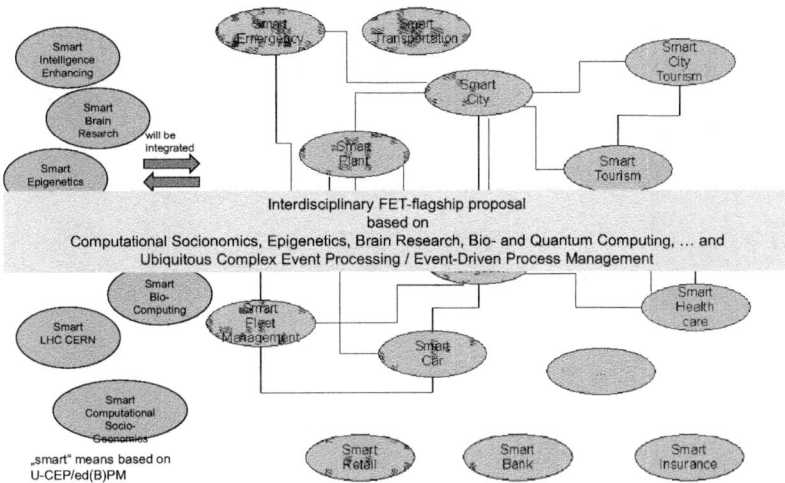

Fig. 2. The different domains of edBPM such as telco, banking, insurance, automotive, logistics, retail, entertainment etc. are enhanced by new domains like brain research, bio-computing, or epigenetics, human enhancements and artificial global intelligence, robotics, cyborgs and socio-economic applications.

This way, processes will be able to change their control flow dynamically and very flexibly according to enterprise-internal or -external Internet services. For this aim a process execution standard like BPEL (OASIS) has to be enhanced by integrating not only simple single, process external events but also complex events. The workshop discussed a reference model for edBPM and used cases for different domains such as telco, banking, insurance, automotive, logistics, retail, entertainment etc. (see Fig. 2).

First experiences in setting up edBPM applications have shown that the potential adopters have major problems to adequately define and implement the underlying complex event patterns. Engineering of such applications remains a laborious trial-and-error process with slow development and change cycles. Therefore the availability of domain-specific reference models for event patterns is an urgent need that businesses have today. Adopters and decision makers need a clear understanding of the alternative event patterns and their applicability to solve certain edBPM problems. They should be able to choose the event pattern which is most suitable for fulfilling the properties and objectives of the intended application in a particular domain. The workshop also discussed how to find and model appropriate event patterns.

The Internet of Service will change the way business processes will be performed, by having them in the form of services on the Internet. Consequently, this opens many challenges, but the most important is managing the interaction between services in such an open environment. Indeed, in such a networked services supply chain, every service produces many events that might be relevant for other services. It is clear that all these influences, due to their ad-hoc nature, cannot be defined in advance explicitly. Real-world reactivity requires a kind of publish–subscribe mechanism that enables relevant events to be pushed to interested parties. It means that the actual data flow (and not predefined workflows) will determine the reactive nature of a Future Internet system.

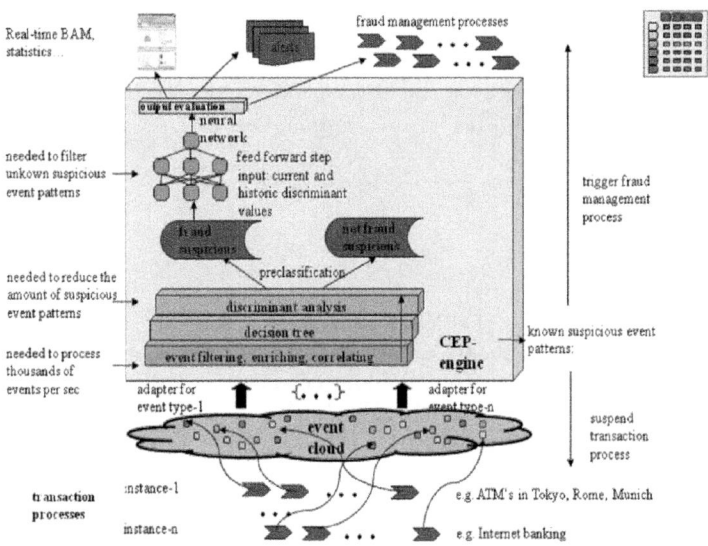

Fig. 3. A reference model for U-CEP as a combination of determistically programmed event patterns and non-deterministic, unknown or suspicious event patterns [4]. Therefore a U-CEP approach must be enhanced by artificial intelligence components.

The last part of the workshop dealt with the "Grand Challenges" of what is summarized under the concept of "ubiquitous complex event processing" and where the concept of the Internet of Services is enhanced according to the FET-F Initiative. Hardly anybody would have forecast 10 years ago that the business world would look like it does today. How will the industrial world look in 10 year's time? Which products and technologies will we use to produce goods, to do business, to learn, to live and to communicate? To better explore the potential that these technologies can offer, the European Commission (Vice-Presidents Antonio Tajani, Neelie Kroes and Commissioner Maire Geoghegan-Quinn) has launched a high-level expert group on key enabling technologies. Key enabling technologies, such as U-CEP in connection with nanotechnology, micro- and nanoelectronics including semiconductors, bio- and quantum computing, biotechnology and photonics, but also brain research, cell biology, epigenetics, robot companions for citizens, cyborgs, exocortex etc., will provide services in a much broader sense. For the modeling and management of such new event types and patterns as so-called smart dust we also need new modeling and execution platforms. In this workshop we started a dialogue between experts and visionary potential adopters.

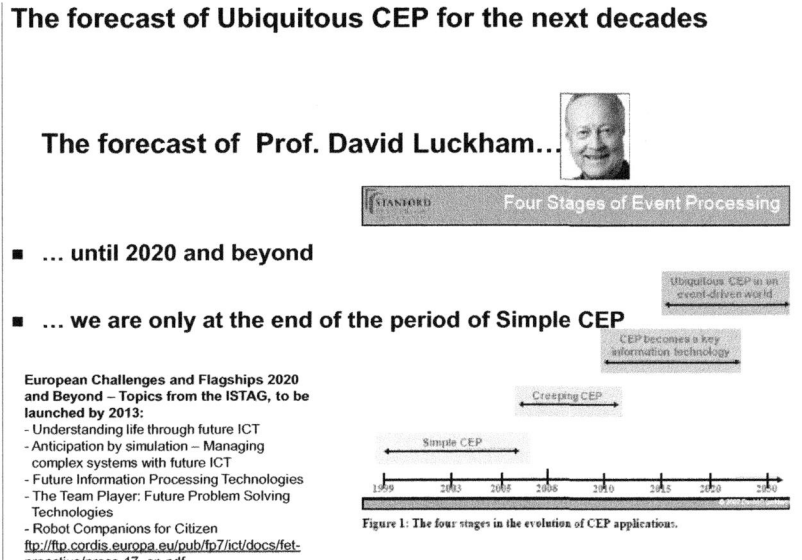

Fig. 4. The forecast of ubiquitous CEP for the next few decades by David Luckham is combined in this workshop with the challenges of the European Future Internet and the FET-F Initiatives.

References

1. European Commission: European Challenges and Flagships 2020 and beyond. Report of the ICT Advisory Group (ISTAG), July 2009,
   ftp://ftp.cordis.europa.eu/pub/ist/docs/istag/flag-fet-july09_en.pdf
2. Ammon, R. v.: Ubiquitous Complex Event Processing. In: CONTRIBUTIONS to the online FET FLAGSHIP CONSULTATION, Status 30 April 2010,
   http://cordis.europa.eu/fp7/ict/fet-proactive/docs/flagshipcons09-01_en.pdf
3. Ammon, R. v.: Event Driven Business Process Management. In Encyclopedia of Database Systems, Ling Liu and M. Tamer Özsu (eds.), Springer (2009)
4. Ammon, R. v., Ertlmaier, Th., Etzion, O., Kofman, A. and Paulus, Th.: Integrating Complex Events for Collaborating and Dynamically Changing Business Processes, In: ICSOC/2nd ServiceWave 2009, Mona+ workshop, Nov 23-24, Stockholm (2009)

EDBPM 2010 Workshop Organization

Organizing Committee

Rainer von Ammon	CITT Regensburg/Germany
Pedro Bizarro	University of Coimbra, Portugal
Mani Chandy	Caltech Pasadena, USA
Opher Etzion	IBM Research Lab Haifa, Israel
Rüdiger Klein	Fraunhofer IAIS, Bonn/Birlinghoven, Germany
Bernhard Seeger	Philipps-Universität Marburg, Germany
Rudi Studer	FZI Research Center for Information Technologies at the University of Karlsruhe, Germany

Program Committee

Atta Badii	University of Reading, UK
Hans-Arno Jacobsen	University of Toronto, Canada
Miriam Leis	TNO Netherlands
David Luckham	University of Stanford, USA
Jorge Marx-Gomez	University of Oldenburg, Germany
Septimiu Nechifor	Siemens Brasov, Romania
James Odell	CSC/OMG Anne Arbor, USA
Themis Palpanas	University of Trento, Italy
Plamen Simeonov	Biomathics Berlin, Germany
Paul Vincent	TIBCO London, UK

Table of Contents

1st International Workshop on Service Modelling and Representation Techniques (SMART 2010)

From Event-Driven Business Process Management to Ubiquitous Complex Event Processing (EDBPM 2010)

Architecturing a Sky Computing Platform

Dana Petcu[1], Ciprian Crăciun[1], Marian Neagul[1], Silviu Panica[1],
Beniamino Di Martino[2], Salvatore Venticinque[2],
Massimiliano Rak[2], and Rocco Aversa[2]

[1] Institute e-Austria Timisoara, Romania
[2] Second University of Naples, Italy

Abstract. Current Cloud computing solutions force people to be stranded into locked, proprietary systems. In order to overcome this limitation several efforts of the research community are addressing issues such as common programming models, open standard interfaces, adequate service level agreements or portability of applications. In this context, we argue about the need for an open-source Cloud application programming interface and a platform targeted for developing multi-Cloud oriented applications. This paper describes the approach that we propose for a platform that allows the deployment of component-based applications in Cloud environments taking into account multiple Cloud provider offers.

1 Introduction

Cloud computing is a model for enabling on-demand access to a pool of dedicated and configurable computing, storage or communication resources that can be rapidly provisioned and released with minimal management effort or service provider interaction. But currently, this model is still in its early stages, with consistent experimentation to come. Cloud computing solutions are currently used in applications that have been developed without addressing a scalable programming model, open standard interfaces, adequate service level agreements or portability of applications. Neglecting these issues the current Cloud computing context forces people to be stranded into locked, proprietary solutions. The developers making an effort in Cloudifying their applications cannot easily port them elsewhere. Unfortunately, non-seamless portability and platform-dependency are only a few of the issues raising doubts about the future of Cloud as a global computing infrastructure.

In this context the mOSAIC project (www.mosaic-cloud.eu) has been initiated in the frame of European Commission's FP7-ICT programme and intends to create, promote and exploit an open Cloud application programming interface and an open-source platform targeted at the development of component-based applications, taking into account multiple Cloud providers. The main benefits of using the mOSAIC platform are firstly a transparent and simple access to heterogeneous Cloud resources avoiding proprietary solutions lock-in, and secondly providing an easy and almost automatic tool for application scalability.

The paper is organized as follows. First we describe in Section 2 the challenges and limitations of the current Cloud ecosystem for which we indicate potential

M. Cezon and Y. Wolfsthal (Eds.): ServiceWave 2010 Workshops, LNCS 6569, pp. 1–13, 2011.

solutions. Section 3 presents the basic concepts behind the API that is under construction, while Section 4 introduces the platform architecture. Thereafter in Section 5 we try to position our proposal in the context of existing Cloud platforms and we draw some conclusions.

2   Cloud Challenges and Limitations

The type of services provided by the current Cloud solutions are very different, ranging from computing, storage, communication, and everything in between, the technology ranges from full virtualization to operating system containers, and the offer from infrastructure (IaaS) to software (SaaS). For example Amazon's EC2 offers Linux virtual machines with full root access, complemented by the S3 distributed storage solution, and SQS/SNS message exchange infrastructure. Nimbus Context Broker enables the use of turnkey virtual clusters. Google's App Engine lets running any program developed in a limited variant of Python or Java (no background threads, file access or communication) allowing only the usage of Google's database. GoGrid offers the widest range of virtual machines but it does not offer many solutions for data storage [1]. Moreover, Cloud interaction and control is accomplished by using proprietary interfaces, limiting the ability to choose any Cloud provider or swapping one provider for another [2].

As a consequence of the current diversity of Cloud solutions there are several limitations on application and data portability, governance and management, monitoring and security (these and other such problems are discussed in depth in Open Cloud Manifesto or [3]). The mOSAIC API and platform intends to address the first category of issues, as we believe that the use of open and standard interfaces enables the flexibility needed to build interoperable applications regardless of specific Cloud providers.

Terms like virtualization, resource provisioning, fault-tolerance, scalability, etc. are overloaded with different meanings in the context of different providers, and to overcome this situation an unified concept dictionary is needed. Therefore we consider that a comprehensive Cloud ontology should be defined to support the need of a common language between the Cloud providers, as well as the application developers.

Another belief that we agree to is that the adoption of a technology is mainly dependent on the degree of its simplicity and similarity with current common models. Therefore we currently investigate the most commonly applied Cloud usage patterns to enable them through the proposed API.

Even the task for selecting Cloud providers for a particular application is an intricate issue due to the complex business model associated with such providers, as the cost depends on many factors, e.g. CPU performance, storage capacity, communication, location, privacy requirements, just to name a few. Therefore a powerful brokering mechanism is required to select the best Cloud offers taking into account the characteristics of the target applications (like less expensive or more performance tradeoffs). Moreover, complex applications are likely to require more than a single Cloud provider, and thus several Cloud offers need to be combined to satisfy their needs. Final application service consumers can require fast response time and distributing requests to multiple geographically spread Cloud providers can be a solution for satisfying such a requirement. Another situation might come from the need of combining unique offers (e.g. a Google AppEngine front end application with an Amazon Hadoop instance as the analytical tool). These and other such situations are consequences of the need for a Cloud environment that enables the interconnection and interoperation of resources from multiple Cloud providers. Thus a new term has emerged recently which implies such a solution: Sky computing [4].

Cloud providers need to support the specification of QoS characteristics customized for each individual application and their negotiation in specific SLAs. They usually deploy traditional system-centric resource management architecture. A market-oriented resource management is instead necessary, according to [2], in order to regulate the provisioning of Cloud resources, and even allowing dynamic re-negotiation of SLAs. Therefore a Cloud must be, but currently is either limited or not at all, able to support application-driven resource management based on application profiles and monitoring (a first attempt of solving this problem is presented in [5]). In this context, new SLA-oriented resource management strategies are needed for providing personalized support to the customers and their applications, as application requirements from users can change over time and thus may require amendments of original service requests.

Unfortunately there are also other issues (like QoS, security, migration, business models, etc.) not discussed in this paper that have to be thoroughly analyzed and if needed addressed in the final version of the mOSAIC solution.

3   Towards a Unified Cloud Programming Interface

One of the benefits of Clouds is the introduction of the concept of programmable infrastructures. We argue that we have at this moment three levels of programmability. As mentioned previously, standard interfaces are needed: (a) at a low level – namely infrastructure programming interface – for Cloud resources (virtualized machines, disks, networks, etc.); (b) at a high level – namely application programming interface – for Cloud services (data-stores, queues, etc.); (c) at a middle level – namely middleware programming interface – for interoperability between multiple Clouds. Concerning the high level, a uniform API needs to reflect the main functionalities necessary for any Cloud-based applications. We consider that the minimal functionalities are those depicted by Table 1.

In order to build an efficient API, a deep analysis, assessment and extraction of the main features of existing platform-dependent programming APIs (e.g. the ones provided Amazon, Google or Force.com) are needed. On the other hand, the additions must be judicious and pragmatic avoiding the creation of a big API, ensuring that standards promote innovation and do not inhibit it. Cloud usage patterns need to be identified beyond the ones recently reported [6] that are reflecting the vendor perspective – instead an application specific view will be followed. These usage patterns will be finally encountered in the proposed API.

Table 1. Minimal functionalities exposed by mOSAIC's API

Type	Model	Production-ready examples
Storage	Distributed file system	GoogleFS, HadoopFS, Amazon S3
	Block devices	Amazon EBS, DRBD
	Distributed databases	Google BigTable, Amazon SimpleDB, Riak
Communication	Message queues	AMQP, Amazon SQS/SNS, JMS
	RPC	Web Services, REST
	Datagram	UDT, Ericsson TIPC
	Synchronization	Zookeeper, Scalaris
Monitoring		Amazon CloudWatch, Ganglia, Nagios
Provisioning		Amazon EC2, Eucalyptus, OpenNebula

At the middle level, the starting point in order to build a comprehensive API is to consider the emerging standards and then to build the missing pieces thus binding them into a unitary component. We mention here only two most important emerging standards: the OCCI (Open Cloud Computing Interface, for remote management of Cloud computing infrastructure, allowing for the development of interoperable tools for common tasks including deployment, autonomic scaling and monitoring), and Google UCI, (Unified Cloud Interface Project) followed by our semantic Cloud abstraction (ontology, under development; our intention is to instantiate a semantic Cloud model beyond the UCIs one that stops at data level). For the low level we mention other standards: OVF (Open Virtualization Format [7]), as hypervisor-neutral, efficient, extensible, and open specification for the packaging and distribution of virtual appliances composed of one or more VMs (the mOSAIC API follows the example of vCloud API [8] in what concerns the integration of OVF), and CDMI (Cloud Data Management Interface [9]) as an interface that applications can use to create, retrieve, update and delete data elements in the Cloud.

We make a series of assumptions related to the way in which the application developer will interact with mOSAIC API and platform.

First of all we underline the need of decoupling the development of the Cloud based application from its deployment. The developer should focus on the development of the application components according to the proposed API and the platform should automate and assist the deployment and execution of the application. Figure 1 suggests the two different views of the same application: the logical one – the developer view – and the infrastructure one – the platform view. The application is composed from several components (rhombs) representing different layers (e.g. business logic, services, user interface etc). They are communicating through asynchronous messages using queues (gray rectangles). Even though the components are depicted as single boxes, these are logical components, and they could and should be embodied by multiple instances at run-time. The application that will reside on the Cloud(s) is supposed to be accessible via Internet protocols. The descriptor of the applications specifies the

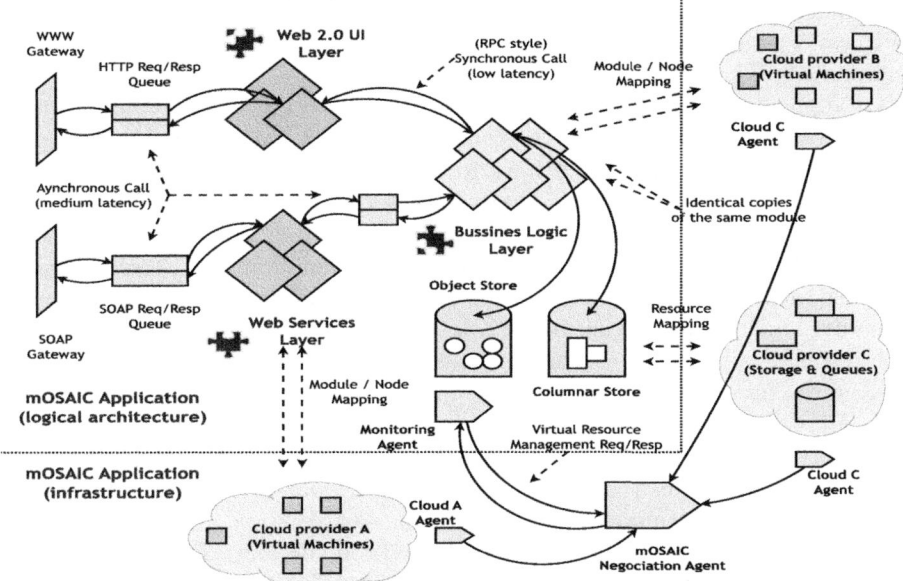

Fig. 1. Application components – logical architecture and infrastructure architecture

components as well as the needs in what concerns the types of resources (without specifying the Cloud provider). In the case suggested by Fig. 1 the business logic requires some objects to be stored and some data to be maintained in a columnar store as well as virtual machines to process the data, while the service layers requires only virtual machines to launched depending on the overload on the application through the web service interfaces. A Cloud Agency ([10] and next section) assists in finding a collection of resources from one or multiple Cloud providers that are matching the requirements of the application as well as in monitoring the behaviour of the resources at run-time (yellow components).

Secondly, we consider that, in order to benefit from the advantages of the mOSAIC's API, application developers have to follow the next steps: develop the application components; specify the resource requirements; submit the requirements to the platform's resource broker that gives back a resource contract committing to meet the requirements; bootstrap the contracted resources by using a specialized tool; deploy and start the application; monitor the application.

Thirdly, we assume that the design of the application will following the guidelines provided by the API: split the application in components based on their purpose; create clear (communication and data) dependencies between components; use the recommended architectural paradigm (service oriented); use the recommended communication patterns: either synchronous or asynchronous remote calls, or message-queue oriented. Furthermore, we also assume that in the development of the application by using the provided API: all the communication and data exchange between components are done through the API; all communications to and from the exterior (i.e. Internet) are using the provided API; avoid using ad-hoc IPC mechanisms that have not been integrated in the environment (like sockets).

An application descriptor needs to be provided to enable the deployment by the mOSAIC platform. Except the component descriptions, the other necessary information for the deployment have to be specified. They can include, beyond the type of the resource, the amount of needed resources, the availability timeframe of the resources (some resources could be asked only for certain stages of the application life-cycle), the QoS needs (like: minimum processor speed or available memory in case of computing nodes), or minimum bandwidth (in case of message queues or Internet access), latency or average down-time, budget for each resource type, trade-offs between performance and costs.

From the previous description one could observe that the mOSAIC API suits more for two kinds of applications: long-running scalable applications (most suitable type of application for the proposed platform) and massive batch- or parallel-processing jobs (these data- or computational-intensive applications although are not our primary target can still be easily and successfully deployed). By long-running scalable applications we envision the kind of applications that are composed of multiple components which communicate one with another to solve the given tasks. These applications, once submitted, should run for undefined period of time, but also scale (upward or downward) as the usage demands it. Some examples of such applications are web-crawlers, forecasting systems (financial, meteorology), economical applications (ERP), etc.

4   Towards a Platform for Deployment/Execution of Applications Using Resources of Multiple Cloud Providers

We propose an architecture for the platform that has two main parts: the deployer, named Resource Broker (responsible of resource negotiation and booking, and denoted RB), and the executor, named Application Executor (AE).

The main goal of the RB component of the platform is to mediate between the client and the providers. This mediation should also try to optimize the costs and maximize the performance of the resulting contract. All the requests and responses (SLA's, bid requests, and contracts) are described according to a specific ontology that governs the brokering domain. Because each involved party could natively have a different ontology, the agents that sit behind them, need to implement a semantic mapping between the native ontology and the brokering ontology; this happens in the semantic layer of the platform, that will also provide ontological validation and translation and will refine the application specification document into a correct and complete SLA on behalf of the user.

The RB has two sub-systems, Client interface and Cloud Agency. The Client interface uses the application descriptor or supplementary resource specification document (for requesting supplementary resources by the AE). The Cloud Agency (denoted by CA and similar to the one reported in [10]) includes a

Monitor, a Negotiator, a Mediator, a Registry, Client semantic engine, and uses Cloud Ontology and Quality of Service Parameters. It validates the application specifications and generates a SLA document (used by the Cloud Agency for resource negotiation and booking). Moreover, it includes Provider Semantic Engines (represented by agents) and generates a Resource contract (document used by the AE subsystem to access the physical resources for application execution).

The agent-based architecture is composed at least of Client Agents, Mediation Agents and Provider Agents. The Client Agent, that acts as access point for the client to the Cloud Agency, offering proactive services, maintains the user profile and the requested SLA and cooperates with the Mediation Agent in order to offer the services with the requested SLA. The Mediation Agent retrieves a list of available Provider Agents (from a Registry Agent), contacts each Provider Agent, and requests a bid for the needed resources (of course it shall request only those resource types provided by the targeted platform). Once it obtains responses from Provider Agents, it assesses the following: the QoS provided and the quality of the provider itself (requesting historical data from an Archiver Agent). After assessing the bid responses, it puts together a contract with the winning providers on behalf of the client. It answers back to the Client Agent with the corresponding contract. The Mediation Agent tries to optimize the contract by applying different trade-offs between performance, availability or costs, but within the bounds specified by the client. The Provider Agent accepts bid requests from the Mediation Agent and tries to propose a contract for the resources it could provides (of course there could be a negotiation iteration between the Mediation and the Provider Agents).

The Application Execution (AE) component is in charge with application execution using the resources booked and stated in Resource contract document. In order for the AE to fulfill its goals it must cooperate and communicate with: the Cloud Agency by using JADE specific XML/HTTP API's, the application itself by providing homogeneous API's, the Cloud-provider itself by consuming heterogeneous cloud API's, and other middleware by consuming middleware dependent API's. The main components of AE are supporting services for deployment, running, monitoring, and scaling. They support the language dependent libraries that expose the mOSAIC API to the developer and providing run-time operations for module configuration and life-cycle management, as well as resource mediation for file system (e.g. wrapping HDFS, S3, etc.), key-value store (e.g. wrapping Riak, S3, etc.), columnar store (e.g. wrapping HBase), message queues (e.g. wrapping RabbitMQ, SQS+SNS).

At the user or Cloud provider site several components of mOSAIC platform need to be deployed. The main services offered are: provisioner, bootstrapper, environment builder, supervisor, controller, statistics collector and aggregator, notifier, and resource drivers.

Provisioner. At the request of other components it mediates the creation of VMs or other Cloud resources, by either contacting the Cloud provider directly (using a Cloud-provider dependent API's) or by delegating the work to the CA.

Deployer. Once a new virtual machine was provisioned (by the Provisioner at the request of the Controller) it must be prepared for running different mOSAIC components. In order to run these components the mOSAIC platform itself must be installed on the targeted virtual machine – this is the task of the Deployer service. Details on how to connect and run an arbitrary command on the targeted node (e.g.: it could use ssh, by receiving an ssh private-key, host IP and username) are given as inputs. The following actions will be performed: connect to the targeted node; create an initial environment needed by the mOSAIC core platform (i.e. copy need binaries, data files, etc. matching the targeted CPU architecture and operating system flavour); start the Bootstrapper process.

Bootstrapper. After a node is provisioned (created and started) the first actual mOSAIC process run there. The bootstrapper starts only after the Deployer which runs (remotely, via ssh) generic commands, e.g. cp, wget, etc. Once started it should connect to the Controller in order to obtain a list of services to be run. Then it delegates the role of preparing the needed environment for services to Environment Builder and delegates their start and monitoring to the Supervisor. The inputs are related to the details on how to connect to the Controller (a TCP socket address or a ZooKeeper ensembly address). The main actions are: connect to the Controller to find out a list of services that must be run; delegate to the Environment Builder the preparation of the environment (e.g. needed files, operating system services, etc.) in which different (mOSAIC) services run in; delegate to the Supervisor the actual starting and monitoring of the services; periodically exchange information with the Controller in order to start/stop/ update the running services, or decommissioning of the node.

Environment Builder. In order for any mOSAIC service or application module to run they need a specific file-system contents (e.g. binary files, libraries, data files, etc.), environment setup (process UID/GID, environment variables), operating system services running, operating system configuration (e.g. firewall). All these items are prepared by this process. The input is a process descriptor which states all of the above details (this process descriptor is derived from the application deployment descriptor, and should be passed by the Bootstrapper).

Supervisor. Once the environment of a service was prepared by the Environment Builder, the actual service process is started and monitored by the current process. The input is a service descriptor (the same as for the builder) which states which is the executable file and arguments that should be run. The actions that are undertaken are: starts the child process (the supervised service process); monitors the process existence, state and resource consumption; based on a policy (described in the process descriptor) it stops/restarts the child process in case of malfunction or excessive resource consumption; periodically communicates with the Bootstrapper (or maybe directly with the Controller) in order to manage the life-cycle of the supervised process (start, stop, etc.); periodically communicates with the Collector sending statistics about the monitored process.

Controller. This service is the brain of the entire run-time. It takes decisions and delegates actions to all the other components: it based on collected and

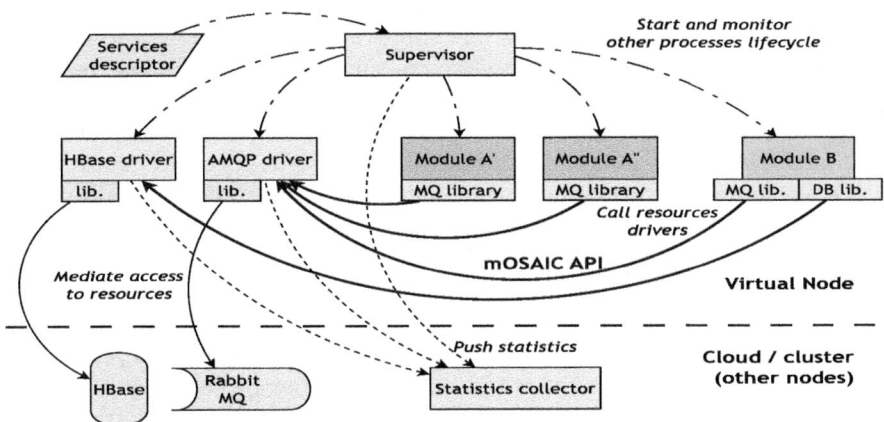

Fig. 2. Service interactions

aggregated statistics it decides if new resources must be provisioned (thus delegating work to the Provisioner and then to the Deployer); based on different services load (again through statistics) it decides whether to and where to start new, or stop running modules (delegating the actual work to the Bootstrapper or Supervisor). As inputs this service receives the application deployment descriptor and the contract (provided by the CA).

Statistics Collector, Statistics Aggregator and Notifier. Based either on a push or pull method the Collector gathers raw statistics from the AE components (mainly from the running processes or middleware). The gathered statistics are deposited in a store that should be available to the Statistics Aggregator. Based on the raw statistics collected from diverse components, the Aggregator consolidates them in meaningful single figures (i.e. starting from means to trends or patterns) and deposit them in a specific repository. Based on a push or pull method from the Statistics Aggregator, and a set of alerting policies, the Notifier contacts interesting parties in case of any such alerts.

Resource Drivers. As mOSAIC offers a language independent and homogeneous programmatic interface to Cloud resources, these resource drivers are the ones that are going to actually implement the resource specific protocol and present to the modules the API, thus wrapping/mediating resource access.

Service interactions. The interactions between the services described above are summarized by Fig. 2. After the virtual node was created by the Provisioner, prepared by the Deployer, and the Bootstrapper started, then next process that comes into play is the Supervisor which, after reading the application descriptor, starts and monitors the needed services. By monitoring we assume that if a service process exceeds its prescribed resources it should kill and restart it; the same should happen also in the case the process suddenly dies. All these actions should be done according with a prescribed policy (e.g. how many times to restart the service before giving up, or how much time to wait between restarts) and should be recorded for further statistics. The supervisor sends various service related statistics as: operating system resource consumption per node and per service (e.g. memory, file handles, processor time, network traffic), operating system resource events per node and per service (e.g. swap usage, virtual memory page-faults), AE related events (e. g. module faults). The resource drivers themselves push statistics as operation metrics (count, time, latency, etc.) or failures.

Once the application modules have been started, they need to access the resources abstracted by the AE. This is done through the following layers. Firstly, the application uses the uniform resource API in the language of his choice provided by language dependent, resource implementation independent libraries. Secondly, the libraries are proxies which transform language dependent API calls into messages to the drivers (an uniform resource access protocol). Third, the drivers understanding the uniform resource access protocol translate the operations into resource implementation dependent API calls. Finally, the actual resource libraries communicate with the resources.

5   Related Work

There are already quite a few research, commercial or community driven projects which enable an integrated consumption of heterogeneous Cloud resources offered by different providers. Thus in what follows we point the most relevant ones and we try to highlight what sets aside our solution.

Most of the initiatives related to the consumption of Cloud resources are addressing the Infrastructure as a Service (IaaS) perspective. RESERVOIR [11] is the first initiative intending to provide an open source solution to enable the deployment and management of complex resources across different administrative domains, and one of its' main components, OpenNebula, is currently providing uniform interfaces for EC2 and ElasticHosts [12]. Eucalyptus, integrated in the Ubuntu Linux distribution, enables building IaaS solutions using an Amazon EC2 compatible interface, while also providing S3 and SimpleDB compatible clones. There are also countless other commercial providers – like Enomaly, GoGrid, RackSpace, etc. – addressing the same IaaS aspect by exposing proprietary interfaces, or projects – like DeltaCloud, OCCI, libcloud, etc. – proposing open IaaS interfaces. All commercial solutions are built from a Cloud provider perspective, none easing the tasks of portability for the developer. Meanwhile mOSAIC intends to tackle the Cloud issues by focusing on the application developer, providing him or her with higher abstractions for Cloud resources, and enabling him or her to easily obtain the desired application characteristics (like scalability, fault-tolerance, QoS, etc.).

As PaaS solution, remarkable is Simple Cloud API (www.simplecloud.org) enabling uniform access to data-oriented Cloud resources and offering an API for developing Web applications. But as of today's state of the art it targets only PHP-based Web applications, exposing just a few functionalities (file storage, key-value stores and queues) and only for a couple of Cloud providers (access to Amazon Storage service, Microsoft Azure Queue System, and planned support for RackSpace). mOSAIC may use some of the proposed solution for setting up the final wrappers between the proposed architecture and the Cloud vendors. In the same category of solutions as Simple Cloud API, targeted at specific and limited set of resource types and providers, there are Google's AppEngine (and its clones), Microsoft's Azure, GigaSpaces XAP, etc. Compared to them, our mOSAIC platform sets itself apart as a programming language neutral solution, targeting not only Web applications, and planning to support a wider range of functionalities and providers.

Closer to our proposal for a Resource Broker is CloudBroker (www.cloud-broker.com), a proprietary platform aiming to provide a Cloud environment tailored according to the customer's needs and enabling the integration of Cloud resources offered by different providers. Unfortunately, the configuration and tuning should be done manually in advance by experts, after consultants analyze the application's requirements, and finally a customized platform is released. On opposite side, mOSAIC aims at integrating inside its platform resource related services – such as resource discovery and brokering, tuning and scalability – all which will be available directly to the Cloud developers, while also providing mechanisms to pro-actively adapt the Cloud configuration according to changes in the application requirements.

Also differentiating our mOSAIC solution from the existing ones is the intention to create SLA-aware components, thus following recent trends in Cloud related business policies. One recent approach reported in [13] is the first attempt to combine SLA-based resource negotiation with virtualized resources in terms of on-demand service provisioning. The proposed architecture consists of: a meta-negotiator that manages SLAs and mediates between the user and the meta-broker, selects appropriate protocol agreements, negotiates SLA creation, and handles fulfillment and violation; a meta-broker having the role to select a broker that is capable of deploying a service with the specified user requirements; brokers requirements; brokers that interact with virtual or physical resources, and in case the required service needs to be deployed it interacts directly with the automatic service deployer; automatic service deployers which install the required service on the selected resource on demand. This architectural approach is close to the one proposed above for mOSAIC's Resource broker and only partial for Application executor (described in the previous section).

Furthermore we fully agree with the challenges in building Sky computing platforms, as described in [4], therefore our architectural proposal tries to address, at least partially, the raised issues. In particular we follow the recommendations from Sky computing proponents by combining the various providers' SLAs thus enabling differentiated QoS at each infrastructure layer. We also follow the recommendations recently proposed in [14] related to storage services, as well as the negotiation mechanisms proposed in [15,16], and the SLA-based adaptive resource management proposed in [17].

6   Conclusions and Future Work

The proposed API and platform are intended to be used by developers of Cloud based applications to build their software using the exposed libraries, tools and documentation, to deploy it on top of multiple Clouds, to delegate the provisioning role to a resource broker, to obtain the best price offers following the recommendation of an Cloud agency, and to monitor and scale the application.

The development of the mOSAIC's API and platform that were described in the previous sections is an on-going task. Note that the first stable implementation of the open-source API and platform implementation is expected to be publicly available in Autumn 2011. Therefore this paper only presenting their basic architecture and positioning in the current context of Cloud computing. But most importantly we are trying to build the first, to our knowledge, open-source solution that supports multiple Cloud providers and targets application developers. If the implementation will be successfully completed, the proposed solution will offer to the application developer the freedom of choice both in terms of Cloud resource providers and of programming environment.

References

1. Wayner, P.: Cloud versus Cloud: A guided tour of Amazon, Google, AppNexus, and GoGrid. InfoWorld (2008)
2. Buyya, R., Yeo, C.S., Venugopal, S., Broberg, J., Brandic, I.: Cloud computing and emerging IT platforms: Vision, hype, and reality for delivering computing as the 5th utility. Future Generation Computer Systems 25(6), 599–616 (2009)
3. Armbrust, M., Fox, A., Griffith, R., Joseph, A.D., Katz, R., Konwinski, A., Lee, G., Patterson, D.A., Rabkin, A., Stoica, I., Zaharia, M.: Above the Clouds: A Berkeley View of Cloud Computing, Tech. Report No. UCB/EECS-2009-28 (2009)
4. Keahey, K., Tsugawa, M., Matsunaga, A., Fortes, J.: Sky Computing. Internet Computing 13(5), 43–51 (2009)
5. Yang, J., Qiu, J., Li, Y.: A Profile-Based Approach to Just-in-Time Scalability for Cloud Applications. In: Procs. IEEE Internat. Conf. on Cloud Computing (2009)
6. Cloud Computing Use Case Discussion Group, Cloud Computing Use Cases, White Paper v0.1 (2009)
7. DMTF, Open Virtualization Format White Paper (2009)
8. VMWare Inc, vCloud API Programming Guide, v0.8 Tech Preview (2009)
9. SNIA, Cloud Storage Reference Model (2009), http://www.snia.org/tech_activities/publicreview/CloudStorageReferenceModelV03.pdf
10. Aversa, R., Di Martino, B., Rak, M., Venticinque, S.: Cloud Agency: A Mobile Agent Based Cloud System. In: Procs. International Conference on Complex, Intelligent and Software. IEEE Computer Press, Los Alamitos (2010)
11. Rochwerger, B., Breitgand, D., Levy, E., Galis, A., Nagin, K., Llorente, I., Montero, R., Wolfsthal, Y., Elmroth, E., Caceres, J., Ben-Yehuda, M., Emmerich, W., Galan, F.: The RESERVOIR Model and Architecture for Open Federated Cloud Computing. IBM Journal of Research and Development 53(4) (2009)
12. Sotomayer, B., Montero, R., Lorente, I., Foster, I.: Virtual Infrastructure Management in Private and Hybrid Clouds. Internet Computing 13(5), 14–22 (2009)

13. Kertesz, A., Kecskemeti, G., Brandic, I.: An SLA-based resource virtualization approach for on-demand service provision. In: Virtualization Technology in Distributed Computing - Procs. of the 3rd International Workshop on Virtualization Technologies in Distributed Computing, pp. 27–34 (2009)
14. Harmer, T., Wright, P., Cunningham, C., Perrott, R.: Provider-Independent Use of the Cloud. In: Sips, H., Epema, D., Lin, H.-X. (eds.) Euro-Par 2009. LNCS, vol. 5704, pp. 454–465. Springer, Heidelberg (2009)
15. Paletta, M., Herrero, P.: A MAS-Based Negotiation Mechanism to Deal with Service Collaboration in Cloud Computing. In: Procs. ICIS 2009, pp. 642–646. IEEE Press, New York (2009)
16. Mietzner, R., Unger, T., Leymann, F.: Cafe: A Generic Configurable Customizable Composite Cloud Application Framework. In: Meersman, R., Dillon, T., Herrero, P. (eds.) OTM 2009. LNCS, vol. 5870, pp. 357–364. Springer, Heidelberg (2009)
17. Iqbal, W., Dailey, M., Carrera, D.: SLA-Driven Adaptive Resource Management for Web Applications on a Heterogeneous Compute Cloud. In: Jaatun, M.G., Zhao, G., Rong, C. (eds.) Cloud Computing. LNCS, vol. 5931, pp. 243–253. Springer, Heidelberg (2009)

Optimising Development and Deployment of Enterprise Software Applications on PaaS: The CAST Project

Dimitrios Kourtesis[1], Volker Kuttruff[2], and Iraklis Paraskakis[1]

[1] South-East European Research Centre (SEERC), City College - International Faculty of the University of Sheffield, 24 Proxenou Koromila, 54622, Thessaloniki, Greece
[2] CAS Software AG, Wilhelm-Schickard-Str. 10-12, 76131 Karlsruhe, Germany

Abstract. Platform as a Service (PaaS) is a concept whereby a computing platform and a software development stack are being offered as a combined service to prospective application developers. This model has been shown to carry a great number of benefits for developers and PaaS providers alike, and represents an important trend within cloud computing today. However, the design of mature platforms to support this model to its full extent remains a complex and challenging undertaking for enterprise application PaaS providers. The aim of this paper is to present the approach that is being undertaken within research project CAST to realise a platform that pushes the envelope of PaaS facilities and addresses the challenges associated with optimising application reusability, extensibility, configurability, integrability, and manageability. The ultimate aim is to create a software platform that fosters the creation of an ecosystem, thus pursuing the PaaS vision to its fullest extent possible.

Keywords: Software as a Service, SaaS, SaaS Platform, Customisation, Platform as a Service, PaaS.

1 Introduction

The concepts of Software as a Service (SaaS), Platform as a Service (PaaS), and Infrastructure as a Service (IaaS), represent new ways of thinking about the delivery of computing capabilities in the context of cloud computing. These concepts have gained significant traction during the past few years and are increasingly becoming the centre of attention for innovation in contemporary IT, in both industrial and academic settings.

The term PaaS refers to the notion of combining a computing platform that can be accessed over the internet (or some private network) with a stack of tools and services for developing and deploying software to be executed on that platform, and offering them as a bundled service to prospective developers.

The model carries a great number of benefits for developers of software applications, because it shifts a significant portion of the traditional effort associated with developing, distributing and maintaining software towards the platform provider's end. PaaS offerings are appealing to a wide range of types of software developers, such as Independent Software Vendors (ISVs), Value-Added Resellers (VARs), System

M. Cezon and Y. Wolfsthal (Eds.): ServiceWave 2010 Workshops, LNCS 6569, pp. 14–25, 2011.
© Springer-Verlag Berlin Heidelberg 2011

Integrators, but also in-house IT teams [1]. The model is theoretically applicable to applications and solutions irrespective of size or domain, but in practice, it appears to have gained widespread adoption especially in the context of enterprise software applications [2], primarily due to their inherent database-centric nature.

Apart from the benefits that the model of PaaS brings for software developers, it also carries a great number of benefits for prospective PaaS providers. Most importantly, it ultimately enables platform providers to pursue the creation of value-added networks and the development of entire business ecosystems around their platforms, in an analogy to the way current mobile phone platforms like iPhone, Android and Blackberry are operating. This, however, remains largely a vision for the time being. With a few exceptions (e.g. force.com [3]), the majority of today's PaaS providers lack the required technical facilities to support this concept to its full extent. The reason is that the design of mature platforms to support this model in an effective fashion is a particularly complex and challenging undertaking for PaaS providers.

CAST is an ongoing research project[1] that is investigating the challenges associated with this vision and aims to develop a commercial platform that can fulfil this objective. The project is seeking to define an approach for the design of a platform that pushes the envelope of configurability and customisability, ecosystem-centric extensibility and native multi-tenancy. In the rest of this paper we discuss the key challenges associated with the design of such a platform, briefly review the state of practice in the area of PaaS offerings relative to those challenges, and provide an overview of the CAST platform's main concepts and architecture.

2 Platform Maturity Levels and the State of Practice

The technology space for PaaS offerings is currently evolving and undergoing changes as it progresses towards higher levels of maturity. As usually happens with concepts that gain wide acceptance before they are fully analysed and understood, the term PaaS has become rather overloaded. Broadly speaking, we can categorise the PaaS offerings available today in two basic types: technology-specific PaaS, such as Google App Engine, Microsoft Azure, Heroku and Engine Yard, and domain-specific PaaS, such as Force.com, LongJump, Zoho Creator and WOLF.

Despite the widespread adoption of PaaS as a model, it might not be an exaggeration to claim that, at the moment, only a few of the technology providers that categorise themselves under 'PaaS' are actually supporting the concept of PaaS to its full extent, i.e. work with a vision to achieve a true "software platform effect" [4] and to support the creation of actual ecosystems around their offerings.

To facilitate comparison between the multitude of offerings and supporting platforms for SaaS/PaaS that are available on the market, attempts have been made to develop maturity models based on sets of key characteristics. The first attempt was by Chong and Carraro of Microsoft [5], who tried to define a maturity model for on-demand/SaaS offerings and their supporting platforms, along the criteria of scalability, multi-tenancy, and customisability through configuration. On the basis of these characteristics they defined a maturity model consisting of four levels:

---

[1] http://www.cast-project.eu

- Level 0 (ad-hoc/custom): No provision is made to serve multiple tenants[2] from a single instance of server software. A separate instance of server software is installed for each customer to be served, including any necessary customisations specific to that customer (such as custom business logic, data schema, UI forms). This is essentially the same as the traditional Application Service Provider (ASP) model.
- Level 1 (configurable): Applications are possible to customise via configuration (i.e. without writing and deploying any custom code) in order to fulfil specific requirements of different tenants. This allows all tenants to be served by the same application codebase. However, a dedicated installation (code-wise identical) is still being maintained for each customer. This type of architecture is not considered multi-tenant since computing resources are still not shared among software instances. Server space/time must be provided for as many instances as the vendor has customers.
- Level 2 (configurable, multi tenant): Applications can be customised solely through configuration, and a single instance of server software can serve all customers. Compared to the previous level, this allows for much more efficient use of computing resources. However, scalability remains a problem, because the only way to scale the application up is by moving it to more powerful hardware, at least for as long as this remains cost-effective.
- Level 3 (scalable, configurable, multi tenant): Applications are featuring all characteristics of the previous level, with the addition of load balancing to address scalability. The number of servers and instances can be adapted to match demand, making applications scalable to arbitrarily large numbers of customers.

Ried, Rymer and Iqbal of Forrester Research proposed an alternative maturity model for cloud computing application platforms comprising six levels [6].

- Level 0 in the Forrester model concerns cases where some form of software outsourcing is inaccurately being referred to as SaaS provisioning. By this the authors are trying to stress that the term should be used with due care to avoid overloading and misinterpretations.
- Level 1 corresponds to the traditional ASP model, i.e. to Microsoft's level 0. A separate instance of server software is installed for each customer served.
- Level 2 in the Forrester model corresponds to level 1 in Microsoft's model. It refers to applications which are customisable via configuration, such that the codebase can be shared, but where dedicated installations are maintained for different customers.
- Level 3 corresponds to levels 2 and 3 in Microsoft's model. Scalability, multi-tenancy, and customisability through configuration are considered prerequisites, similarly to Microsoft's level 3. However, the Forrester model adds an additional characteristic: the fact that platforms/vendors at this level of maturity offer single well-defined SaaS applications (e.g. a CRM solution).
- Level 4 is for platforms where applications can be extended by additional business logic through custom extensions (beyond configuration) and by third-party packaged SaaS solutions, thus making it possible to build SaaS applications for entire business domains.

---

[2] The term tenant refers to a whole customer organisation/company, not to a single user.

- Finally, level 5 refers to platforms that satisfy all criteria for level 4, and moreover, are pre-populated with numerous business applications or business services which can be dynamically composed to create tenant-specific or even user-specific SaaS business applications.

Considering the state of practice in the contemporary PaaS technology and market space [7, 8, 9] relative to the above maturity criteria, it can be noted that most of today's PaaS providers are lacking with regard to support for one or more of the following platform capabilities, which are central to a mature PaaS offering:

1. Support for sharing of an application's codebase or runtime instances by multiple tenants in order to minimise operational costs for the provider (multi-tenancy)
2. Support for modifying/tailoring applications already deployed on the platform (through metadata-driven configurability and/or code-driven customisability)
3. Support for reusing applications that were developed by third parties as building blocks for creating completely new applications (ecosystem-centric extensibility)
4. Support for creating applications without restrictions to a particular business domain such as CRM only (multi-domain applicability)

Lacking with respect to the first platform capability, i.e. enabling a multi-tenant infrastructure, severely limits the platform provider's potential to achieve economies of scale, and inevitably becomes a roadblock for growth in a cloud computing context. Lacking with respect to the other three platform capabilities limits the platform provider's potential with regard to the emergence of a technology and business ecosystem around the platform.

3 Summary of Challenges in the Design of the CAST Platform

The CAST project is working towards the direction of a fully-fledged PaaS model. It is investigating techniques, methods and tools for the realisation of a software platform that overcomes the abovementioned deficiencies in the current state of practice, and enables efficient and effective development, deployment and provisioning of on-demand enterprise software applications.

To achieve this goal, the design of the CAST platform needs to address two distinct (but complementary) sets of challenges, which shape the platform's model of operation and its technical architecture:

- Challenges which are generic with regard to *cloud infrastructures*, such as enabling multi-tenancy, scalability, reliability, security;
- Challenges which are specific to *application platforms*, such as facilitating application reusability, extensibility, configurability, integrability, manageability.

The first set of challenges is fundamental to providing any cloud-based service. The second set is fundamental to providing a service on the basis of a PaaS offering. The focus here is supporting application development specifically in the context of a 'software platform' [10, 11, 12], and achieving the 'platform effect' that has already become very popular outside the cloud computing domain by mobile phone platforms such as Apple's iPhone. Fundamental to this, is to provide facilities which will act as catalysts for the emergence of an actual ecosystem around the platform.

In practical terms, these facilities include enabling application developers to reuse existing applications found on the platform, adapt them to their needs, integrate them with external systems, combine them into new solutions and resell them, while keeping the platform provider's effort for maintaining the platform and managing the application development/deployment process as low as possible.

4 Main Concepts and Terminology

Before going into further detail with regard to the platform's model of operation and architecture, it is best to provide an overview of the main concepts and associated terminology. We explain how we use the terms platform, solution, customisation, app, and external service, in the context of the CAST project and this paper.

Platform
The platform is defined as a software environment used for developing, deploying, and provisioning enterprise software applications. The usage of the platform is offered as a service to developers who are looking to create Web-based on-demand applications. Those developers can be Independent Software Vendors (ISVs) who are looking to create new solutions addressable to entire markets, or IT teams looking to create solutions for specific needs within their own organisations.

The platform consists of an execution stack (hardware, server software, databases, application containers, etc), a set of core and optional "building blocks" which are used for developing new applications/solutions, and a set of specialised tools to support the activities of developers and administrators.

The platform adheres to the open/closed principle: it is open for extensions through changes at explicitly declared components of the architecture, and closed for any other modifications that could affect its stability and reliability.

Solutions
A solution is defined as an enterprise software application which is based on the platform and is targeted at a specific market segment (e.g. CRM for insurance companies). Solutions are therefore intended to be marketable to a great number of potential end users. A solution accounts for domain specific characteristics within its domain model, its business logic and its user interface.

Customisations
A customisation is defined as an application that is based on an existing solution and has been tailored to address the needs of one specific customer. There exists a one-to-many relationship between platform, solutions and customisations: A platform hosts many solutions, and for each solution, it is possible to provide several customer-specific customisations.

Apps
Solutions and customisations can be regarded as "bundles" consisting of finer-grained components which are called apps. Each app within a solution or customisation provides a highly-specialised functionality. An app can be data-centric, e.g. providing the implementation for a new data type, or it can be process-centric, e.g. supporting a sales employee for performing mass imports of customer addresses.

Apps can (but may not always) affect all of the platform's runtime layers, i.e. by defining new data object types on the data layer, new business operations on the business logic layer, and new user interface elements on the presentation layer.

An app's behaviour can be extended by creating so called app extensions which interface with the app at designated extension points. An app extension is not a standalone component, but functions as a plug-in to one or more apps. Apps as well as app extensions can be configurable. Predefined functionality can be enabled, disabled or adjusted to a certain extent.

External Services

Apps and app extensions may rely on external services to deliver part of their functionality. By external services we refer to systems that are deployed externally to the platform and are accessible over the Web, and through a programmatic interface (i.e. Web services).

The ability to use Web services enables the developers of solutions and customisations to leverage already existing (and tested) solutions for particular highly-specialised tasks within their apps, instead of having to reinvent the wheel. For example, an app or app extension for contact management could invoke an external service to perform postal address validation for a particular contact, or to obtain stock quote information for a contact's company.

Even more importantly, the use of Web services in conjunction with apps opens the possibility of integrating solutions that are deployed on the platform with external organisations and service providers, or even with legacy systems.

5 CAST Platform Outline

We could outline the synthesis of the CAST platform by distinguishing among three main elements within its architecture: the platform's execution infrastructure, the platform's governance infrastructure, and the platform's end-user directory. In the following we outline the main functionalities of each element.

5.1 Runtime Infrastructure

The runtime infrastructure of the CAST platform comprises three layers:

- Data layer: The data layer provides an abstraction over the physical database and facilitates secured access to the data objects stored therein. It provides basic CRUD (Create, Retrieve, Update, Delete) operations on objects, while enforcing permissions, checking constraints and creating journal entries. The stored objects instantiate the platform's standard domain model, whose schema can however be manipulated through a set of standard operations in order to create new data types. Schema customisations are stored in a way which ensures that multi-tenancy does not prohibit upgradability and scalability.
- Business logic layer: The business logic layer is where domain-specific business functions are implemented. The platform's business logic can be extended by creating Event-Condition-Action rules that realise custom logic and are evaluated by a rule engine at runtime, or by providing customised business logic through

Web services that are external to the CAST platform. For the first option, the platform provides a set of predefined events and a set of predefined actions. For the second option, the platform provides a configurable framework for external service invocation which can also be extended through custom plugins.

- Presentation layer: The presentation layer facilitates interaction with the user: it presents information from the data layer, offers actions to execute business logic operations and accepts user input for creating, editing or deleting data. It is conceptually part of the platform's runtime infrastructure, but it is actually executed completely on the client's side. The RIA framework that is used for its implementation is Microsoft Silverlight. Silverlight emphasises the concept of separating user interface structure and presentation logic, and adopts a declarative approach to defining user interfaces as compositions of standard and custom controls in an XML-based language (XAML).

5.2 Governance Infrastructure

The governance infrastructure comprises a registry/repository system that serves as a central location in which entities and artefacts that are necessary to the operation of the CAST platform are stored, organised, and managed throughout their lifecycle. It provides a space and a set of functions for enabling the effective governance of entities and artefacts from creation to retirement.

Governance is supported by providing specialised tools which assist the users of the system (i.e. platform administrators and solution/customisation developers) in performing standard (manual) quality assurance tasks, but also, by providing tools that automate a number of quality controls by applying conformance checking and data validation with regard to platform governance rules.

Specifically, the registry/repository system supports the following functions:

- Central cataloguing of solutions, apps, and external services, and storage of their associated artefacts in platform-wide accessible location.
- Versioning of managed entities and artefacts to reflect significant changes and to designate new states in development.
- Controlling the evolution of managed entities and artefacts, by modelling lifecycle states and associating validation checks with state transitions.
- Tracking dependencies among solutions, apps, and services and allowing for impact analysis.
- Performing conformance checking to ensure that managed entities and artefacts are compliant to the platform provider's ground rules regarding valid structures.
- Monitoring of the external Web services on which apps are dependent to ensure appropriate levels of availability and performance, considering SLAs.

5.3 App/Solution Directory (Store)

An app/solution directory is an end-user facing Web application that allows customers to view the solutions and apps that are available on the CAST platform. Users can select a solution, view all apps that are compatible with the particular solution, enable/disable optional apps, and install them to their account, triggering all necessary licensing/billing/configuration steps through standardized wizards. Input for these wizards can be extracted from app metadata (app/solution manifest) that were written to the registry/repository during app deployment.

Installation of an app in the CAST context does not mean that native code and artefacts are deployed / installed to a special location. Installation means unlocking the functionality of an app for a specific user. During installation of an app, the database schema specifications will be applied (e.g. new tables will be created or existing tables will be extended). Furthermore, other artefacts of the app will be interpreted from this point on. This also holds for native code: dispatchers in the CAST platform core will call the associated native code components after an app has been unlocked for the user. This also means that native code parts of an app are always part of the CAST platform's code base, but they will not be invoked until an app is explicitly installed.

6 CAST Platform Packaging Model

Apps are the basic blocks for creating enterprise software solutions and customisations within the CAST platform. There can be apps that are pre-fabricated by the CAST platform provider (e.g. built-in apps for basic functionalities like contact management or document management) and are subsequently configured by a platform partner for a particular solution or customisation, or apps which are developed by a platform partner from the ground-up, and subsequently added to the platform for other partners to reuse and customise for their own solutions.

Every solution or customisation is a package which consists of a set of apps, as well as a number of artefacts that determine how these apps are to be combined and executed by the platform's runtime infrastructure. Those artefacts are primarily used for defining solution-specific constraints on the apps involved. Since an app can be part of more than one solution, different constraints can be active for a particular app depending on the execution context. An example for such a constraint is a domain-specific or tenant-specific reduction of the valid range of a value (which may be unbounded in the general data model for an app).

Figure 1 shows an example of a CRM solution addressed to insurance companies. The solution reuses four pre-fabricated apps (Address management, Document management, Email management and Calendar management) which have been developed by the provider of the CAST platform. Additionally, the solution developer creates four solution-specific apps: two data-centric apps for the new Insurance policy and Seminar data object types, and two process-centric apps for Insurance Policy Re-negotiation and Importing of Insurance Policy Data (for performing mass imports from third party systems).

In addition, two app extensions are employed to extend the functionality of the Address management, Document management and Email management apps. The Organisation structuring app extension automatically links address objects that belong together (e.g. for a subsidiary company) within the Address management app. The Coverflow app extension extends the user interface of the Document management and Email management apps by allowing the user to visually flip through snapshots of the contents of the corresponding data objects using three-dimensional animation.

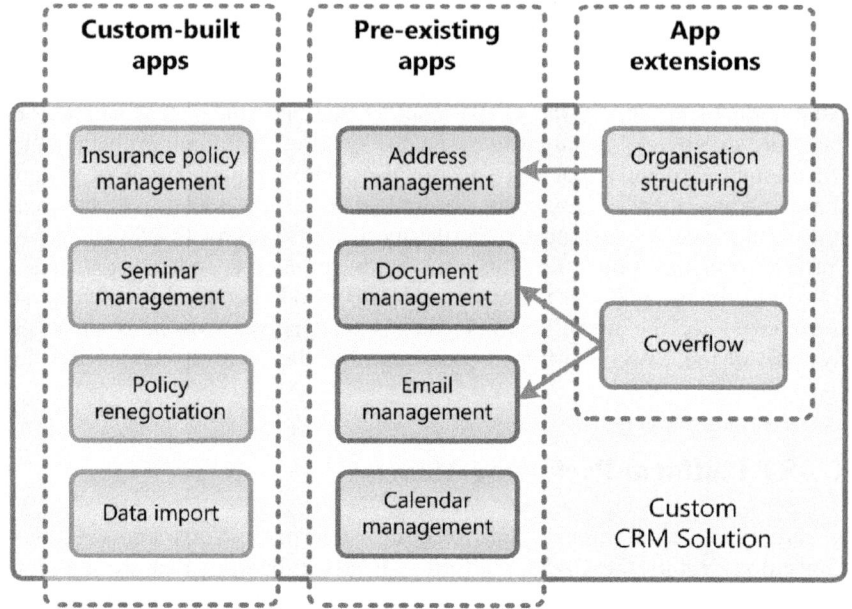

Fig. 1. Example of packaging a CRM solution for insurance companies

7   CAST Platform Deployment Model

The way in which solutions and customisations are deployed on the platform differs, depending on the artefacts/code that come with their associated apps, and how the latter are deployed to the runtime infrastructure.

Within CAST, we distinguish between three types of apps with respect to their method of deployment: purely declarative apps (type 1), apps that involve code execution at the client-side (type 2), and apps that involve code execution at both client-side and server-side (type 3). The increasing numbering of app types denotes increasing capabilities but also increased deployment complexity. This concept applies not only to apps, but to app extensions as well.

7.1   Type 1: Purely Declarative Apps

A major objective for the CAST platform is to promote declarative configurations over native code. If an app is created using declarative specifications only, it is classified as type 1. Such apps can be deployed during normal execution of the CAST platform, without the need to stop and resume any subsystems or affect any active users. During deployment to the platform's runtime infrastructure, a type 1 app comprises the following (not necessarily all) types of XML-based artefacts:

- Database schema descriptions, for extending already existing data object types or defining new ones.
- Declarative specifications of data validators employed to enforce constraints on data object types.

- Definitions of custom UI elements (XAML-based), page flows, and mappings from page types to forms.
- Extensions to business logic through definitions of data-centric rules, or declarative specifications of invocations to external Web services.
- Definitions of translation/localisation resources.
- Specifications of app extension points.

In addition, each app comes with a manifest that describes additional important properties, such as dependencies on other apps, version information, provider information, licensing information, pricing information, etc.

7.2   Type 2: Client-Side Code Apps

Type 2 apps offer all of the possibilities that are provided by apps of type 1, and in addition, include the possibility to use native code which is deployed and executed at the client's machine. In the CAST platform, this is C# code that is intended for runtime deployment to a Silverlight runtime instance within the client's browser (making use of Silverlight's ability for dynamic loading of libraries from a Web server). This allows the deployment and execution of customised command handlers for implementing new custom client logic, customised Model/ViewModel implementations and new custom controls.

Since the presentation layer of the CAST platform executes on the user's machine within a Silverlight plug-in, security risks are lower compared to code that runs within the CAST platform's application servers. In case a type 2 app crashes, the only user that is affected is the one currently using the app. However, to prevent potential problems with bugs causing crashes to client machines and creating a negative impact with regard to the platform's reputation, type 2 apps need to undergo a review and certification process by the platform provider for quality assurance. Due to the presence of native code to be reviewed, this requires substantially more effort compared to conducting review and certification for purely declarative apps (type 1).

7.3   Type 3: Client-Side and Server-Side Code Apps

Type 3 apps enable customisation and extensibility to the fullest extent possible with the CAST platform. In addition to declarative customisations and native code to be executed at the client's side, type 3 apps include the possibility to write native code to be executed by the CAST platform's application servers. To that end, the CAST platform runtime defines dedicated extension points to enhance the existing functionality that is built-in to the platform.

This further allows developers to implement customised business logic for their apps that is impossible to express using the platform's facility for data-centric rules, and providing totally new business operations that are registered within the CAST platform application servers and can be called from clients upon request.

Since the server-side code of type 3 apps runs within the same execution context as the core CAST platform, the latter's stability can be seriously threatened. Thus, apps of type 3 can only be deployed to the CAST platform application servers by the platform provider. Prior to this deployment, type 3 apps need to be reviewed and certified, similarly to apps of type 2.

The deployment of a type 3 app is a lengthy process. On the one hand, this is due to the review, testing and certification processes. On the other hand, a deployment of new native server code requires a shutdown of the application servers. Shutting down and restarting the platform can only happen when it is necessary to perform important maintenance activities, or to deploy new platform releases.

8 Conclusions

The model of Platform as a Service (PaaS), whereby a computing platform and a software development stack are being offered as a combined service to prospective application/solution developers, represents an important trend within cloud computing today. The PaaS model carries a great number of benefits for developers and PaaS providers alike. However, the design of a mature platform to support such a model to its fullest extent possible is a rather complex and challenging undertaking in which the majority of today's PaaS providers face several difficulties.

In this paper we introduced the approach that is put forward in the CAST project for the realisation of a platform that overcomes the deficiencies in the current state of practice around PaaS offerings. The project works towards the direction of a fully-fledged PaaS model and is tackling problems beyond the classic challenges associated with cloud infrastructures (multi-tenancy, scalability, reliability, security), going into platform-specific challenges such as optimising application reusability, extensibility, configurability, integrability, and manageability, such that an ecosystem can eventually emerge around the platform.

The paper provides an overview of the main concepts associated with the CAST platform and the development of applications based upon it, an outline of its core elements and their functionalities, a discussion about the model by which solutions and customisations are packaged, and an analysis of the model by which applications are deployed on the platform.

Acknowledgments. This work has been carried out in the context of research project CAST, co-funded by Eureka Eurostars (E! 4373), the European Community, the Greek General Secretariat for Research and Technology (15627/4-8-09), and the German Federal Ministry for Education and Research.

References

1. Natis, Y.V.: Introducing SaaS-Enabled Application Platforms: Features, Roles and Futures. Gartner Inc. (2007)
2. Knipp, E., Natis, Y.V.: The Coming Enterprise Shift to an APaaS-Centric Web. Gartner Inc. (2009)
3. Force.com: Create and Run any Application, On Demand. Salesforce.com Inc. (2007)
4. Evans, D.S., Hagiu, A., Schmalensee, R.: Invisible Engines: How Software Platforms Drive Innovation and Transform Industries. MIT Press, Cambridge (2006)
5. Chong, F., Carraro, G.: Architecture Strategies for Catching the Long Tail. MSDN Library, Microsoft Corporation (2006)

6. Ried, S., Rymer, J.R., Iqbal, R.: Forrester's SaaS Maturity Model. Forrester Research (2008)
7. Lawton, G.: Developing Software Online With Platform-as-a-Service Technology. IEEE Computer 41(6), 13–15 (2008)
8. Leavitt, N.: Is Cloud Computing Really Ready for Prime Time? IEEE Computer 42(1), 15–20 (2009)
9. Natis, Y.V., Knipp, E., Pezzini, M., Valdes, R.: Cool Vendors in Application Platforms as a Service. Gartner Inc. (2010)
10. Meyer, M.H., Seliger, R.: Product Platforms in Software Development. Sloan Management Review 40(1), 61–74 (1998)
11. Evans, D.S., Hagiu, A., Schmalensee, R.: A Survey of the Economic Role of Software Platforms in Computer-based Industries. CESifo Economic Studies 51(2), 189–224 (2005)
12. Wainewright, P.: Redefining Software Platforms: How PaaS Changes the Game for ISVs. Procullux Media Limited (2009)

The Bullwhip Effect and VM Sprawl
in the Cloud Supply Chain

Maik Lindner, Philip Robinson, Barry McLarnon, and Fiona McDonald

SAP Research (UK) Ltd, The Concourse, Queen's Road,
Queen's Island, Titanic Quarter, Belfast BT3 9DT, UK
{m.lindner,philip.robinson,barry.mclarnon,
fiona.mcdonald}@sap.com

Abstract. The Bullwhip Effect is the result of problems occurring throughout nearly any type of supply chain. Whether it is surges in internal or external defects, every participant in a supply chain need to avoid it. This paper discusses the Bullwhip phenomenon and how it applies to the world of Cloud Computing. Comparisons are made between a traditional supply chain and the Cloud supply chain in order to observe how these relate with each other. This leads to the realisation of the main problem areas within the Cloud supply chain and its main defect, the VM Sprawl. Also we derived indicators for each of the problem areas, which can be seen as a sign of the Bullwhip Effect in a specific Cloud supply chain. Automation and monitoring are also considered, and a prototypical implementation has been developed to support this.

Keywords: Virtualisation, Virtual Machine, VM Sprawl, Monitoring, Automation, Indicators, Mitigation.

1 Motivation

Cloud Computing can be defined as a model for enabling convenient, on-demand network access to a shared pool of easily usable and accessible virtualised resources [1],[2]. The Cloud supply chain, like any other, is a system involving business processes that allow consumer demand to be met. It is the steps involved in manufacturing a product/service from the supplier level to the customer level. In terms of Cloud computing, the supply chain involves the process of transferring funds and information down the supply chain in order to meet the demands of the user. A critical problem in a supply chain known as the Bullwhip Effect negatively influences the business processes causing problems along the supply chain for suppliers and more importantly customers. [3]. "The Bullwhip phenomenon creates large swings in demand on the supply chain resulting from relatively small, but unplanned, variations in consumer demand that escalate with each link in the chain." [4]

Research was carried out around the topic of problems within traditional business supply chains and we decided to use Toyota Motor Corporation as an example of this. We examined their supply chain and its processes in order to extract problem areas and identify how these were solved. This process provided a direction to compare the

M. Cezon and Y. Wolfsthal (Eds.): ServiceWave 2010 Workshops, LNCS 6569, pp. 26–37, 2011.
© Springer-Verlag Berlin Heidelberg 2011

traditional supply chain problems with problems in the Cloud supply chain and in turn lead to the recognition of the problem involved with virtualisation.

The remainder of the paper is structured as follows: In Chapter 2, we analyse the problem of the Bullwhip Effect in a traditional supply chain and identify the problem areas, indicators of these and the mitigation techniques to adapt in order to avoid these problems. These problem areas, indicators and mitigation techniques are then transferred to the Cloud supply chain in Chapter 3. Chapter 4 provides a systems approach to addressing the Bullwhip Effect in the Cloud supply chain, with an emphasis on monitoring and mitigation of VM Sprawl indicators. A prototype is then explained in Chapter 5 and how this can be used to combat the Bullwhip Effect. Finally in Chapter 6, the summary and outlook of future research is provided.

2   Bullwhip in Traditional Supply Chains

2.1   Explanation of Bullwhip

Following a commonly shared definition, a supply chain consists of "two or more parties linked by a flow of goods, information, and funds" [5]. The Bullwhip Effect is a phenomenon described in 1961 by Jay Forrester. The idea behind the Bullwhip Effect illustrates that when a customer places an order, the order fluctuations grow upstream along the supply chain [6]. The Bullwhip Effect suggests that demand uncertainty and variability increases as one moves up a supply chain, decreasing efficiency and profits.

2.2   Identified Problem Areas

Table 1. Problems in Traditional Supply Chains

Problem Area	Indicator	Mitigation
1. Season-caused low demand	High unit costs Too much stock at particular time	Adapt JIT (Just-In-Time) system
2. Lack of effective communication	Delays in transportation of goods and information	Moves geographically close to customers and suppliers
3. Defects in products	Corrective actions required	Adapt continuous improvement (Kaizen)
4. Dispersed supply chain structure	High costs and inefficiency	Suppliers located closer to manufacturing plants
5. Internally dispersed communication structures	Internal communication difficulties	Staff are consolidated into one single communications department
6. Various suppliers for single supply parts	Lack of efficiency on supplier side High communication effort along the supply chain	Same suppliers supply various parts

The Toyota Motor Corporation provides the most prominent case study of the Bullwhip Effect in literature, but it should be noted that other well-known companies like Procter and Gamble and HP (Hewlett and Packard) have also been studied with similar problems reported [6]. Table 1 summarises the problems, indicators and mitigation strategies extracted from this case study. Given that there are established patterns of problems, indicators and mitigation strategies for the Bullwhip Effect, it would be beneficial if a transfer to the problem domain of the Cloud supply chain were identified. This would lead to systematically preventing and recovering from instances of these problems in practice.

3   Bullwhip in Cloud Supply Chains – The Transfer

This section describes how the identified problem areas from the traditional supply chain can be related to the Cloud supply chain by suggesting indicators that may cause Bullwhip Effect, using Fig. 1 as a reference.

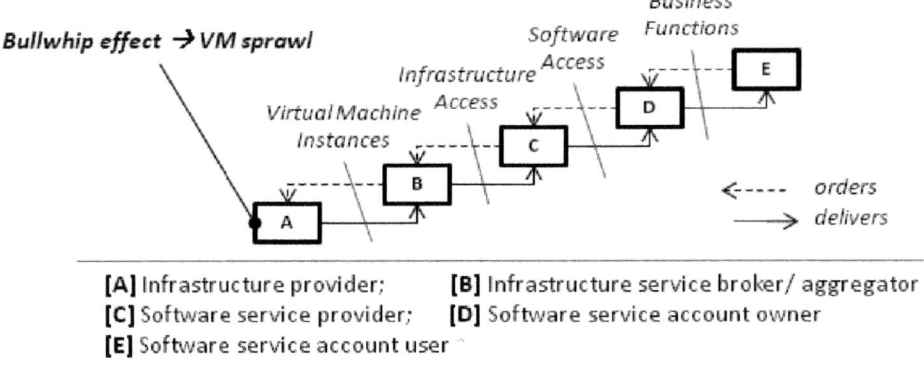

Fig. 1. A generalised Cloud Supply Chain showing upstream and downstream trade between participants

Fig. 1 shows the Infrastructure Provider [**A**] as the most downstream participant in the Cloud Supply Chain. [A] provisions VMs based on the demand from an aggregator [**B**]. Continuing upstream, [**B**]'s decisions for VM orders are based on infrastructure access orders coming from a software service provider [**C**] required to support software access orders from a software service account owner [**D**], who is dedicated to support the business functions of a set of users [**E**]. As the demand from [**E**] dynamically varies, the overall inefficiency of resources consumed in the supply chain propagates downstream to [**A**], arising in a phenomenon known as *VM sprawl*, brought about by the nature of virtualisation.

3.1   Transfer of Problem Areas, Indicators and Mitigation Techniques

Virtualisation is a fundamental enabler of Cloud Computing. It enables individual physical computational resources – storage, memory, compute cycles (CPU) and networking – or machines to be shared amongst several users while still maintaining operational isolation. Virtualisation is now a well understood and frequently-applied technology. It however turns out to be a major contributor to Bullwhip in Cloud supply chains, as discussed in the following. The problem areas derived from the example of the traditional supply chain resulted in a list of Cloud supply chain problem areas and associated indicators that describe the factors that affect virtualisation and therefore contribute negatively to Bullwhip Effect.

1. Problem Area: The ease of creating new Virtual Machines (VMs)

VMs can be created easily to meet last minute and short-term needs and demands [7]. Owners tend to create new machines instead of editing an existing machine to meet their needs.

Indicators:

- Number of VMs: The more VMs created (existing, running, unused), the harder they are to manage.
- Number of running VMs: Some VMs are created for short-term purposes and when no longer required, still exist wasting valuable resources.
- Number of running unused VMs: Lack of monitoring can result in unused VMs existing within the data center, using storage and resources.

Mitigation Technique: With the use of a request portal users can specify a length of time the virtual machine is required for. This would act as a lease and expire when the time is reached to allow for the VM to be decommissioned after confirmation from the owner.

2. Problem Area: Efficiency of data collection and distribution

There tends to be a lack of knowledge concerning where data is being geographically processed, as a result of global networks, as well as processing speeds.

Indicators:

- Value contribution of virtual IT components: This indicator provides an impression of how much a company depends on virtualisation to give an insight into the impact Bullwhip Effect may have on them.
- Affinity of data and computing: To comply with Data Protection regulations, certain data must run on a local Cloud. More complications arise with more affinity such as monitoring, processing speeds and costs.
- Response time of the system: Depending on the location of data and compute, the response time can be affected, therefore affecting the user experience.

Mitigation Technique: This focuses on the geographic location, so choosing a data center geographically close to the system being used would help speed up response times and reduce delays between processing in different locations.

3. Problem Area: Design of virtual machines and processes

Lack of thought on deployment of VMs results in machines not meeting user requirements. This results in the user abandoning their current VM and creating a new machine in order to meet their requirements.

Indicators:

- Percentage of VMs changed post deployment: As a result of user requirements changing, when new machines are created, the old machines are not being used and are utilising valuable resources.
- Percentage of over-provisioned VMs: With no defined procedure put in place for the deployment of virtual machines, they can be over-provisioned and under-utilised, therefore wasting valuable resources.
- Number of VM taking snapshots: VM users tend to keep snapshots of their system, so they can return to a particular state of the system, but this uses a lot of storage capacity within the data center.
- Frequency of snapshots: Saving snapshots frequently can result in a lot of storage being taken up within the data center causing VMs to run slow.

Mitigation Technique: Instead of creating another machine, the user should stop, edit and restart the current machine to suit their needs. This will extend the virtual image by additional pre-installed software.

4. Problem Area: **Supply chain Structure**

This is in relation to where applications or data are located globally. This has an effect on costs, the speed of processing and communication.
Indicators:

- Location of private IT environment: This is important as several Cloud components may be used within the same IT environment which affects response times depending on location of compute and storage capacity.
- Number of public Cloud providers used: The more Clouds used to run virtual machines, the more difficult it is to monitor all of the machines.
- Location capacity of public Cloud providers used: Depending on the location, the costs for running virtual machines on Cloud service providers can vary. It is important for users to know where their data is and how much they are meant to be paying for their service.

Mitigation Technique: Be sure to define in the Service Level Agreement where the data must be processed to ensure local data stays close to the user. This is important to comply with Data Protection Laws and ensure the user is fully informed.

5. Problem Area: **Intra-Cloud Communication Structure**

Effective communication is a key influence for success in any business.
Indicators:

- Heterogeneity of IT environment: The size of the environment as well as the amount and location of VMs affects the transmission of communication and can have a negative impact on the supply chain.
- Structural match of requirements and used resources: Users need to be specific when requesting VMs as this can cause a lot of problems. Using Clouds outside the region of the users can cause difficulties with communication and monitoring.

Mitigation Technique: A shared information model for constant review of the entire IT landscape will make monitoring the environment a lot easier. Problems can be identified and resolved as there is a clear view of the overall activity.

6. Problem Area: **VM image repository management**
Users tend to create new images for VMs depending on what they require when setting up a virtual machine instead of using a base image that is already made.
Indicators:

- Number of identical base images: Base images are being duplicated so the same image may exist several times causing image overload which is unnecessary.
- Match of user requirements and software setup of base images: When users develop further requirements, they may create new base images to meet these needs, which is wasteful.

Mitigation Technique: Use a catalogue of predefined images in fixed sizes (S, M, L, XL) so users can copy, clone and customise these base images instead of creating new base images. If a user requires a new image that is not in the catalogue, approval should be requested before the image can be created.

3.2 Explanation of Bullwhip Effect Indicators for the Identified Problem Areas

Each of the indicators relate to different problem areas that have been identified within the Cloud supply chain. The indicators are both qualitative and quantitative and have been converted into questions for the user to understand what is being asked. Each of the answers of these questions have weighted values depending on the overall importance of the influence it has on Bullwhip Effect. Overall, the indicators have different benchmarks depending on the size of the IT environment that is being assessed. Some of the indicators would hold a higher value for a small company, at the same time holding an average value for a large company. The indicators are designed to address all of the issues and factors that cause problems for IT environments or for virtual machines to perform properly.

The quantitative indicators are the questions that prompt the user to answer with a number. These quantitative answers provide the data for the calculations in order to determine the scale of Bullwhip Effect. The qualitative indicators prompt the user for an insight into the factors affecting their IT environment, such as the value of IT components to their work. Depending on the answers to these questions, the value of the answer varies. It is important to ask both quantitative and qualitative questions in order to be able to offer a reliable, accurate indication of the risk of Bullwhip Effect to an IT environment. Each of these indicators exist to evaluate the affect virtualisation has on an IT environment. Virtualisation has the benefit of providing virtual resources to meet user's needs; however the drawback of this is the amount of storage space that is usually wasted. Security is also an issue, as it is more difficult to enforce measures with a lot of machines.

4   A Systems Approach to Tackling Bullwhip Effect in Practice

This chapter describes how Bullwhip Effect can be systematically reduced in the Cloud supply chain, focusing on how the prevention, detection and mitigation of Virtual Machine (VM) Sprawl can be managed within IT environments.

4.1   VM Sprawl as a Sub-Effect of Bullwhip

VM Sprawl is a major negative side-effect of virtual infrastructures. It occurs when many unused VMs continue to consume resources (energy, CPU, memory, storage, licenses). It is a consequence of VM creation being straightforward and lacking control which results in over-provisioning or VMs using resources and storage that they no longer need [8], and without explicit mapping to a specific business need [9]. Due to the ease of creating VMs and the unrestricted storage capacity available, they tend to increase in quantity over time and can cause VM Sprawl. Bourdeau also identified this as a problem in his paper "Controlling VM Sprawl" [10]. He identifies the root of VM Sprawl and adapts the concept "Reduce, Reuse, Recycle". Every VM has a resource cost, therefore costs are a considerable problem caused by VM Sprawl. The costs include infrastructure, software, licensing and operational costs [11]. Desai [13] also identifies a number of best practices to prevent and manage VM Sprawl, which are consistent with our systems approach. These include creating and enforcing deployment policies, detecting and addressing unauthorised VMs, managing security and compliance in virtual environments and managing the entire VM lifecycle.

Several companies have released virtual machine managers that monitor and report on virtual machines, as well as automate mitigation strategies. Embotics [12] appears to be leading the market currently, based on independent reports, with respect to explicit solutions for tackling VM Sprawl in virtualisation management. Their solution can also be integrated with many of the leading virtualisation technology vendors. We hence treat them as representative of the industry. Their solutions enforce policies on virtual machines and alert members of management of problems via e-mail. There are other companies on the market that have solutions to virtual machine management such as BMC Software [13], EMC [14] and Jamcracker [15].

4.2   Initialisation of VM Sprawl Monitoring and Assessment with Organisational and Technical Factors

Any organisation using virtualisation can experience Bullwhip Effect. Depending on the size of the IT environment, the indication of Bullwhip Effect will vary. For e.g. to state that a company should have no more than 300 VMs is too general. The implications are different based on the size, IT dependency and activities of the organisation in question. Consider the operational difference between a small organisation (10 – 50 personnel) with 250 active VM instances versus a large company (500 – 1000 personnel) with 350 instances. The generic indicator would inaccurately resolve that the large company was experiencing VM Sprawl, when it is the case for the small organisation. The template in Figure 2 is defined to initialise the process of information gathering and Bullwhip indicator assessment.

A similar problem would occur if the indicators were not tuned against the activity, usage and operational profiles of the organisation and resources under study. We make the assumption that these preliminary variables are inserted manually at the beginning of an assessment, but we can imagine them being automatically acquired from traces or on-line observation over time.

```
$userbase=?        #{small, medium, large}
$app-variance=?    #{simple, normal, abnormal}
$time-unit=?       #{ss, mm, hh, dd, ww, mm, yy}
$cpu-prof=?        #Estimated CPU Utilisation peaks per
                   time-unit
$access-prof=?     #Estimated Access peaks per time-unit
$storage-prof=?    #Storage growth per time-unit
$retention=?       #Legal retention in time-unit
$redundancy=[y/n]  #Indicates if it is a mirror or
                   backup for other instances
$dependents=[y/n]  #Indicates if there are other
                   dependent instances
```

Fig. 2. Initialisation template with preliminary variables for VM Sprawl Assessment

The $userbase variable denotes the size of the organisation and its IT usage profile. The $app-variance gives an idea of how variant the IT needs and functions are in the organisation. There are then 3 usage profile variables - $cpu-prof, $access-prof and $storage-prof- for CPU, I/O and storage usage respectively. The $time-unit variable is necessary, as every organisation monitors and evaluates its IT usage with different frequency cycles. These profiles assist the correctness of the determining if a VM instance's idleness period is contributing to sprawl or if this is a natural consequence of its intended usage. However, there are also legal reasons to keep VMs active, including contractual and auditory obligations. The $retention variable is used to capture this. An instance might also be in an idle state as it is part of a recovery or scalability strategy, indicated by the $redundancy flag, or holds state information that is critical for other instances, indicated by the $dependents flag.

The manual analysis and assessment of VM Sprawl is not trivial and includes many different variables. The above variables help to move the assessment from being general to a point where it is tailored for a specific environment. There is therefore a need to employ automated techniques for monitoring, information gathering and visualising indicators.

4.3 Architecture for Monitoring and Assessment of VM Sprawl Risk

Monitoring and assessment of VM Sprawl risk supports ongoing prevention and mitigation of VM Sprawl occurrences. The architecture in Figure 3 includes the systems components required for implementing these processes. It is an automated architecture but could also be developed in an "offline" mode that allows users to start with a high-level assessment of the VM Sprawl situation for the IT environment under study. Moreover, a combination of offline and online monitoring and assessment covers the entire lifecycle of VMs and virtual infrastructure, as planning and post-runtime auditing typically occur before or after VM instances are operational. Secondly, the information provided by such a tool needs to be tailored to the capabilities and needs of the receiver.

The Bullwhip Effect Indicator is the presentation layer of the architecture. The presentation layer connects to the management layer via two APIs for initialisation/tuning (Init API) and for execution of specific queries (Query API).

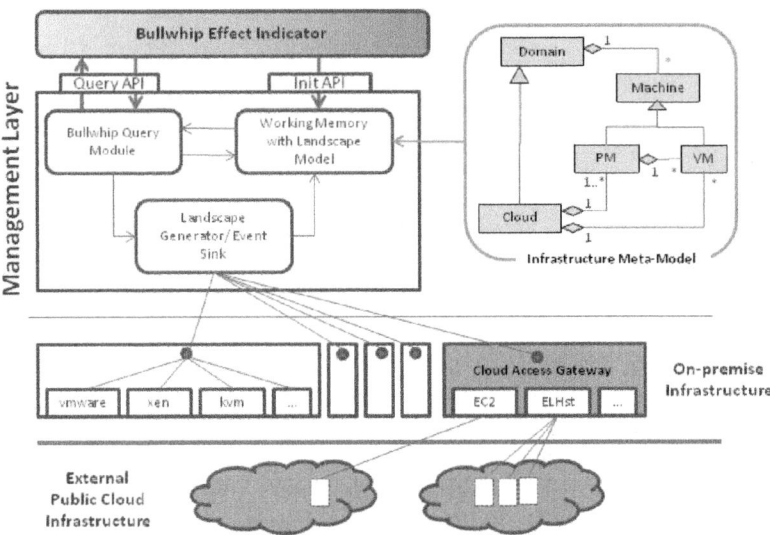

Fig. 3. High-level monitoring architecture for the monitoring and assessment of VM Sprawl

The Init API is used to set the variables in the initialisation template of Figure 3. The Query API allows predefined and extended queries to be pushed to the management layer, where there is a Bullwhip Query Module for handling these queries. This module retrieves state information from the Working Memory of the management layer for specific managed elements.

The managed elements are classified using the Infrastructure Meta-Model in Figure 3 and the operational instance of the meta-model is called the Landscape Model. The meta-model states that a Domain consists of multiple Machines, where a Machine can be physical (PM) or virtual (VM). A PM then hosts multiple VMs and a Cloud is a specific instance of a Domain. All queries used to address the questions in the Bullwhip Effect Indicator can be answered using this data model. The details of these objects are not provided here, but can be understood as descriptive and qualitative attributes of these components including instances, users, capacity and utilisation.

The Landscape Generator is a central Event Sink that is connected to various probes and event generators in the on-premise IT environment and Infrastructure. For each class of object in the meta-model there exists a probe. However, given that there are multiple technologies used to realise virtualisation in an IT environment, different probes or extensions have to be written for the different technologies involved. For example, as shown in Figure 3, the probe access point is connected to specialisations for VMware, XEN and KVM, or any other type of virtualisation technology to be included in the infrastructure. Within the Cloud supply chain organisations are users and providers of virtualised resources.

In the same way that different probe extensions are required for different virtualisation technologies, different extensions are required for different Cloud providers, bar a standard for Cloud monitoring is established. We currently assume that the capabilities of Amazon's EC2 CloudWatch web service allows Cloud consumers to monitor their instances [16]. This allows a number of metrics to be monitored and reported, although there is a degree of uncertainty introduced that is not present in the purely on-premise case. There are numerous tools on the market that could be used to enhance the collation of data from external and private sources. The details of these are not critical for the description of the architecture and the prototype.

5   Bullwhip Effect Indicator Prototype

The indicators are used to structure the design of a dash-board for decision makers in a Cloud supply chain. They can be addressed in either an offline or online manner. The offline mode offers the tool as a questionnaire, while the online mode connects it to the Init and Query APIs of the management architecture described in Section 4.3.

5.1   Transfer of Indicators to Prototype

In order to make the tool more interactive and effective Business Objects Xcelsius was used for the development of the prototype as shown in Figure 4.

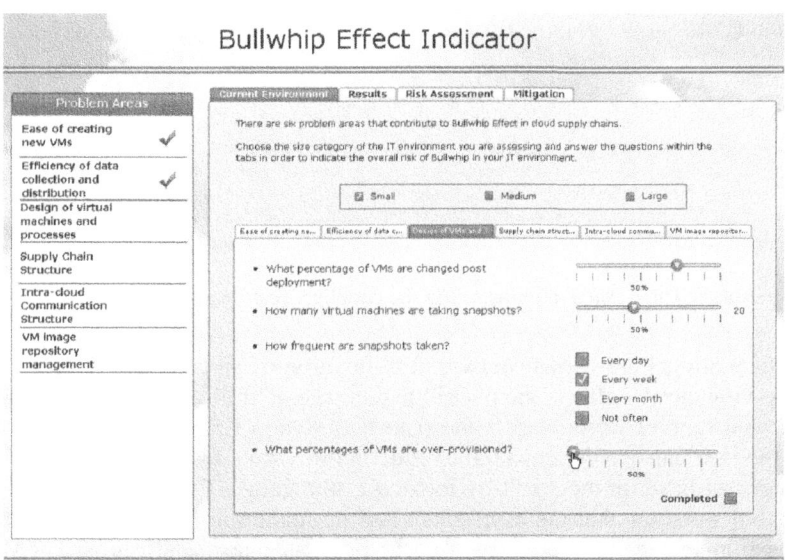

Fig. 4. Screenshot of Indication tool created using Xcelsius

Instead of the user manually entering the number of VMs to answer the question, the application provided features such as, tabs, check boxes, spinners and sliders. With the use of these features, options were given where the user could select only one or multiple answers. Most of the questions provide the user with a slider, so they can input the estimated answer as a percentage of their overall VMs. This ensures that the tool does not rely on specific data that would be difficult for the user to retrieve in a short period of time. Some of the qualitative questions provide check boxes with a selection of options for the user to choose from. Depending on which size category the user selects, the questions will appear with different defined values for each question.

5.2 Bullwhip Effect Equaliser Indicator

The results tab gives the user an overall percentage of Bullwhip Effect. It is designed to give users the knowledge of what mitigation is through the equaliser facility.

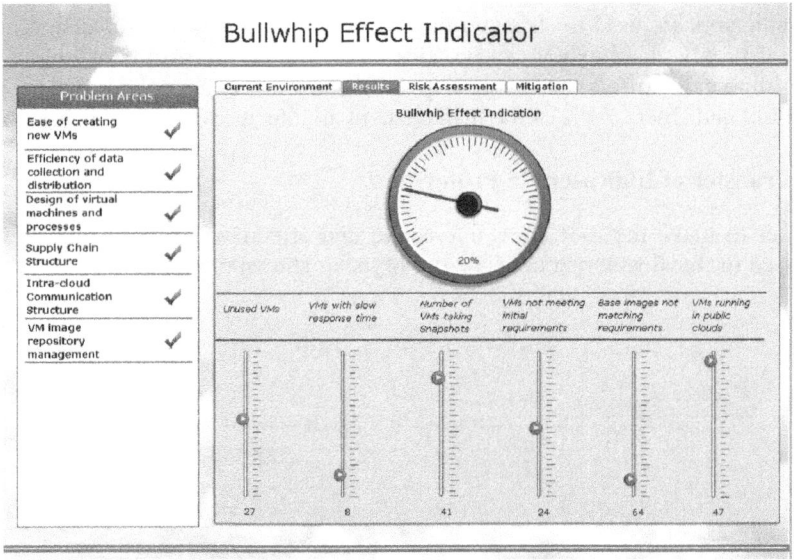

Fig. 5. The *Results* tab illustrating the equaliser feature and overall indication

Vertical sliders are used to provide the function of an equaliser. Users can adjust these to view how it affects the overall percentage of Bullwhip Effect and understand better what type of factors affect the risk of Bullwhip Effect. Simply by moving the slider the user can see the impact the reduction in virtual machines within a particular indicator can have on the result by looking at the gauge. Even with the offline mode of the tool we show that the assessment and mitigation are tuned to the needs of the organisation increasing their capability to prevent, detect and mitigate VM Sprawl and the Bullwhip Effect in their Cloud supply chain.

6 Summary and Outlook

By extracting problem areas from a traditional supply chain, we were able to develop problem areas, indicators and therefore mitigation techniques for the Cloud supply chain. We will carry out further research into this topic, in order to develop a system that automatically monitors Bullwhip Effect in a live environment. This would be a method of continuous improvement, as the environment would be constantly being monitored and the indication of Bullwhip Effect would change accordingly. We will also conduct research into automating the mitigation techniques that have been identified, developing a fully live and automated system for the management and elimination of Bullwhip. By adapting these mitigation techniques, where and when needed, Bullwhip Effect can be managed easily. Also establishing a cross supply chain information system can aid to the elimination of Bullwhip Effect in IT supply chains.

References

[1] Mell, P., Grance, T.: The NIST Definition of Cloud Computing (July 2009)
[2] Lindner, M.: A Break in the Clouds: Towards a Cloud Definition (January 2009)
[3] Wangphanich, P., Kara, S., Kayis, B.: A Simulation Model of Bullwhip Effect in a Multi-Stage Chain (2007)
[4] Griffin, D.: Define the Bullwhip Effect (2010), http://www.ehow.co.uk/about_6465225_define-bullwhip-effect.html
[5] Paulitsch, M.: Dynamic Coordination of Supply Chains (2003)
[6] Lee, H.L., Padmanabhan, V., Whang, S.: The Bullwhip Effect In Supply Chains (1997)
[7] Combating Virtual Machine Sprawl — EnterpriseStorageForum.com, http://www.enterprisestorageforum.com/management/features/article.php/3772841/Combating-Virtual-Machine-Sprawl.htm
[8] Sprawl Control | DynamicOps, http://www.dynamicops.com/solutions/sprawl-control/default.cfm
[9] Virtualization FAQ: What is VM Sprawl, http://www.virtualizationadmin.com/faq/vm-sprawl.html
[10] Rich Bourdeau, Controlling VM Sprawl - How to better utilize your virtual infrastructure (2010)
[11] The Costs of Virtual Sprawl, http://www.forbes.com/2009/12/01/embotics-computers-enterprise-technology-cio-network-virtualization.html
[12] Embotics Eases Management of Virtual Environments, http://www.eweek.com/c/a/Virtualization/Embotics-Eases-Management-of-Virtual-Environments-306988/
[13] BMC Software - Business Runs on IT, http://www.bmc.com/index.html
[14] EMC, http://uk.emc.com/index.htm
[15] Jamcracker | Unifying Cloud Services, http://www.jamcracker.com/
[16] Amazon CloudWatch, http://aws.amazon.com/cloudwatch/

Using Service Level Agreements for Optimising Cloud Infrastructure Services

Andy Lawrence[1], Karim Djemame[3], Oliver Wäldrich[2],
Wolfgang Ziegler[2], and Csilla Zsigri[1]

[1] The 451 Group, London, WC1E6HH, United Kingdom
{csilla.zsigri,andy.lawrence}@the451group.com
[2] Fraunhofer Institute SCAI, 53754 Sankt Augustin, Germany
{oliver.waeldrich,wolfgang.zieglerl}@scai.fraunhofer.de
[3] School of Computing University of Leeds, Leeds, United Kingdom
karim@comp.leeds.ac.uk

Abstract. Current Cloud environments are offered to their customers in a best effort approach. Instead of guarantees a statistical uptime expectation is communicated to the user with minimal compensations in case of unexpected downtime. In contrast, a service provider intending e.g. to extend his own resources dynamically with Cloud resources in case of peak demands of his customers needs a reliable Service Level Agreement with the Cloud infrastructure provider. This Service Level Agreement must cover aspects like cost, security, legal requirements for data-placement, eco-efficiency and more. The European project OPTI-MIS is focussing on optimisation of cloud infrastructure services meeting demands from service providers, e.g. when public and private Clouds are federated in different configurations. This paper describes the approach of OPTIMIS for negotiating and creating Service Level Agreements between infrastructure providers and service providers.

1 Introduction

So far, electronic Service Level Agreements are rarely used in Clouds to define and agree upon the QoS the Cloud provider will deliver to its customers regardless whether the customer is an end-user or a service provider. Instead Cloud environments are offered to their customers in a best effort approach. Instead of guarantees a statistical uptime expectation is communicated to the user, e.g. 99.95%in case of Amazon EC2, with minimal compensations in case of unexpected downtime. In contrast, a service provider intending e.g. to extend his own resources dynamically with Cloud resources in case of peak demands of his customers needs a reliable Service Level Agreement with the Cloud infrastructure provider. This Service Level Agreement must cover aspects like cost, security, legal requirements for data-placement, eco-efficiency and more. The European project OPTIMIS [9] is focussing on optimisation of multi-cloud infrastructure services meeting demands from service providers, e.g. when public and private Clouds are federated in different configurations, e.g. busting into the cloud, federation of a private and a public Cloud, federation of two public Clouds. This

M. Cezon and Y. Wolfsthal (Eds.): ServiceWave 2010 Workshops, LNCS 6569, pp. 38–49, 2011.

paper describes the approach of OPTIMIS for negotiating and creating Service Level Agreements between infrastructure providers (IP) and service providers (SP).

The remainder of the paper is organised as follows. Section 2 presents related work. Section 3 discusses general aspects of Service Level Management (SLM) and where SLM is used in OPTIMIS. Section 4 presents the technology for creating the Service Level Agreements in OPTIMIS. Relevant properties identified in OPTIMIS for describing QoS and elasticity are described in Section 4.1 and three examples for term languages are presented in Section 4.2, 4.3 and 4.4. The paper concludes with a summary and plans for future work.

2   Related Work

Only limited research has been focusing on SLAs for Clouds. In [11] an approach for using SLA in a single cloud scenario is presented. In case of SLA violation a penalty mechanism is activated rather than dynamically extending the hardware resources provided. Moreover, despite the fact the authors complain about missing standards in this area they propose using IBM's proprietary solution developed 5 years ago. In 2010 [3] addresses challenges for IaaS, identifying Service Level Agreements as one of them which attracted little attention so far. IBM recently published a review and summary of cloud service level agreements [5] as part of their Cloud Computing Use Cases Whitepaper [6], which suggests SLA requirements and metrics for Cloud environments. However, this is not linked to any concrete implementation. To our best knowledge currently there is no related work on using Service Level Agreements between a service provider and an infrastructure provider to maintain the agreed upon QoS of the infrastructure services and those of the service provider depending on the infrastructure.

3   Service Level Management

The management of Service Level Agreements (SLA) is a key aspect in distributed resource management. SLAs represent a contractual relationship between a service consumer (e.g. the Service Provider) and a service provider (e.g. the Infrastructure Provider). SLAs describe the service that is delivered, the functional and non-functional properties of the service, and the obligations of each party involved (e.g. which party is the provider of the service). Additionally, SLAs define guarantees for the functional and non-functional service properties. These guarantees specify a service level objective that must be met in order to fulfil a guarantee, and they define compensations in form of penalties and rewards which are charged in case the guarantee is fulfilled or violated respectively. The WS-Agreement standard of the Open Grid Forum (OGF) is a well-accepted standard for creating and monitoring SLAs in distributed environments. The WSAG4J framework [12] is an implementation of the WS-Agreement standard [1]. It provides comprehensive support for common SLA management tasks such as SLA template management, SLA negotiation and creation, and SLA monitoring and accounting.

The OPTIMIS Service Level Management (SLM) component integrates with multiple components of the OPTIMIS toolkit. These components are in particular Admission Control, the Service Monitoring, the Service Optimizer, and the Cloud Optimizer.

- Admission Control (actors involved SP, IP)
  In order to negotiate and create SLAs with a service consumer (in case of OPTIMIS the SP), the service provider (in case of OPTIMIS the IP) must assert that the agreed service can be provided. When a SLA is created with the service consumer, the SLA management component of the service provider initiates the service deployment process.
- Service Monitoring (actors involved SP, IP)
  Each provider that offers SLAs for a particular service should also perform SLA aware service monitoring in order to detect possible SLA violations and to take appropriate counter measures. The SLA monitoring component therefore integrates with the Service Monitoring, which provides the required monitoring data to assess the fulfillment of the service level objectives defined in a SLA at runtime. SLA monitoring is a continuous process during the lifetime of an SLA and is performed on regular base. The evaluation of the SLA guarantees results in corresponding events, which are then processed other components, such as SLA accounting (penalties and rewards), the service optimizer, or the cloud optimizer.
- Service Optimizer (actor involved SP)
  The service optimizer consumes events generated by the SLA monitoring of the SP. According to the event type and its importance, the service optimizer takes appropriate measures in order to fulfill the guarantees given in the SLA. These measures may include starting up or shutting down a VM using the elasticity engine.
- Cloud Optimizer (actor involved IP)
  The cloud optimizer consumes events generated by the SLA monitoring of the IP. According to the event type and its importance, the cloud optimizer takes appropriate measures in order to fulfill the guarantees given in the SLA. These measures may include starting up or shutting down a VM using the elasticity engine, or to migrate a VM using the fault tolerance engine.

4   Service Level Agreements

The OPTIMIS Cloud SLM component is based on the WS-Agreement for Java implementation (WSAG4J) of the Fraunhofer Institute SCAI. Figure 1 depicts the components of WSAG4J, which are briefly described in the following paragraphs.

- The API Module
  This module contains interface definitions and implementations that are shared by the different modules of the framework (not shown in the Figure 1 since it is used by all modules).
- The WSAG4J Client Module
  This module is an implementation of the client API defined in the API module. It is implemented for accessing the WSAG4J web service stack.
- The SLA Engine Module
  This module is the core of the WSAG4J framework. It provides a generic implementation of a WS-Agreement based SLA engine. It implements the standard functionality for processing agreement offers, creating agreements, monitoring the agreements' runtime states, and evaluating and accounting agreement guarantees. Agreement acceptance policies and business logic for instantiating and monitoring SLA aware services can easily plugged in.
- TheWSAG4J Web Service Module
  This module implements the remote frontend for the WSAG4J engine. It implements the WS-Agreement port types and delegates the calls to the WSAG4J engine, if necessary. The web service module is implemented on the base of the Apache Muse framework [8]. This framework provides the WSRF [13] container required by the WS-Agreement specification.
- The Server Distribution
  This module comprises the WSAG4J server including the web service stack, the SLA engine and all required configurations. It is a packaged web application archive which can easily deployed in a wide set of application servers.

An agreement consists of the agreement name, its context and the agreement terms. The context contains information about the involved parties and metadata

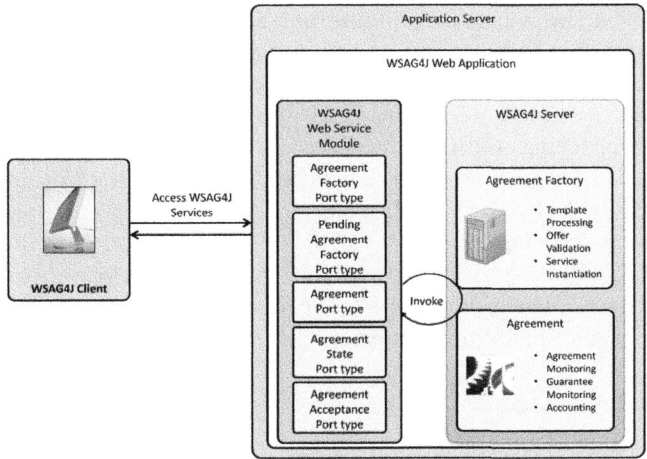

Fig. 1. Components of WSAG4J

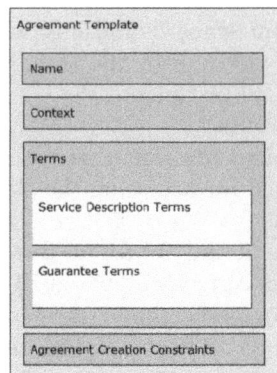

Fig. 2. Agreement Template

such as the duration of the agreement. Agreement terms define the content of an agreement: Service Description Terms (SDTs) define the functionality that is delivered under an agreement. A SDT includes a domain-specific description of the offered or required functionality (the service itself). Guarantee Terms define assurance on service quality of the service described by the SDTs. They define Service Level Objectives (SLOs), which describe the quality of service aspects of the service that have to be fulfilled by the provider. The Web Services Agreement Specification allows the usage of any domain specific or standard condition expression language to define SLOs. The specification of domain-specific term languages is explicitly left open. Figure 2 shows the structure of an Agreement template, which is basically the same as that of an Agreement, except that the final Agreement does not contain Agreement Creation Constraints. Agreement templates are provided by the respective service provider and capture the services and their properties a provider is offering. SLA Negotiation [2] and creation of agreements are based on agreement templates that will be refined in the process and finally used to create the agreement.

Once an agreement is in force it is possible to query the individual agreements to retrieve monitoring information based on the states of the agreement terms. To that end the service provider must feed the relevant information collected and made available by the OPTIMIS Service Monitoring component. Based on the evaluation of the individual service term states it can be decided whether an agreement is fulfilled or risks to be violated if no appropriate countermeasures are taken. The sequence diagram shown in Figure 3 summarises the necessary steps to query monitoring information from an agreement.

4.1   Term Languages

In order to provide SLA-aware infrastructure services with extended QoS capabilities the SLA management layer requires capabilities to detect resources underperforming with respect to the SLAs defined or just failing completely. In case of resource performance degradation the infrastructure service should

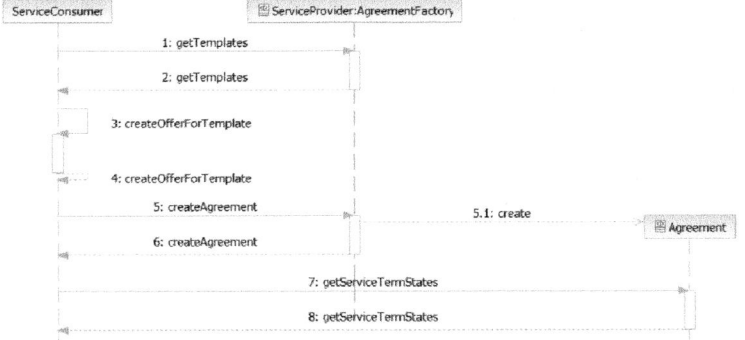

Fig. 3. SLA monitoring

be migrated to a new hardware resource in order to adhere to the guarantees defined in the SLA. Migration could for example be realised on the base of the checkpoint-restart model or using the functionalities of the virtualisation layer. When an infrastructure service is instantiated, it should be possible to define the required checkpoint interval. The OPTIMIS VM placement supports the migration of VMs (e.g. in case of performance degradation) as well as the restart of VMs (e.g. in case of resource failures). Infrastructure monitoring services will provide the required monitoring data for determining resource failures and performance degradation. To be able to decide whether the guarantees for terms of a Service Level Agreement have been fulfilled or have been violated the Service Level Agreement service needs monitoring information. Depending on the terms agreed upon in a Service Level Agreement the monitoring information required concerns different QoS parameters. In OPTIMIS we initially consider the following parameters

- Eco-efficiency
- QoS parameters of the computing infrastructure
- Application specific parameter
- Cost
- Legal constraints (e.g. for VM and data placement)
- Trust
- Scurity

Term languages to express the different types of QoS parameters according to the areas Service Level Agreements are created in OPTIMIS and to express guarantees, respective penalties and rewards will be defined based on requirements of IPs and SPs and the end-users. For some of the term languages we use existing ones while term languages that do not exist wil be defined in OPTIMIS and fed into a standardisation process around WS-Agreement at the Open Grid Forum. In the following sections we present the initial parameters we identified for use in OPTIMIS SLAs to express hardware parameters and parameters of VMs, parameters for eco-efficiency and parameters for the expression of risk.

Table 1. Monitoring information of the physical IT infrastructure

Parameter	Description	Data type	Example
IP address	IP address of a physical node	String	x.y.z.w
Virtual domains	A list of the virtual domains of a node	List	<dom0, dom1>
Architecture	The node's architecture	String	amd64
# CPUs	The number of CPUs of a node	Integer	8
CPUs' speed	The speed of the CPUs (in MHz)	Integer	3000 MHz
Memory	The amount of memory (in megabytes) of a given node	Integer	8000 MB
Free Memory	The amount of free memory (in megabytes)	Integer	2000 MB
Bandwidth	The bandwidth available on the node (in Kbytes/sec)	Integer	10 Kbytes/sec
Disk space	The amount of disk space (in megabytes) available in a node	Integer	1000000 MB

4.2   Hardware Parameters

The end-user of services deployed in an OPTIMIS enhanced Cloud environment is expected to express its requests concerning the QoS delivered by the service provider in an abstract, high level language. This language then needs to be mapped to technical terms the service provider can enter in his service manifest that describes the capabilities requested from the infrastructure provider. On the level of the communication with the infrastructure service provider it seems most appropriate and unambiguous to use terms describing properties of hardware or virtual machines needed to fulfil the performance requirements of a service provider (and its client in the background). As a good starting point the information initially provided by the OPTIMIS monitoring is considered. The information expected to be available from the monitoring is described in Table 1.

Besides the properties of the hardware OPTIMIS also considers the characteristics of VMs when creating SLAs between infrastructure provider and service provider. Again, we will use information expected to be available from the monitoring as described in Table 2.

As potential formats to be used for the machine processable description two different approaches have been evaluated:

- the Job Submission Description Language (JSDL), a standard of the Open Grid Forum [7]
- the Open Virtualization Format Specification (OVF), a specification of the Distributed Management Task Force [10]

JSDL was originally developed to describe resource requirements for job requests . As such, JSDL contains several attributes, which are also applicable

Table 2. Set of virtual IT-infrastructure parameters

Parameter	Description	Data type	Example
State	The VM's state	String	Running
IP address	IP address of a VM	String	x.y.z.w
Virtual domain	The virtual domain where a VM is running	String	dom0
Architecture	The system's architecture of a VM	String	x86
# CPUs	The number of CPUs available on the VM	Integer	4
CPUs' speed	The speed of the CPUs (in MHz)	Integer	3000 MHz
CPU allocated	The CPU capacity (i.e. #CPUs*100) dynamically assigned to a VM	Integer	300
CPU usage	The current usage of CPU (in %)	Float	0.25
Memory	The amount of memory (in megabytes) allocated to a VM	Integer	1000 MB
Memory Usage	The current usage of memory (in %)	Float	0.118
Bandwidth	The bandwidth of a VM (in Kbytes/sec)	Integer	10 Kbytes/sec
Disk space	The amount of disk space (in megabytes) available in a given VM	Integer	2000 MB

describing hardware properties. JSDL can also be extended using profiles addressing specific hardware properties such are not covered by the default schema.

In contrast the Open Virtualization Format Specification describes an extensible format for the packaging and distribution of software to be run in virtual machines. The specifications allows describing properties of virtual machines and similar to JSDL provides extension points.

Since both specifications are defined in form of XML documents both fit well in WS-Agreement. After evaluation the project decided to use OVF with OPTIMIS specific extensions because of its origin in and focus on virtualisation.

4.3 Eco-Efficiency Parameters

The core measurable for eco-efficiency are standard: Energy (in kilowatts per hour per process) and Carbon (in CO2e) associated with operational energy. In addition, there are a number of ways, beyond basic energy use, that datacenter operators can demonstrate eco-efficiency. Some of these are appearing in contracts and could appear in legal contracts. Conformance to these should, therefore, be considered. The following are likely to be commonly used:

- PUE (power usage effectiveness). This measures the infrastructure overhead of the facility and is a measure of the energy efficiency of the datacentre (but not the IT equipment).

Table 3. Basic parameters that will be used in the SLA relating to eco-efficiency

Terms and parameters	Metric
Energy used for task or resource	KWh
CO_2 per task or resource	KG CO_2
Kg of CO_2 offset	KG CO_2
Kg of CO_2 covered by renewable energy certifcates	KG CO_2
The centres annualized average PUE? (last 12 months)	Range 1 - 2.5
Is the centre European Code of Conduct for Datacentre compliant?	Yes/No
Does the centre have an Energy Star for Datacentre rating?	Points range or star rating, no
Is the centre LEED (or BREEAM) for datacentre rated?	Platinum, Gold, Silver, Bronze, no

- Conformance to the EU Code of Conduct (COC) for Datacenters. This sets out best practices and operators must endorse the code or be a full signatory.
- Energy Star for Datacentres. This US driven certification of energy efficiency will be promoted across the world.
- LEED or BREEAM for datacentres. These two competing standards rate a datacenter for the positive impact on the environment.

Table 3 summarizes the initial set of basic terms that will be used in the SLA relating to eco-efficiency.

The Need for Further Sustainability Fields. It may be necessary to add to extra criteria to the SLAs to establish participation in wider standards efforts. For example, ISO 14064 greenhouse gas reporting and verification, or conformance to other reporting protocols (CDP, GHG protocol). However, at present, this is not likely to be required during the lifetime of the OPTIMIS project. It will also be advisable to allow for development of new Green Grid datacenter and IT efficiency standards. Further complications that have to be considered when federarion comes into play: The use of multiple datacentres may complicate the SLA, because eco-efficiency factors can change dramatically from datacenter to datacenter. This may affect overall construction of the SLA, but will most likely not affected the terminology.

Optimising for Energy Efficiency. It may be necessary to add to the SLA for providers or consumers who want to optimize energy efficiency. It is not clear if this is fully within the initial scope of OPTIMIS and will need further discussion. Currently this is discussed in OPTIMIS and will require further exploration. For example:

1. The service provider is able to offer the consumer a choice of datacenters, or halls, within their service; or even a choice of servers in order to save energy. (This choice may be required for privacy and other legal reasons anyway).
2. The service provider is able to offer reduced performance or demand-sensitive low energy or low carbon options, which may involve, for example, the task taking longer, or being scheduled when demand is low.
3. The service provider is able to offer a premium service that involves the use of low energy equipment, renewable energy, carbon offsets etc.

At this stage, it is not yet clear how these will be represented in the SLA. OPTIMIS and the European project FIT4Green [4] that addresses energy aware ICT optimization policies will cooperate on the definition of a meaningful standardised set of terms. OPTIMIS will then come up with a consolidated list of terms and the corresponding XML schema relevant to express eco-efficiency requirements in the SLAs.

4.4   Expressing the Risk Level

The following high-level descriptions of the core OPTIMIS actors, relevant to the Risk Assessment tools, provide an overview of the term language to be found in SLAs with respect to risk assessment:

End-user. The end-user can specify the risk expressed in a 3 colour traffic-light system, which green corresponding to a low probability, orange to a medium probability and red to a high probability.

Infrastructure Provider. From the perspective of the IP, SLAs represent commitments to meet the objectives specified therein. Without a means of formally evaluating the risk and expected impact of potentially negative events, an IP provider faces serious difficulties and potential risk in deciding upon the feasibility of admitting a new service following a request for quotes from the SDO. Therefore, IP's risk assessment will enable the identification of infrastructure bottlenecks and mitigate potential risk, in some cases by identifying fault-tolerance mechanisms to prevent SLA violations. Risk is represented by the Probability of Failure (PoF), which is the probability estimated by the infrastructure provider's Admission Controller (AC) that the SLA might fail. It is expressed in five levels: very low, low, medium, high and very high, which are corresponding to a very low, low, medium, high and very high PoF respectively . The values are specified by the Service Provider. Note that the SLA is constantly monitored during the service operation, especially the risk associated with its failure, which may be caused by risky events as identified in the IP's risk inventory. In such situation, risk management takes place: risk reduction by initiating fault tolerance (FT) mechanisms, risk transfer by outsourcing to a third party, or risk acceptance by violating the SLA.

Service Provider. The Service Deployment Optimizer (SDO) provides the functionality to evaluate the risk associated with an offer returned by the Infrastructure Provider's Admission Controller (AC). It is necessary to incorporate provider reliability into this risk assessment process, in order to verify the expected integrity of an IP's guarantees when they make any offer. Consequently, the SP's role can determine the reputation and trustworthiness of an IP.

The Risk Assessor component provides the logic used by the Confidence Service to compute a reliability measure and if necessary a risk assessment. It does this using a Data Access Object (DAO) component and the IP's Distinguishing Name (DN) to retrieve past and present SLA, Trust, Risk, Eco-efficiency, and Cost (TREC) factors and Monitoring data from a historical database. The Risk Assessor uses this data to determine the reliability of the offered PoF value from the IP's SLA and pass this to the SDO for evaluation. It returns a reliability object which contains the IP's name, the number of SLAs, TREC factors and monitoring data on which the reliability is based, a reliability measure and an adjusted PoF.

The Adjusted risk Probability of Failure (PoF) is the probability that the provider may fail, but estimated by an independent and non-biased third party (the Service Provider risk assessor). Note that the SLA is constantly monitored during the service operation, especially the risk associated with its failure, which may be caused by risky events as identified in the SP's risk inventory. In such situation, risk management takes place by notifying the SDO, which, by considering other factors of TREC together, may invoke risk reduction by initiating FT mechanisms, risk transfer by outsourcing to a third party, or risk acceptance by violating the SLA.. In case such risky events take place, the corresponding management tools are also notified.

5   Conclusions and Future Work

We presented an approach for Service Level Management in a multi-cloud environment. The SLA technology used is based on WS-Agreement using the Java implementation WSAG4J. Next steps of the OPTIMIS project are full definition of the missing term languages and their rendering as XML schema. Once these steps have been completed the integration with the OPTIMIS monitoring, Admission Control, Service Optimiser, and Cloud Optimiser will be tackled. The SLA framework is already available at [12] for download. A first version of the integrated OPTIMIS toolkit will be available mid of 2011 through the OPTIMIS web-site.

Acknowledgements. Work reported in this paper has been co-funded by the European Commissions ICT programme in the FP7 project OPTIMIS under grant #257115 and by the German Federal Ministry of Education and Research in the D-Grid project under grant #01AK800A.

References

1. Andrieux, A., Czajkowski, K., Dan, A., Keahey, K., Ludwig, H., Nakata, T., Pruyne, J., Rofrano, J., Tuecke, S., Xu, M.: Web services agreement specification (ws-agreement). Gwd-r (recommendation), Open Grid Forum, GFD.107 recommendation (2010), http://www.ogf.org/documents/GFD.107.pdf
2. Battré, D., Brazier, F.M.T., Clark, K.P., Oey, M., Papaspyrou, A., Wäldrich, O., Wieder, P., Ziegler, W.: A proposal for WS-Agreement Negotiation. In: IEEE Grid 2010 Conference (2010)
3. Dawoud, W., Takouna, I., Meinel, C.: Infrastructure as a service security: Challenges and solutions. In: The 7th International Conference on Informatics and Systems (INFOS), pp. 1–8 (March 2010)
4. FIT4Green Energy aware ICT optimization policies. FIT4Green project website, http://www.fit4green.eu/
5. Review and summary of cloud service level agreements. Accessible on IBM's web-site, http://public.dhe.ibm.com/software/dw/cloud/library/cl-rev2sla-pdf.pdf
6. Cloud Computing Use Cases Whitepaper Version 4.0, http://www.scribd.com/doc/18172802/Cloud-Computing-Use-Cases-Whitepaper
7. Job Submission Description Language (JSDL) Specification, Version 1.0, Accessible on OGF's web-site: http://www.ogf.org/documents/GFD.136.pdf
8. Apache Muse Project web-site. Project Website, http://ws.apache.org/muse/
9. OPTIMIS - Optimised Infrastructure Services (October 30, 2010), http://www.optimis-project.eu
10. Open Virtualization Format Specification Version 1.1.0, Accessible on DMTF's web-site: http://www.dmtf.org/sites/default/files/standards/documents/DSP0243_1.1.0.pdf
11. Patel, P., Ranabahu, A., Sheth, A.: Service Level Agreement in Cloud Computing. In: Cloud Workshops at OOPSLA 2009 (2009)
12. WSAG4J - Web Services Agreement for Java (October 28, 2010), http://packcs-e0.scai.fraunhofer.de/wsag4j
13. OASIS Web Services Resource Framework (WSRF) TC, http://www.oasis-open.org/committees/wsrf

Process-Aware Information Systems for Emergency Management

Massimiliano de Leoni[1], Andrea Marrella[2], and Alessandro Russo[2]

[1] Technical University of Eindhoven, Eindhoven, The Netherlands
m.d.leoni@tue.nl
[2] SAPIENZA - Università di Roma, Rome, Italy
{marrella,arusso}@dis.uniroma1.it

Abstract. Nowadays, Process-aware Information Systems (PAISs) are widely used in many business scenarios, e.g., by government agencies, by insurance companies, and by banks. Despite this widespread usage, the typical application of such systems is predominantly in the context of business scenarios. Nevertheless, emergency management can also benefit from the use of PAISs; for instance, the metaphor of a business process fits very good with the concept of emergency recovery plan. This paper summarizes an invited talk given by the first author for the EMSOA'10 workshop that has been co-located with the ServiceWave 2010 Conference. This paper starts the basic PAIS' requirements for the domain of emergency management, then it gives an overview of the nowadays' literature on using PAISs for Emergency Management. Finally, the paper proposes an architecture and a system to support the execution of emergency management processes.

1 Introduction

Nowadays organisations are always trying to improve the performance of the processes they are part of. It does not matter whether such organisations are dealing with classical static business domains, such as loans, bank accounts or insurances, or with pervasive and highly dynamic scenarios. The demands are always the same: seeking more efficiency for their processes to reduce the time and the cost for their execution.

According to the definition given by the Workflow Management Coalition[1], a workflow is "the computerised facilitation of automation of a business process, in whole or part". The Workflow Management Coalition defines a Workflow Management System as "a system that completely defines, manages and executes workflows through the execution of software whose order of execution is driven by a computer representation of the workflow logic".

So a PAIS is driven by some process model. The model may be implicit or hidden, but the system supports the handling of cases in some (semi-)structured form. PAISs also have in common that they offer work to resources (typically people). The elementary pieces of work are called *work items*, e.g., "Approve travel request XYZ1234". These work items are offered to the users by the so-called *work-list handler*. This system component takes care of work distribution and authorization issues. Typically, PAISs

---

[1] Workflow Management Coalition Web Site - http://wfmc.org

M. Cezon and Y. Wolfsthal (Eds.): ServiceWave 2010 Workshops, LNCS 6569, pp. 50–58, 2011.

use a so-called "pull mechanism", i.e., work is offered to all resources that qualify and the first resource to select the work item will be the only one responsible for its execution.

On the basis of several studies of emergency plans [7,9] and some end-users interviews we have conducted [8], it becomes evident that emergency plans are, in fact, similar to business processes. Therefore, a correct introduction of a PAIS during emergency management can result in improving the efficiency and effectiveness in dealing with the emergency's aftermath, thus reducing the event's consequence. As a further confirmation of the equivalence of emergency plans and usual processes, we can compare the life cycles of a typical PAIS [14] and of the emergency management [12]. The phases of a PAIS life-cycle can be roughly mapped onto emergency management as follows:

1. *Process Designing*, i.e. when the process schemas are prepared by experts, coincides with the *Preparedness Phase*, where contingency plans are create to manage the aftermath of emergencies
2. *System Configuration* can be mapped partially upon the *Preparedness* for the definition of the skills the process requires, and partially upon the *Response Phase*, for what concerns the configuration of the running instances as regards to the actual emergencies. The *Response Phase* during Emergency Management concerns the period when prepared plans are enacted to manage actual emergency occurrences.
3. *Process Enactment and Monitoring* corresponds particularly to the *Response Phase*, but also the Long-term Recovery. The *Long-term Recovery Phase* is the period after *Response Phase*, when all urgencies have been managed and, subsequently, it is aimed to restore the living condition to a situation comparable to that before the emergency breaks out. However, it is worthy highlighting that the most of the *Long-term Recovery Phase* is usually executed with no support of PAISs. Indeed, this phase involves so many external entities and services that a central PAIS would be strongly limiting.
4. The *diagnosis phase* is very similar to the planning phase and the *Mitigation Activities*. Indeed, during the Diagnosis Phase, the execution logs are analyzed in order evaluate the management of the past emergency, thus finding bottlenecks and, hence, proposing process improvements.

In sum, the process metaphor is suitable for dealing with emergencies and, as stated in [15] "*past and future objective remain the same in crises: providing relevant communities collaborative knowledge systems to exchange information*".

2   User Requirements

In work [9], Jul reflects the American disaster management practices, investigating how the emergency size influences the response type and how collaboration should occur on the spot to deal with the aftermath of an emergency. The American disaster management requirements reported in this work are also confirmed by the experience of the WORKPAD project [2] and a joint analysis with a German civil-protection officer [7].

Jul starts classify calamities in three groups: *(i)* simple local emergencies that are short-lived event whose effects are localized in a single community; *(ii)* disasters, i.e.

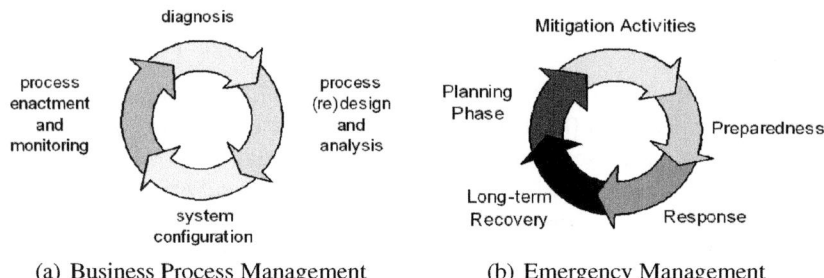

(a) Business Process Management   (b) Emergency Management

Fig. 1. The comparison of the respective life cycles

long-lived event affecting many communities, but community and response infrastructures are affected by few damages; *(iii)* catastrophes, long-lived event affecting hundreds of communities, destroying almost every infrastructure and damaging the response systems. For example, the three category comprise respectively an house explosion, 9/11 terroristic attack and 2005 Hurricane Katrina. From this moment on, we are not going to consider any longer local emergencies, since they do not require an extensive PAIS support: the necessity of some collaboration is quite limited, due to the local nature of the happening.

As far as the Response and Communication Infrastructure, this can be characterized by local damages (medium-size disasters) or extensive destruction (large catastrophes). Even if it is not disrupted, past experiences suggest the existing infrastructure should be used as less as possible. For instance, the Katrina catastrophe has shown that if all civil-protection units use the existing infrastructure, it is destined to collapse or to experience a too low performance level, due to the overload. Indeed, it was not designed to support so many users at the same time. Therefore, **it is advisable to opt for Mobile-ad hoc Networks** (Requirement 1), which are wireless networks in which hosts act both as end points sending/receiving packets and as relays forwarding packets along the correct nodes' paths towards the intended recipients [1].

The support for context awareness is crucial: this is confirmed by [9]: "*context can be characterized by their similarity to environment known to the user, with individual contexts being very familiar, somewhat familiar or unfamiliar*". Moreover "*a given user, particularly in larger events, is likely to work in a variety of contexts, either because of physical relocation or because of changes in the context itself*". Therefore, users cannot be assumed to have local knowledge of the geography and resources of the area. Consequently, **PAISs should be integrated with Geographic Information Systems (GISs), which allow users to gain a deep knowledge of the area, or, more in general, with Geographic-aware Information Systems** (Requirement 2).

As from [9], "*context may be more or less austere*" and "*operations may be established in novel locations*", as well as "*response activities may be relocated*". Hence, "*uncertainty and ambiguity are inherent to disaster*", from which it follows that response technology must allow for flexibility and deviation in their application, while imposing standard structures and procedures. So, **PAISs should allow for large process**

specifications that are specialized time by time according to the specific happenings (Requirement 3), as well as **they need to foresee techniques to adapt the process execution to possibly changing circumstances and contingencies** (Requirement 4).

Last but not least, PAIS Client Tools must be extremely usable and intuitive. As from [9], *"the response typically involve semi-trained or untrained responders ... and the proportion of semi-trained and untrained responders increases with the scale of the event, and they assume greater responsibility for response activities."*. As Emergency Management Systems are not used on daily basis but in exceptional cases, even experts could be not very trained: training sessions could be helpful, but a real emergency is totally different. From this, follows that the **Emergency Management Systems should be so intuitive that they can be easily mastered after few interaction sessions** (Requirement 5).

3   Survey of the Current-Day PAIS' Approaches for Emergency Management

Current approaches based on the adoption of PAISs in the emergency management domain mainly aim at providing support for the *preparedness*, *response* and *recovery* activities. In order to support emergency operators in quickly and efficiently defining process models, in [10] the authors propose a domain-driven process adaptation approach based on configurable process models. Configurable process models capture and combine common practices and process variants related to specific emergency domains, which can be configured in a specific setting leading to individualized process models. In a configurable model, different process variants are integrated and represented through *variation points*, enabling process configuration. Variation points allow removing part of a large process specification that are irrelevant for the current enactment, thus meeting Requirement 3 of Section 2. During process configuration, the requirements stemming from a specific emergency scenario reduce the configuration space, but due to the number of variation points and constraints, the model is in general too difficult to be manually configured. Process configuration is thus performed using interactive questionnaires which allow process experts to decide each variation point by answering a question

A different approach based on design-time synthesis from scenarios is proposed in [5]. Under this approach, small processes, named *scenarios* and modeled as Petri Nets, are dynamically merged upon request. Thus, a large emergency management process is synthesized by composing several fragments. Specifically, in each process representing a *scenario*, places are associated with labels, which determine the points where scenarios can be concatenated: places with the same label can be merged. This is a different approach for Requirement 3, but it is also useful for meeting Requirement 4: if needed, new scenarios can even be appended at run-time as a mechanism of adaptation of system and process behavior.

The support of process adaptation needs for emergency management is crucial (as for Requirement 4); a similar requirement already exists for classical business process management. Therefore, there is a large body of work on this topic. The only existing approaches that are applicable for emergency management are the *automatic* approaches, since *manual* ones, where an expert adapts manually the process upon contingencies, would delay the execution in a way that can lead to consequences (e.g., death of people, collapsing of buildings).

Inside the category of the automatic approaches, the *pre-planned* strategies foresee that, after designing the process schema, the designers describe the policies for the management of all possible discrepancies that may occur. As a consequence, the number of possible discrepancies needs to be known a priori, as well as the way to deal with their occurrence. Therefore, *pre-planned* adaptation is feasible and valuable in static contexts, where exceptions occur rarely, but it is not applicable in dynamic scenarios where policies for too many discrepancies should be designed. On the other side, *unplanned* automatic adaptation approaches try to devise a general recovery method that should be able to handle any kind of event, including those unexpectable. The process is defined as if exogenous events (i.e., contingencies) cannot occur. Whenever discrepancies are detected thus leading to no successful process termination, the control moves to a single exception handler in charge of activating a general recovery method. Such a method is intended to modify the failing executing process into a new one that achieves all goal of the old but such that it terminates in the changed environment.

Nowadays, commercial and open source PAISs use a *manual* adaptation approach (e.g., ADEPT2, ADOME, AgentWork), a *pre-planned* approach (e.g., YAWL), or both (e.g., COSA, Tibco, WebSphere, OPERA), and there exists no PAIS using an *unplanned* adaptation approach (for a more comprehensive analysis see also [4]). An interesting previous case study for using PAISs for emergency management has been carried on using the AristaFlow BPM Suite [11]. AristaFlow, the commercial version of the ADEPT2 framework, allows for verification of the process structure and it features an intuitive approach to adapt process instances at run-time to deal with contingencies. This enables non-computer experts to apply changes and adapted processes are checked for soundness. But, unfortunately, the approach is still manual, even though interesting work has been conducted to simplify the work of adapting process instances. AristaFlow aims also at meeting Requirement 2 of Section 2: relevant information linked to tasks is visualized on geographic maps of the area where the emergency has broken out.

AristaFlow provides also a mobile version for the Work-list Handler [13] that can be installed on Smartphones based on Windows Mobile. The idea is that rescue operators connect to the server to retrieve the tasks they are assigned to and, later, they execute such tasks while disconnected from the PAIS server. Finally or at any point in time, end users can synchronize their work with the server. The problem of this approach is that tasks are executed off-line and, hence, previous tasks can modify at any time the list of tasks that need to be executed afterwards. Consequently, users can be assigned to and carrying on tasks that, when synchronizing after finishing executing them, are learnt to be no more required. The most appropriate solution is that the server itself is constantly being available on the spot and running on mobile devices, so that off-line solutions are prevented. Section 4 describes ROME4EU, a mobile Process-aware Information System that allows for on-line task assignment and execution.

An automatic process adaptation approach based on execution monitoring has been proposed in [4]. Adaptation through execution monitoring requires to define: *(i)* techniques for monitor and possibly predict discrepancies between the internal *virtual* reality built by the PAIS and the external *physical* reality built "sensing" the real world; *(ii)* techniques for identification of corrective actions to deal with the new execution context; *(iii)* techniques for automatic process restructuring in order to successfully terminate the adapted process in the new context. According to the proposed approach, the PAIS assigns tasks to resources considering execution context and resources' capabilities. For each execution step, an *execution monitor* aligns the internal *virtual* reality built by the PAIS with the *physical* reality and data retrieved from external world by sensors (intended as any software and/or hardware component able to get contextual information), possibly adapting the process to unforeseen exogenous events and producing an adapted process to be executed.

4   The WORKPAD Approach

In complex emergency/disaster scenarios teams from various emergency-response organizations collaborate with each other to achieve a common goal. In these scenarios the use of smart mobile devices and applications can improve the collaboration dynamically. The WORKPAD project [8], finished in 2009, aimed at the development of an Adaptive Peer-to-Peer Software Infrastructure for supporting the collaborative work of human operators in Emergency Management Scenarios.

According to the initial user requirements collected [8], WORK-PAD has developed a two-level infrastructure: a first level is deployed on the spot and includes the diverse rescue teams that are sent to the area in order to be actively included in providing assistance to the involved people and in mitigate the aftermath. There are several front-end teams on the field, each composed by rescue operators and headed by a "leader operator", who coordinates the intervention of the other team members.

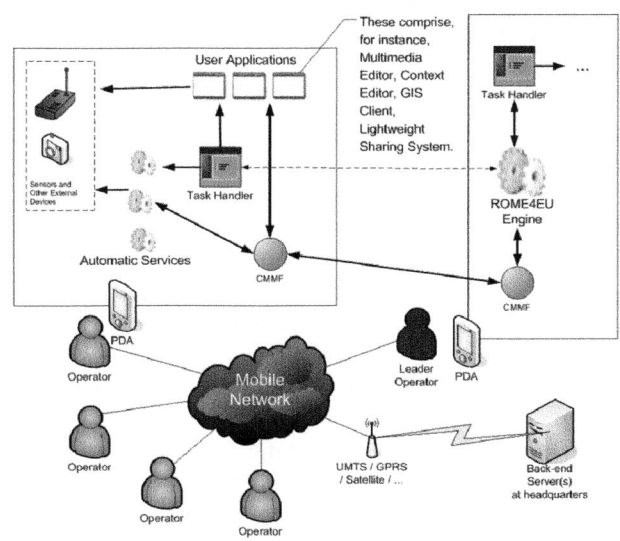

Fig. 2. The High-Level Infrastructure of the WORKPAD System

Rescue operators are equipped with PDAs and their work is orchestrated by a WfMS named ROME4EU [3] hosted on the most powerful device (which is typically the team leader's device). The ROME4EU engine manages the execution of emergency-management processes by orchestrating the human operators with their software applications and some automatic services to access the external data sources and sensors. At the back-end side data sources from several servers are automatically integrated and the result is a single virtual data source that front-end devices can query, thus obtaining information aggregated from several sources. From an organizational perspective, back-end includes the control rooms/headquarters of the diverse organizations that have rescuers involved at front-end. These control rooms provide instructions and information to front-end teams to support their work. Collaboration strictly depends on the possibility that operators and their devices can communicate with each other. Communication is executed on top of ad-hoc networks, such as MANET or Mesh Networks [15,1], as from Requirement 1 of Section 2. Such mobile networks provide gateways to connect to back-end servers. Figure 2 shows an overview of the front-end WORKPAD infrastructure. The figure refers to one single (front-end) team with different operators who are coordinated in an emergency.

It is worthy observing that WORKPAD deals with the coordination inside the single teams but does not concern the synchronization of activities of processes carried on by different teams. This is a possible continuation of the WORKPAD work; for instance, Franke et al. [6] are being conducted some work on this topic.

For what concerns front-end teams, when a certain task is assigned to a specific operator, the ROME4EU server interacts with the Work-list Handler, which is informed about each assignment made to the respective operator. Both the server and the Handlers are built on top of a Web-service middleware and communicate with each other through web-service endpoints. Each message (e.g., for the notification of a task assignment) is sent through an one-way invocation of a certain method of such endpoints. Once the Work-list Handler Handler receives notification of a certain task assignment to respective users, it displays the name of the task together with relevant information. At any time users can decide to start a task by accepting the offer. In fact, Work-list Handlers do not execute process tasks: tasks are executed with the support of external applications. The Task Handler is only in charge of informing the users about the task assignments and, later, invoking the right applications for task performances.

The development of ROME4EU and, in general, of the entire WORKPAD project has been following an user-centered methodology [8], according to which the development has been carried on in concert with the end users. These have always been confronted with the alternative architectural and implementing choices for the different system releases to evaluate what they considered as best. Such a kind of approach has guaranteed the architecture and the entire system to meet the actual requirements and provide a really efficient and effective system. The goodness of the WORKPAD outcomes is also proven by a showcase held in June, 2009. An earthquake was simulated to occur in the abandoned town of Pentidattilo in southern Italy, and rescue operators were requested to simulate rescue operations with the current means, previously, and, later, by using the entire WORKPAD system, including ROME4EU. From the comparison of the results with and without the system, we have discovered that more efficiency is actually provided with WORKPAD. Moreover, the end users learnt very quickly how to deal with that system, which complies Requirement 5 of Section 2 (see [2] for more details on the analysis with end users).

5   Conclusion

According to our experience and main project outcomes, PAISs are useful during emergency management to improve the effectiveness of first responders and emergency organizations. The process metaphor is generally well understood by end users and the usage of PAISs forced civil protection departments to systemize the procedures to manage emergencies and solve the inherent inefficiencies, thus resulting in a response-time improvement, which is not a direct consequence of the PAIS introduction. Stemming from the experience acquired during the WORKPAD project, in emergency management, information processing and task execution is fully integrated with the physical environment and its objects. The physical interaction with the environment increases the frequency of unexpected contingencies with respect to classical scenarios. So, providing a higher degree of operational flexibility/adaptability is a key requirement of every PAIS for emergency management. From a visualization viewpoint, Task Handlers and other client applications supporting the execution of tasks should be conceived for being used in extreme conditions and under direct sunlight. Therefore, the use of highly-contrasting colors is important (e.g., white on black, yellow on blue). Moreover, users might not have free hands to use PDA's stylus. Therefore, the GUI widgets should be sized in a way that the use of styluses can be avoided (e.g., participants should be able to touch and press buttons by fingers).

References

1. Bertelli, G., de Leoni, M., Mecella, M., Dean, J.: Mobile Ad hoc Networks for Collaborative and Mission-critical Mobile Scenarios: a Practical Study. In: WETICE 2008: Proceedings of the 17th IEEE International Workshops on Enabling Technologies: Infrastructure for Collaboration Enterprises. IEEE, Los Alamitos (2008)
2. Catarci, T., Mecella, M., de Leoni, M., Marrella, A., Bortenschlager, M., Steinmann, R.: The WORKPAD Project Experience: Improving the Disaster Response through Process Management and Geo Collaboration. In: Proceedings of the 7th International Conference on Information Systems for Crisis Response and Management, ISCRAM 2010 (2010)
3. de Leoni, M., Mecella, M.: Mobile process management through web services. In: SCC 2010: Proceedings of the 2010, IEEE International Conference on Services Computing. IEEE Computer Society, Washington, DC, USA (2010)
4. de Leoni, M., Mecella, M., De Giacomo, G.: Highly Dynamic Adaptation in Process Management Systems Through Execution Monitoring. In: Alonso, G., Dadam, P., Rosemann, M. (eds.) BPM 2007. LNCS, vol. 4714, pp. 182–197. Springer, Heidelberg (2007)
5. Fahland, D., Woith, H.: Towards process models for disaster response. In: Business Process Management Workshops. LNBIP, vol. 17. Springer, Heidelberg (2009)
6. Franke, J., Charoy, F., Ulmer, C.: A Model for Temporal Coordination of Disaster Response Activities. In: Proceedings of the 7th International Conference on Information Systems for Crisis Response and Management, ISCRAM 2010 (2010)
7. Hagebölling, D., de Leoni, M.: Supporting Emergency Management through Process-Aware Information Systems. In: Business Process Management Workshops. LNBIP, vol. 17. Springer, Heidelberg (2009)
8. Humayoun, S.R., Catarci, T., de Leoni, M., Marrella, A., Mecella, M., Bortenschlager, M., Steinmann, R.: The WORKPAD User Interface and Methodology: Developing Smart and Effective Mobile Applications for Emergency Operators. In: Stephanidis, C. (ed.) UAHCI 2009. LNCS, vol. 5616, pp. 343–352. Springer, Heidelberg (2009)

9. Jul, S.: Who's Really on First? A Domain-Level User and Context Analysis for Response Technology. In: Van de Walle, B., Burghardt, P., Nieuwenhuis, C. (eds.) Proceedings of the 4th International Conference on Information Systems for Crisis Response and Management, ISCRAM 2007 (2007)
10. La Rosa, M., Mendling, J.: Domain-Driven Process Adaptation in Emergency Scenarios. In: Business Process Management Workshops. LNBIP, vol. 17. Springer, Heidelberg (2009)
11. Lanz, A., Kreher, U., Reichert, M., Dadam, P.: Enabling Process Support for Advanced Applications with the AristaFlow BPM Suite. In: Proceedings of the Business Process Management 2010 Demonstration Track. CEUR-WS, vol. 615, Hoboken, New Jersey, USA (September 2010)
12. Leitinger, S.H.: Comparision of GIS-based Public Safety Systems For Emergency Management. In: UDMS 2004: Proceedings of 24th Urban Data Management Symposium: Information Systems and the Delivery of the Promised Societal Benefits (2004)
13. Pryss, R., Tiedeken, J., Reichert, M.: Managing Processes on Mobile Devices: The MARPLE Approach. In: Proceedings of the CAiSE 2010 FORUM. CEUR-WS (2010)
14. ter Hofstede, A.H.M., van der Aalst, W.M.P., Adams, M., Russel, N.: YAWL and its Support Environment. Springer, Heidelberg (2009)
15. Turoff, M.: Past and future emergency response information systems. Communication of the ACM 45 (April 2002)

Semantic Services
for Information and Management Support
in Mass Casualty Incident Scenarios

Uwe Krüger, Aygul Gabdulkhakova,
Birgitta König-Ries, and Clemens Beckstein

Institute of Computer Science, Friedrich-Schiller-University Jena, Germany
{uwe.krueger,aygul.gabdulkhakova,birgitta.koenig-ries,
clemens.beckstein}@uni-jena.de
http://www.speedup.uni-jena.de

Abstract. Operation managers in *mass casualty incidents* (MCI) are easily overwhelmed by the highly dynamic scenario. Today, they are often supported by paper-based checklists that help ensure that nothing important gets overlooked. In this paper, we present our approach to dramatically increase the support offered by such checklists: We suggest to replace them by IT-based intelligent checklists that will not only display information the manager should collect and tasks he might perform, but directly support semi-automatic information gathering, propagation and task-execution.

Keywords: checklists, semantic services, service composition.

1 Introduction

In large scale scenarios up to *mass casualty incidents* (MCI), the rescue forces at the scene are overwhelmed by the number and severity of casualties. In order to successfully handle MCIs, operation managers in situ have to manage the gap between available and necessary resources [1]. In *regional rescue coordination centers* special plans and checklists are used to guide through lists of tasks to be done, because in stressful situations such lists prevent dispatchers from forgetting important steps. But checklists are also useful for operation managers in the field — if certain items are skipped or missed, the result can be harmful or even fatal.

Let us look at an example of a classical paper-based checklist containing the following entry addressed to a MCI manager: "*If hazardous substance is involved, inform all leaders about this fact!*". This entry does not specify *who* the addressee of this information are and *how* they can be informed about the danger. These decisions can only be made in the specific MCI situation where hazardous substance was detected and therefore are left to the manager — however busy and stressed he may be in such a dynamic situation. First investigations of real MCI incidents have shown that an electronic assistant, in the form of an intelligent checklist handler, taking over part of this responsibility, allows the manager to

M. Cezon and Y. Wolfsthal (Eds.): ServiceWave 2010 Workshops, LNCS 6569, pp. 59–66, 2011.

better focus on the core problems which tremendously improves the MCI management process. This is also confirmed by the requirements studies [2, 3].

In this paper we present the concept of an intelligent checklist support for the management of MCIs. This work is part of the SPEEDUP[1] project which aims to build up an information and communication system for the operations managers. Section 2 introduces intelligent checklists and explains how they can be used in MCI management processes. Section 3 develops our proposal for an architecture that allows to build *intelligent electronic checklist support systems* (IECSS). This architecture is related to other approaches to the problem at hand in Section 4. The paper concludes with a summary and a discussion of the role that this architecture plays in the overall SPEEDUP project.

2   From Checklists to Intelligent Checklists

In the MCI area checklists typically are not just simple verifiable questions. Rather, they are more or less abstract descriptions of tasks that govern how humans act and communicate in the MCI process. These tasks often leave open important details which are necessary for their successful completion because they can only be realized with the full knowledge of the specific situation at hand.

MCI-checklist entries are of a dual nature: on the one hand they describe a task to be done and on the other the goal that the task is to accomplish. These entries usually are given as natural language orders to the checklist addressee. In order to be usable in an IECSS they therefore first have to be formalized: the semantics (correct usage) of the concepts addressed in the entries (their ontology) has to be fixed and made available for the formulation of pre- and postconditions that control the interplay of the tasks and specify the effects (goals) that the task execution has (should have) in the real world.

Checklists for MCIs typically exhibit a hierarchical structure. This structure may be given explicitly by a higher level checklist entry referring to a lower level checklist implementing this entry or just implicitly by an abstractly formulated entry where the details of its (situation specific) implementation are left to the checklist user. In the SPEEDUP project these implicit relationships were made explicit and formalized as *hierarchical task networks* (HTNs) via a detailed analysis of the strategies used by professionals to handle complex MCIs. Depending on the current situation a suitable subset of these HTNs can therefore now be selected either by man or machine to control how abstract tasks are realized.

In contrast to classical paper-based checklists, entries in MCI-checklists need and often must not be executed in a rigid a priori given order. Different tasks corresponding to different entries of the same checklist and even entire checklists typically are pursued concurrently and therefore hard to manage. The user has to continuously monitor and orchestrate their execution according to the dependences between the tasks involved. This is also the primary design goal for our intelligent electronic checklist support system.

[1] SPEEDUP is funded within the Federal Government's program *Research for Civil Security* by the German Federal Ministry of Education and Research.

MCI managers are bound by law to document the important steps of the MCI development in an event log. Assuming that the intelligent checklist handler logs the completion of any task triggered by a checklist a substantial part of the MCI event log can be generated automatically. This relieves the mission commanders from tedious administrative routine tasks and allows them to fully concentrate on the real problem. The event log entries will not just be predefined blocks of natural language text but machine understandable assertions (like "*heliport established*" or "*no turntable ladder available*") about the formally specified goals for the corresponding tasks. These assertions can then be stored in a knowledge base resembling the tactical situation and reasoned about with a suitable inference machine.

3   An Architecture for Intelligent Checklist Support

In order to build an IECSS for MCIs, we started to implement an architecture that combines knowledge representation, automated planning techniques and semantic service technology (see Fig. 1). The knowledge base contains a formal representation of the situation at hand which can then be used by a planning process to generate activity schemata as (formal) task realizations. Subsequently, the service component will find concrete resources needed to execute these atomic tasks. Figure 1 shows the interplay between the planner, the service component and the execution engine: At planning time the planner uses the service component to goal-directedly retrieve planning operators based on the semantic descriptions of the services they belong to (see ① in Fig. 1). As KUTER et al. [4] and NAU [5] propose, the planner uses information gathering services (IGS)[2] to collect situation specific knowledge necessary for the completion of a working plan (see ② in Fig. 1). If an error occurs during checklist processing, e. g., because the service that implements a plan operator is unexpectedly unavailable or not applicable to the current situation, then the execution component first attempts to resolve the failure without involving the planner — e. g., by providing an alternative service for the same basic task (see ③ in Fig. 1). If the execution engine can not resolve the problem locally, it gives back control to the planner. The planner then searches for alternative plans that accomplish the same overall goals but do not involve the failing operation.

The combination of these technologies provides a suitable basis to deal with checklist support in highly dynamic situations as we will explain in further detail in the remainder of this section.

3.1   Representation of the Situation

We use description logics (DLs) to represent knowledge about the rescue domain in general and about the specific incident in particular. This representation allow us to describe the goals for the checklist items and the situation itself in a formal (semantic) way. For SPEEDUP the domain of interest has been logical modeled via a domain-specific MCI ontology (see Fig. 1). This formal ontology describes

---

[2] According to the *information-gathering actions* in [6].

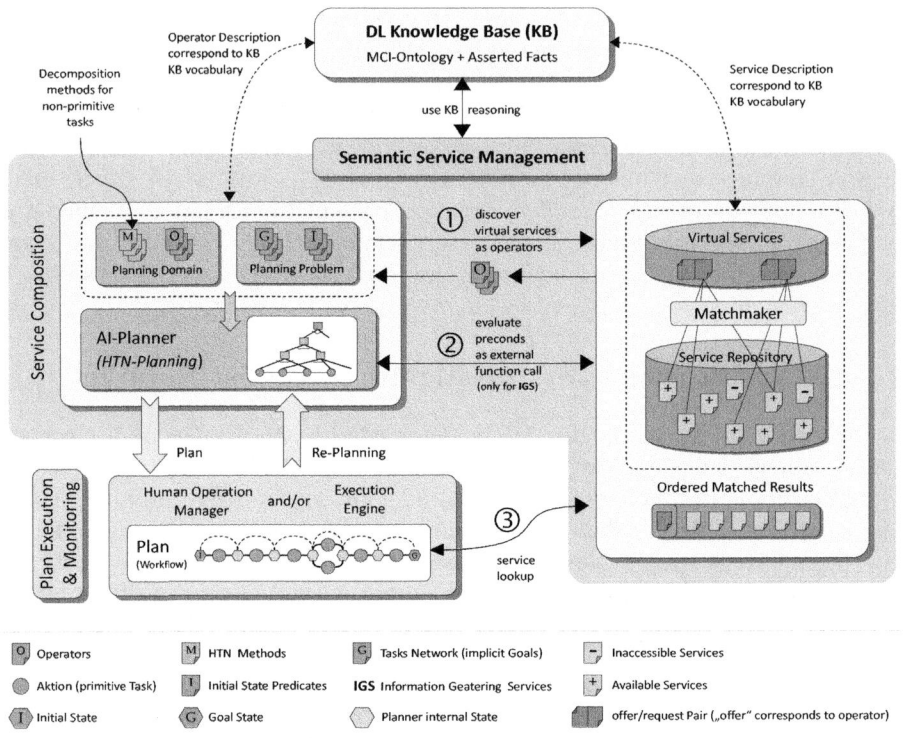

Fig. 1. Core techniques of the solution architecture

the main vocabulary used by German rescue and fire brigades. It serves as the central data repository for the components that plan and control the dynamics of the system with the help of the reasoning services provided by DL-based KBs [7]. This model is also used as a basis for the semantic descriptions introduced below.

At the present time, the SPEEDUp MCI-Ontology[3] defines around 300 concepts which represent classes of rescue workers, technical equipment, special leading structures, the rescue organizations and data collected about injured people. It is still under construction and will be adjusted to fulfill all application requirements.

In addition to the TBox containing the relevant context, the knowledge base's ABox contains instances of these concepts (e. g., individual rescue workers or vehicles) representing the current situation.

3.2   Grounding Checklist Execution

In our architecture semantic services implement the elementary tasks corresponding to primitive checklists entries. We have decided on a service oriented

---

[3] http://users.minet.uni-jena.de/~ukrueger/mci-ontology

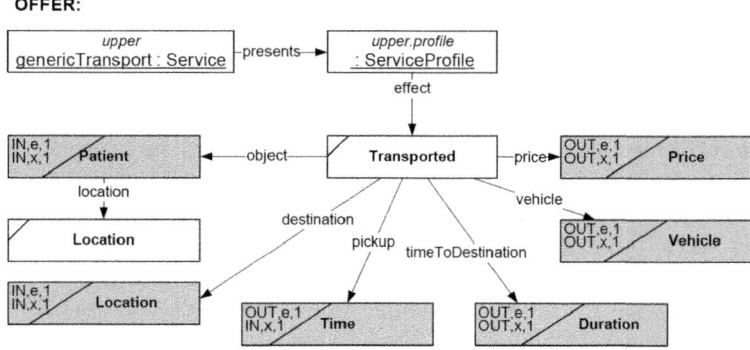

Fig. 2. A generic transport service in the graphical DSD notation

architecture with semantic, i. e., machine-processable service descriptions, as this is an ideal architecture to support flexibility and robustness in dynamic situations. It enables the automatic, dynamic, runtime allocation of resources needed for the execution of tasks, thereby allowing for adjustment to currently available and most suitable resources.

In SPEEDUP, we use the DIANE Service Description language (DSD) and its matchmaker [8] to provide such descriptions and to automatically match service requests and offers in order to find the most appropriate offer for a given checklist item (request). In DSD, *Service offers* are described as sets of required preconditions and achieved effects based on a domain ontology, in this case the MCI-ontology. DSD descriptions of both offers and requests are directed graphs. The matchmaker traverses the request graph and tries to find and configure matching offers by implementing a subset test. Figure 2 shows a somewhat simplified example of a service offer in the graphical DSD notation.

The description tells that the effect of the service execution will be that something (or rather someone) will be transported from their current location (this information needs to be provided as an input) to a destination (again provided as an input). The requester can specify a desired pickup time. In a first step, the estimation phase, the service provider will deliver some additional information about the service: It will tell the requester how much the transport will cost, which vehicle will be used and how long it will take to reach the destination. Based on this information, the requester (or an automatic matchmaker on her behalf) can decide whether to use this service or not. This allows for a good support for highly dynamic situations, as up to date situation information is used for the matchmaking process.

While service offer descriptions will typically be rather concrete, checklist items and the tasks they represent will often be more abstract to make them applicable in different situations. For instance, a checklist entry may be to inform the squad leader about something. The checklist will not specify how this transfer of information is supposed to happen. Concrete services, on the other hand, might provide the possibility to *"send an SMS"* or to *"have a messenger deliver a note"*. Depending on the current situation one or the other of these services will be better suited to fulfill the task required by the checklist. The same is true in the transportation scenario below. Service offers by different providers might offer transport by a vehicle owned by a certain organization. The checklist will only say *"transport patient"*. In order to bridge these differences in an abstraction layer, we introduce the concept of *virtual services* in our architecture.

A virtual service is a service that is not directly implemented but relies on other, more specific services to achieve the functionality it promises. A generic transport service like the one described above is an example for such a virtual service. To the service composition component, it is presented as a service with a service offer. This virtual service communicates with the planner for correctly scheduling currently available suitable services. It is presented as an operator specified by pre- and postconditions. Internally, instead of an implementation, it contains possibly context-dependent service requests which can be mapped to appropriate concrete service providers at runtime. The evaluation of the context can be either hardcoded, e. g., by storing a list of associated service requests and the respective context in which they are suitable, or can be realized via an adapted matchmaking process. This approach is more powerful than the commonly used late binding approach: Like the latter, it allows to hide some of the dynamics and uncertainty of the rescue situation from the planning component. From the point of view of the planner, a virtual service is an operator that promises a certain effect and can thus become part of a plan. But, in contrast to late binding, it also allows to bridge different levels of granularity.

3.3   Realizing Abstract Checklist Entries

In order to decompose complex tasks that result from abstract entries into primitive subtasks a special automated planning component is needed. As described in Section 2, in SPEEDUP, the hierarchical nature of checklists is supported by explicitly modeled HTNs. Thus, we decided to use a planner based on the HTN paradigm [5]. Similar to humans HTN planners use task decomposition as the basic planning method making them a canonical choice for complex and human centric application domains. Setting up an HTN planner amounts to specifying a collection of recipes (so called *methods*) describing how a complex task can be hierarchically decomposed into directly executable elementary activities (*operations*). In this way HTN methods provide the basis for the specification of standard operating procedures [9] and complex checklist support. With the help of the planner the IECSS can provide the desired assistance to the operation commanders: dependent on the current situation (retrieved from the KB) it suggests task specific checklists at different levels of abstraction, maintains the assumptions underlying planning decisions, and helps in adjusting checklists fragments that can not be executed as they were intended to be.

4   Related Work and Open Problems

In the last twenty years, many projects dealt with support in MCI and other emergency scenarios and many used a similar combination of technologies as

SPEEDUP does. Examples include SHARE [10], CoSAR-TS [11], MobiKat [12] and the *Emergency Management System* [13]. However, despite clear indications for the need [2, 3], to the best of our knowledge, none of these projects suggested intelligent checklist support as we understand it. [14] discusses techniques for the runtime adaptation of predefined processes to highly dynamic environments. While this is interesting from a technical point of view a workflow perspective on crisis management does not seem adequate for the typical MCI scenario.

The work in [14], discussing the application of process management techniques for highly dynamics situations, is also an interesting approach.

There are projects aiming to support standard operating procedures (SOPs) in emergency scenarios (e. g., SIADEX [15]). However, a detailed analysis of the organizations involved in emergency operations by our project partners from the working group on intercultural communication, revealed, that — contrary to common belief — such SOPs in general do not exist, at least not explicitly and not on a level of detail that lends itself to automation in dynamic situations. This is also confirmed by [16] which states that *"SOPs should provide only broad procedural guidelines, not specific details of task performance"*.

Checklists on the other hand, are commonly used and widely accepted and can be supported by an architecture as described above. The EU FP6 project OASIS[4], e. g., intended to support a form of intelligent checklists (*general crisis plans*). Unfortunately, no details about the results are available.

5   Conclusion

In this paper we have presented a novel architecture which provides intelligent electronic checklist support for operation managers confronted with dynamic and large-scale MCIs. In our approach, a DL-based domain description builds the semantic foundation for service management, automated service composition, and execution agents. Within the SPEEDUP project, the ideas discussed in this paper are combined with work on inter-organizational communication, on user interfaces for emergency personnel and organizational leaders, and work on the technical basis for communication in disaster situations, to build a comprehensive framework for the support of rescue managers in MCIs.

This framework will be developed in close cooperation with our partners from different rescue organizations and will be evaluated in real-life MCI situations. Such a cooperation among users and scientists is an absolute necessity for the development of useful systems, that one day may help to save life.

References

[1] Peter, H.: Die Leitstelle beim MANV. Stumpf + Kossendey Verlags. mbH (2001)
[2] Robillard, J., Sambrook, R.: USAF Emergency and Incident Management Systems: A Systematic Analysis of Functional Requirements (2008),
     http://www.uccs.edu/~rsambroo//Research/EIM_REQS.pdf

---

[4] http://www.oasis-fp6.org

[3] Lanfranchi, V., Ireson, N.: User requirements for a collective intelligence emergency response system. In: BCS-HCI 2009: Proceedings of the 23rd British HCI Group Annual Conference on People and Computers, pp. 198–203. British Computer Society, Swinton (2009)

[4] Kuter, U., Sirin, E., Parsia, B., Nau, D., Hendler, J.: Information gathering during planning for Web Service composition. Web Semantics: Science, Services and Agents on the World Wide Web, 183–205 (2005)

[5] Sirin, E., Parsia, B., Wu, D., Hendler, J., Nau, D.: HTN planning for Web Service composition using SHOP2. Web Semantics: Science, Services and Agents on the World Wide Web 1(4), 377–396 (2004)

[6] Golden, K., Etzioni, O., Weld, D.: Planning with Execution and Incomplete Information. Technical report, Department of Computer Science and Engineering. University of Washington (1996)

[7] Baader, F., Calvanese, D., McGuinness, D., Nardi, D., Patel-Schneider, P.: The Description Logic Handbook: Theory, Implementation and Applications, 2nd edn. Cambridge University Press, Cambridge (2007)

[8] Kuester, U., Koenig-Ries, B., Klein, M., Stern, M.: DIANE - A Matchmaking-Centered Framework for Automated Service Discovery, Composition, Binding and Invocation on the Web. Special Issue of IJEC (International Journal of Electronic Commerce) on Semantic Matchmaking and Retrieval (2007)

[9] Nau, D.S., Au, T.C., Ilghami, O., Kuter, U., Murdock, J.W., Wu, D., Yaman, F.: SHOP2: An HTN Planning System. Journal of AI Research 20, 379–404 (2003)

[10] Konstantopoulos, S., Pottebaum, J., Schon, J., Schneider, D., Winkler, T., Paliouras, G., Koch, R.: Ontology-Based Rescue Operation Management (2009)

[11] Tate, A., Dalton, J., Bradshaw, J.M., Uszok, A.: Coalition Search and Rescue - Task Support: Intelligent Task Achieving Agents on the Semantic Web. Technical report, Artificial Intelligence Applications Institute The University of Edinburgh and Florida Institute for Human & Machine Cognition, IHMC (2004)

[12] Danowski, K.: MobiKat - Integriertes System zur Unterstützung der Katastrophenbewältigung und der alltäglichen Gefahrenabwehr. Fraunhofer-Institut fur Verkehrs- und Infrastruktursysteme IVI (2007) Infoblatt

[13] Rausch, A., Niebuhr, D., Schindler, M., Herrling, D.: Emergency Management System. In: Proceedings of the International Conference on Pervasive Services 2009 (ICSP 2009), Clausthal University of Technology, Department of Informatics - Software Systems Engineering Research Group (2009)

[14] De Leoni, M., De Giacomo, G., Lespèrance, Y., Mecella, M.: On-line adaptation of sequential mobile processes running concurrently. In: Jacobson Jr., M.J., Rijmen, V., Safavi-Naini, R. (eds.) SAC 2009, pp. 1345–1352. ACM, New York (2009)

[15] Asunción, M.D.L., Garcaprez, O., Palao, F.: SIADEX: A Real World Planning Approach for Forest Fire Fighting Introduction (2004)

[16] IOCAD Emergency Services Group Inc.: Developing Effective Standard Operating Procedures - Guide To Developing Effective Standard Operating Procedures For Fire And EMS Departments. Federal Emergency Management Agency, United States Fire Administration, USA (1999),
http://www.usfa.dhs.gov/downloads/pdf/publications/fa-197-508.pdf

Information Conceptualization for Emergency Management

Ouejdane Mejri

Dipartimento di Elettronica e Informazione, Politecnico di Milano
Piazza Leonardo da Vinci, 32. 20133 Milano
mejri@elet.polimi.it

Abstract. Emergency management information systems are increasingly requiring flexibility and interoperability and their design should not be only based on the conceptualization of information provided and accessed during the recovery stage. In fact, analyzing the entire workflow of emergency management, namely, preparedness, response and recovery we can identify a significant intersection of concepts present in on and another stage. In this paper we will focus on the informational function of contingency management workflows proposing a conceptual structure of this domain through the use of ontologies. More than a simple classification of the kinds of information read, produced, modified, memorized and shared, we would like to capture into the emergency management field which are the specific classes of information objects and the relations that exist among them.

Keywords: Information Systems, Ontology, Emergency Management, Conceptualization.

1 Introduction

On one hand, it is conventional to define risk and emergency management as the natural sequence of the activities of preparedness, response, recovery, and mitigation of disasters. Actually, we can consider the crisis management process in its entirety as a unique workflow, i.e. a pattern of a sequence of connected activities enabled by a structured organization of resources, defined roles and information flows, into an effort process that can be documented and learnt [5]. Contrariwise, each sub-process (i.e. preparedness, response, recovery and mitigation) may be considered in turn as a self-regulating workflow. On the other hand, constructing shared ontologies permit to build specific knowledge bases which describe specific domains and hugely increases the potential for knowledge reuse, a major need in emergency management. Indeed, ontology specification has a domain factual knowledge dimension which provides knowledge about the objective realities in the domain of interest (objects, relations, events, states, causal relations, and so on) [1]. These properties may be combined with Web Services rationale putting together the flexibility, reusability, and universal access that typically characterize a Web Service, with the expressivity of semantic markup and reasoning offered by ontologies for constructing flexible Emergency Management Information Systems (EMISs).

M. Cezon and Y. Wolfsthal (Eds.): ServiceWave 2010 Workshops, LNCS 6569, pp. 67–73, 2011.
© Springer-Verlag Berlin Heidelberg 2011

In recent years, some works were proposed to provide data interoperability through standardizing messages and data elements (e.g., Common Alert Protocol (CAP) [23] and Emergency Data Exchange Language (EDXL) [5]). Other works implemented formal ontologies for Emergency Management purposes, in order to standardize semantic concepts that can be generically applied to different emergency response systems. Li et al. [8] proposes a practical emergency response ontology useful for the development of emergency response applications (i.e., emergency evacuation planning system). Di Maio 1] delineates an open ontology theoretical approach providing design and implementation methodology to developers and users of information systems designed to support Emergency Response operations. Yu et al. [11] introduced the technology of ontology into the knowledge reorganization processing of Emergency Decision Support System. They used the Activity-First Method (AFM) proposed in [9] to construct an emergency ontology from existing documentation. In a more specific way, Ngo et al. [11] proposes ontological enhancements for data exchange languages for ensuring effective communications during emergencies in order to augment availability of emergency personnel.

To the best of our knowledge, the related works dealt exclusively with ontologies applied to emergency handling focusing on the specific activities of emergency response and relief. In this paper, we propose to encode the information flow existing into the contingency management workflow supporting not only singularly the activities of emergency planning, response and recovery but also the entire integrated workflow. We aim to create a shareable knowledge about the likely exploited information and its use during the whole process in order to support components and functions of EMISs.

More specifically, in this paper we will focus on the informational function of contingency management workflows proposing a conceptual structure of this domain through the use of ontologies. More than a simple classification of the kinds of information read, produced, modified, memorized and shared, we would like to capture into the emergency management field which are the specific classes of information objects and the relations that exist among them [1].

2   Emergency Management Information Systems

Crises generate the necessity for different Emergency Operation Centers (EOCs) compound of hundreds of individuals to be able to exchange information without restraint, delegate authority, and conduct oversight [12]. The key obstacle to effective crisis response is the communication needed to access relevant data or expertise and to piece together an accurate understandable picture of reality. Faced with extreme uncertainty, decision makers tend to increase their search for information while simultaneously shutting down some channels of communication, and relying on familiar or formal information and channels [12]. This constant dynamicity coupled with a necessity to access to relevant data may be faced by constructing flexible Emergency Management Information Systems (EMISs). These information systems should cover the entire workflow of contingency management in order to construct knowledge during the whole process accessible by different stakeholders.

Service Oriented Architectures could facilitate the definition of contingency scenarios (preparedness stage), the adaptation of various scenarios in order to generate a realistic emergency plans involving different EMISs (emergency stage) and finally construct a realistic vision of the available resources and how to involve them (Recovery stage). This type of architecture separates the infrastructure from the provided services. As a consequence, all the EMISs installed in the EOCs could be considered as members of a peer-to-peer network where each node provides a set of services and can potentially communicate with all the others. These EMISs need factual knowledge about the domain of discourse (i.e., emergency management) [1], that may be constructed through the conceptualization of information using ontologies. Our vision of such tool and an illustration of a part of the ontology developed is presented in the next section.

Our analysis of information flow into contingency management workflows is related to the factual knowledge providing facts about the domain objective realities. In fact, we analyze the information objects, their properties, states and inter-relations over time in the contingency global process and its sub-processes identifying operational information exchanges between various parties, i.e., interdependencies between them. Hereafter we present a summarized description of the information we identified as essential for dealing with the sub-processes of the emergency management workflow, namely, planning, response and recovery. After that, we integrate the knowledge about the global flow of information through the entire emergency management workflow by developing a unique ontology.

2.1 Emergency Planning

The validity and use of risk assessment is determined by the quality and availability of data. Emergency plans must be synthetic documents, organised in working sheets and forms, containing the crucial information mostly needed to handle a crisis [9]. Emergency plans are also considered as a valid tool to keep collective memory active, by saving it and making it available to the largest number of stakeholders in charge of a crisis.

In order to generate emergency plans we need information about past events, their quantitative recognition and operational historical contents. Information about vulnerability and hazard factors associated with strengths and opportunities for coping and rebuilding. Essential information may be obtained through monitoring systems about the natural phenomena by recognizing its premonitory signals and relative warnings. Furthermore an emergency plan should consider impact information referring to domino effect and interscalar relations and deem about all the kinds of resources useful for possible scenarios. In fact, the available resources and means (i.e., human and material) have to be geo-referenced including the indication of proprietary and usage conditions.

2.2 Emergency Response

During contingency response, information may be produced in the operative processes but it is useful for decisional ones. It may also be produced in the decisional level and furthermore re-used into the operational processes. Conceptually, this information corresponds to instances of some classes of information identified during the emergency preparedness stage when constructing an emergency plan. In fact, we notice that the information needed by stakeholders during an emergency are related to direct consequences of a disaster, resources requests and availability, relief information (e.g., roads, bridges, airports and railways state) and the main features of the involved areas. Furthermore, the communication aspects are crucial to be controlled from informational point of view, either for information about the communications states or their proper contents.

2.3 Emergency Recovery

The relief information may be conceptually mapped on response information adding that information with which we deal during peace time, i.e., indirect disaster consequences, recovery resources, residual risk assessment, and fundraising. After crisis information is related also depends on crisis duration (short or prolonged crisis situations), their gravity and the scale on which they happened.

3 Ontologies for Emergency Management

Under the appellation of "ontology" are found many different types of artifacts created and used in different communities to represent objects and their relationships for purposes including annotating datasets, supporting natural language understanding, integrating information sources, semantic interoperability and to serve as a background knowledge in various applications [6]. Moreover, ontologies represent a significant resource for web applications, as they make available a knowledge representation language and a lexicon of classes and relations that Web services can use to describe content and produce facilities. The main objective after the development of a shared ontology is to build specific knowledge bases which describe emergency management domain, increasing the potential for knowledge reuse. In fact, our proposed ontology permits to conceptualize information produced and accessed by different stakeholders during the different stages of contingency management creating a common emergency information vocabulary regardless of the kind of cause or effects of a disaster. Furthermore, it offers machine-interpretable definitions of the concepts in the contingency management domain and relations among them useful for designing flexible EMISs.

3.1 Information Source

A complete picture of the domain may be obtained through theories and applications for emergency management literature (i.e., sociology, organization and information systems) and domain experts. Indeed, we addressed the ambiguities and gaps in information through questionnaire and interviews.

Various modeling techniques, such as Unified Modeling Language (UML) or Entity-Relationship (ER) were used during the information collecting step in order to represent different viewpoints of the systems, such as functional view or logical view respectively.

3.2 Developed Sample

We choose to develop as a first step a domain ontology through a taxonomy, i.e., tree structure of classifications for a given set of objects (containment hierarchy).

The degree of granularity of the ontology needs to be generic and application independent as possible for share-ability and interoperability and expressive as possible to define a precise conceptualization. In figure 1 we present a part of the ontology related to the information identified into the emergency preparedness sub-process as a description of emergency consequence. This fraction of the ontology describes a classification of data that should be defined into a contingency plan describing a classification of information through relationships (i.e., IS-A relationships and other specific relationships). In figure 1 we illustrate how the object injury of the ontology may have properties defined through ad-hoc relationships, e.g., Has-Cause, Has-Severity and Has-Treatment. These information are shared all over the contingency process involving some or other concepts in one or other stage.

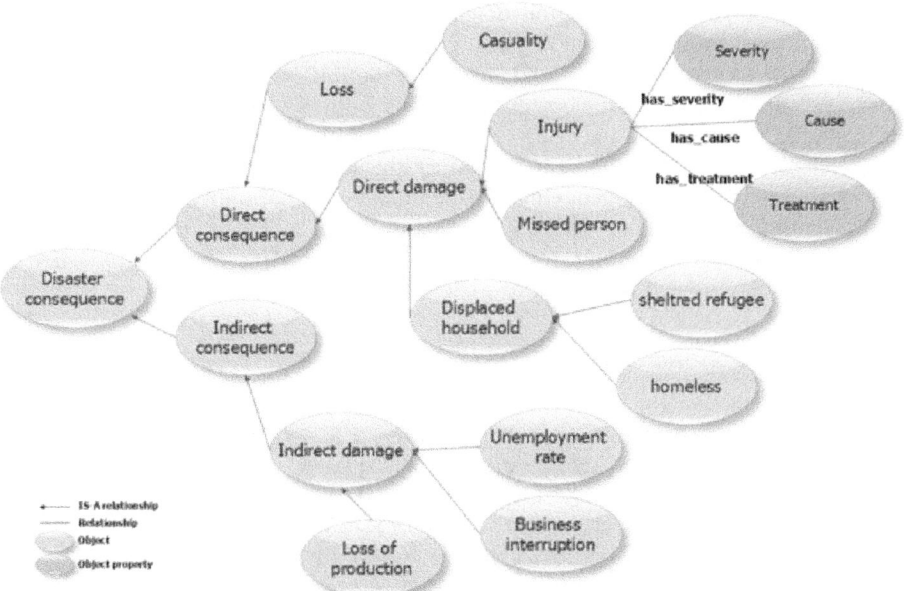

Fig. 1. Ontology fraction on disaster consequences

In fact, in figure 1, all the represented concepts are useful for developing an emergency plan by combining historical data (e.g., direct damages) with estimated properties relatively to different vulnerability scenarios (e.g. causes and severity of injuries). The same fraction of ontology may be used during emergency response stage by producing and accessing to the information relatively to loss and direct damages considering for example the displaced household only in a second emergency response step. Regarding the recovery stage, loss and casualty should not be used as relevant information as other damages as injuries and displaced household and in a following step the indirect consequences useful for a long-term relief process.

Not only for emergency circumstances but also for preparedness and recovery, it is critical that every bit of quantitative or qualitative data brought into the system dealing with the emergency be identified by its human or database source, by its time of occurrence, and by its status. Also, where appropriate, by its location and by links to whatever it is referring to that already exists within the system12]. The use of ontology is consequently useful for tracing these relationships and intrinsic properties of concepts.

4   Conclusions and Further Work

The further work consists of the completion of the ontology with adding the relationships related to communication interactions, i.e.,"*Who communicated what and when?*" considering the entire emergency management workflow. After that the second step should be the evaluation of the obtained ontology. To assess the quality of the design, we will consider the principles from software engineering (i.e., abstraction, modularity, separation of concerns, generality, anticipation for change, and rigor and formality), ontological criteria (i.e., construct overload, construct redundancy, construct excess, and construct deficit). To assess the coverage of concepts and the ease of understanding of the ontology, we will consider doing it through questionnaire and interviews with multidisciplinary users.

Practically speaking, this conceptualization is unlikely to cover all possible potential uses in the contingency management and does not imply any commitment to implementing a related knowledge system. However it may be more appropriate, than ad hoc information modelling, for designing flexible EMISs, particularly when they pursue Service Oriented Architecture's (SOA) design.

References

1. Chandrasekaran, B., Josephson, J.R., Benjamins, V.R.: What are ontologies, and why do we need them? IEEE Intelligent Systems 14, 20–26 (1999)
2. Common Alerting Protocol, v.1.1, OASIS Standard CAP-V1.1 (2005)
3. Common Alerting Protocol Version 1.2, OASIS Standard (2010)
4. Di Maio, P.: An Open Ontology for Open Source Emergency Response System, http://opensource.mit.edu/papers/ TOWARDS_AN_OPEN_ONTOLOGY_FOR_ER.pdf
5. Emergency Data Exchange Language (EDXL) Distribution Element, v. 1.0 OASIS Standard EDXL-DE v1.0, 1 (2006)
6. Executive summary, Ontology, Taxonomy, Folksonomy: Understanding the Distinctions. In: Ontology Summit (2007)
7. Georgakopoulos, D., Hornick, M.F., Sheth, A.P.: An Overview of Workflow Management: Process Modeling to Workflow Automation Infrastructure. Distributed and Parallel Databases 3(2), 119–153 (1995)
8. Li, X., Liu, G., Ling, A., Zhan, L., An, N., Li, L., Sha, Y.: Building a Practical Ontology for Emergency Response Systems. In: International Conference on Computer Science and Software Engineering, pp. 222–225 (2008)
9. Menoni, S.: Encyclopaedia of Natural Hazards, Emergency Planning (2010) (to be edited)

10. Mizoguchi, R., Ikeda, M., Seta, K., Vanwelkenhuysen, J.: Ontology for Modeling the World from Problem Solving Perspectives. In: Proc. Of IJCAI-1995 Workshop on Basic Ontological Issues in Knowledge Sharing, pp. 1–12 (1995)
11. Ngo, P., Wijesekera, D.: Using Ontological Information to Enhance Responder Availability in Emergency Response,
    http://stids.c4i.gmu.edu/papers/STIDS_CR_R5_NgoWijesekera.pdf
12. Rice, R.E.: Information, Computer Mediated Communications and Organizational Innovation. Journal of Communication 37(4), 65–94 (1987)
13. Turoff, M., Chumer, M., Van de Walle, B., Yao, X.: The design of a dynamic emergency response information system. JITTA 5(4), 1–35 (2004)
14. Yu, K., Wang, Q., Rong, L.: Emergency Ontology construction in emergency decision support system. In: IEEE International Conference on Service Operations and Logistics, and Informatics, vol. 1, pp. 801–805 (2008)

Simulator for PROSIMOS (PRiority communications for critical SItuations on MObile networkS) Service

Roberto Gimenez[1], Inmaculada Luengo[1], Anna Mereu[1], Diego Gimenez[2],
Rosa Ana Casar[2], Judith Pertejo[2], Salvador Díaz[3], Jose F. Monserrat[3],
Vicente Osa[3], Javier Herrera[4], Maria Amor Ortega[4], and Iñigo Arizaga[4]

[1] HI-iberia Ingenieria y Proyectos
{rgimenez,iluengo,amereu}@hi-iberia.es
[2] ISDEFE
{dgimenez,racasar,jpertejo}@isdefe.es
[3] Universidad Politecnica de Valencia, iTEAM
{saldiase,jomondel,viosgi}@iteam.upv.es
[4] ROBOTIKER-Tecnalia
{jherrera,mortega,inyigo}@robotiker.es

Abstract. Public Mobile Networks (PMN) are at the very heart of nowadays communications. They are not only used by individuals, but also by a large number of Agencies committed to Security and Safety. This will be even more common in near future, when cities become crowded with real time sensors scattered in every corner of our lives. The ability from this data (and others from First Responders teams) to reach its assigned Command and Control Centers in time can be determinant in a large number of incidents. PROSIMOS project aims at researching on business cases for the implementation of a priority communications system on public mobile networks (PMN). The objective of this system is to enable critical users to communicate during emergency situations, in a time when PMN services may be restricted due to damage, congestion or faults. The scope of the project is to identify the best business case to be adopted to cope with this requirement, guaranteeing its short term implementation in Europe. In order to accomplish this goal a Business Model Simulator has been designed including both economical and network performance features. In this paper we present the Simulator that has been designed in order to identify the most suitable business model and technology to be adopted for the implementation of PROSIMOS service. When taking into consideration enabler technologies for EMSOA PROSIMOS is a not to be missed one.

Keywords: EMSOA Enabler Technology, Priority Communications, Wireless Emergency Communications, Business Models.

Disclaimer. PROSIMOS project has been funded with the support of the Prevention, Preparedness and Consequence Management of Terrorism and other Security-related Risks Programme of the European Commission - Directorate-General Home Affairs". This publication reflects the views only of the authors, and the Commission cannot be held responsible for any use which may be made of the information contained therein.

M. Cezon and Y. Wolfsthal (Eds.): ServiceWave 2010 Workshops, LNCS 6569, pp. 74–81, 2011.
© Springer-Verlag Berlin Heidelberg 2011

1 Introduction

Private Mobile Radios (PMR) like TETRA, TETRAPOL and many other constitute the backbone of nowadays First Responders' Communications. This realization under the shape of different private networks entails, however, several inconveniences: high deployment and maintenance costs and interoperability problems are the most notorious ones.

On the other hand, Public Mobile Networks (PMN) have a penetration ratio superior to 99% of EU territory, interoperability always guaranteed. Nevertheless its public conception has, so far, discouraged its usage during emergencies, since day-to-day experience has shown how, after a catastrophe, increase in service demand brings PMN to default due to the dramatic increase in service demand.

Some countries have been working on how to make available to First Responders Priority Services in their PMN. It is in United States where most serious advances have been made with the implementation of WPS: Wireless Priority Service, introduced in 2002, for public mobile networks. But, other countries such as UK, Peru, Canada, and Sweden have also taken steps in this direction.

In the use case of Spain analyzed in PROSIMOS, priority communications through PMNs are neither available nor planned in the short-term. Communications for safety issues are handled through a plethora of PMR, deployed at national, regional or local scope, with the aforesaid problems of cost and interoperability.

Fig. 1. PMR maze in Spain

The idea of implementing priority services in public mobile networks for First Responders may overcome some of these problems. Even more, now with the hot controversy going on about net neutrality, PROSIMOS concept is to be born in mind. But in order to become a reality, a deep analysis of user requirements, cost and associated business models is erstwhile needed.

This paper introduces a Business Model Simulator (BMS), for addressing this problem, that is being at present moment developed in the frame of the PROSIMOS Project. It does not only include an economical simulator but also a traffic network one to evaluate the technological aspects like congestion side-effects leading to calls drop and maximum network capacity. The BMS takes into account an extensive set of variables basically belonging to three different domains: User Requirements, considered Scenarios, CAPEX and OPEX costs and applicable Radio Access Technologies (RATs).

2   User Requirements and Scenarios

First phase in PROSIMOS project requires a correct definition of user requirements. After in-depth inquires with several First Responders Agencies, PROSIMOS project has been able to sift major needs and translate them into technical understandable parameters. Prioritization (prioritization mechanisms permanently activated, levels of priority, automatic authorized users set-up…), interoperability, high network resilience, availability, trust and ruggedized terminals are the most remarkable ones. These requirements have been reflected into input variables to the BMS. This consideration will allow end-users to verify the fulfillment level of their requirements among the thousands of possible realizations of PROSIMOS.

Also a definition of use cases and emergency scenarios has been performed. For the sake of the project simplicity, four synthetic test scenarios for the validation of PROSIMOS BMS have been defined. These scenarios are: Incident in a Critical Infrastructure (Metro); Natural disaster in a rural area (Forest Fire); Aircraft crash in an airport and a mass gathering event (like a football match).

3   CAPEX and OPEX Costs

In order to estimate the economical impact that the implementation of PROSIMOS service could have on PMN Operators, First Responder Agencies and Government, a deep study of non-recurrent (CAPEX) and operating (OPEX) costs has been needed; in particular, the estimation of these costs in Spain has been performed.

CAPEX costs are mainly (60%) constituted by the update or replacement of the mobile network equipment, that is Mobile Switching Centers (MSC) and Home Location Registers (HLR). In order to compute these costs, the following information is necessary for each mobile operator: number of total MSC and HLR; number of network component that have to be updated on the basis of their lifetime; components unit cost. This information is not available for the public; hence, it has been estimated starting from the information of total number of mobile users, approximate MSC and HLR user capacity and update/replacement costs, and market share of each PMN.

Other CAPEX costs are the following: design and engineering tasks (that cover the cost of consultants); transport, installation and configuration; costs of management and control platform for call priority, that have been estimated starting from other mobile portability platforms; costs of the management and control platform website for user registration and other functionalities for First Responders.

On the other hand, OPEX costs can be classified into fixed and variable costs. Fixed OPEX costs are the structural, personnel and allowance costs related to the new departments founded, and costs related to the operation and maintenance concept. They are the following: priority service management department, that cover the structural and personnel costs; priority service information and training department costs, that cover the structural, personnel and allowance costs; hosting and O&M (Operation and Maintenance) of management and control platform website.

Variable OPEX costs depend on the priority calls routed by the service, in fact it is composed of the quantity: Gross per-minute cost * Priority call length * Number of priority calls: the latter element is quite difficult to estimate at emergency scenario level, but above all, it is difficult to estimate at annual level. One of the goals of the simulator is also the estimation of this quantity.

4 Radio Access Technologies

The ability of PMN to support Priority Services is basic enabler in PROSIMOS. Foundation pillars for this ability are Call Admission Control (CAC) and Congestion Control (CC). CAC is used to control the users' access. CC methods are used to manage the network load in order to ensure the minimum required QoS.

At PROSIMOS considered RAT are GSM/GPRS/EDGE Radio Access Network (GERAN), Universal Mobile Telecommunication System (UMTS) and Long Term Evolution (LTE) technologies. The reason is that the actual public radio technologies deployed in Europe are GERAN and UMTS, while LTE is now considered as the next step forward in the development of 3G networks and its massive roll-out is expected during 2011.

With respect to GERAN RAT and PROSIMOS, three different 3GPP specifications can be used as possible CAC solutions: TS 43.022, TS 22.011 and TS 22.067. The CAC proposed for UMTS are TS 25.304, TS 25.33, TS 22.011 and TS 22.06. Finally, the CAC proposed for LTE is TS 22.011.

When considering CC, one of the first challenges to be solved is determining when the system is overloaded to counteract this state. First step is to know, in average, the load introduced by one user depending on the service. Identifying this load in a GSM system is simple neither for UMTS or LTE. Second, it is important to know the maximum load supported by the network with a specific configuration.

The knowledge of users load is attained thanks to system simulations, conducted to extract the main behavior of users. Extensive simulations have been run in different scenarios and with increasing system loads. Concerning maximum load, this will depend on the business model and the levels of QoS that the operator specifies. PROSIMOS has studied different solutions for the CC implementation in a range of load thresholds that act as inputs for the business simulator described in following section.

In order to determine the technical aspects of the business models, PROSIMOS makes use of a standalone RAT simulator, SPHERE. SPHERE is a novel, ambitious and scalable radio simulation platform for heterogeneous wireless developed in the framework of PROSIMOS. The platform currently integrates five advanced system level simulators, emulating the GERAN, HSDPA, WLAN and LTE RATs.

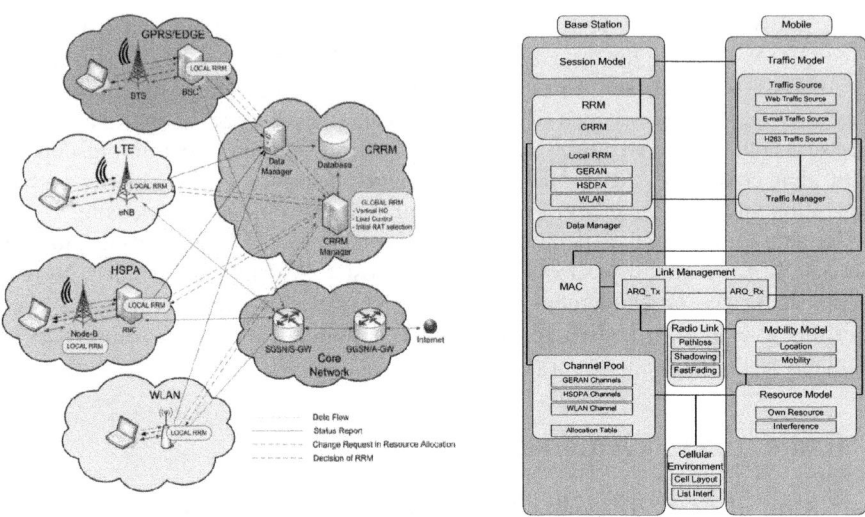

Fig. 2. SPHERE heterogeneous scenario and logic structure

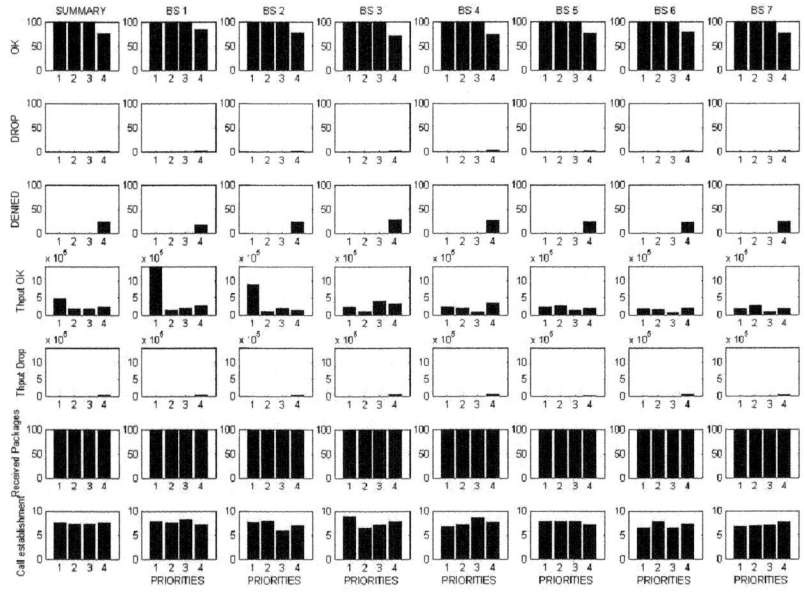

Fig. 3. SPHERE results

SPHERE is a unique simulation platform that emulates all five RATs in parallel and at the packet level, which enables an accurate evaluation of the final user perceived QoS through the implementation of novel Congestion Radio Resources Management (RRM) and RRM mechanisms. The radio interface specifications of these five technologies have been faithfully implemented in the SPHERE simulation platform, which works with a high time resolution. This modeling approach validates the capability of the SPHERE simulation platform to dynamically and precisely evaluate the performance of RRM/CRRM techniques devised in PROSIMOS.

An example of SPHERE simulator results is depicted in Figure 3. We can see that different network performance indicators are shown in correspondence of different Base Station, and then the overall performance. The indicators are: probability of successive calls, probability of dropped calls, probability of denied calls, call establishment time, etc..., for the different priority class. Note that three priority levels have been defined for First Responders, whereas the fourth level is the one assigned to civilians.

These parameters corresponding to the different emergency scenarios, RAT technologies and user requirements, are then given as input to the Business Model simulator.

5 Business Models

PROSIMOS project outcome is expected to foster the development and favorable regulatory for a set of new services for First Responders across Europe. In order to reach this point it is necessary, however, that the corresponding business models are defined. The basic starting point is the costs analysis, since it will impact the whole business model chain. In PROSIMOS different schemes can be applied in order to translate non-recurrent (CAPEX) and operating (OPEX) cost to the three actors that are considered to be economically supporting the system: Government, First Responder Agencies and finally PMN Operators. In following lines we will produce the three business models that have been considered in PROSIMOS. It has to be noted that these Business Models have been produced after an extensive analysis and synthesis of the different implementation of PROSIMOS service worldwide (in USA, UK, Peru...).

In the first approach it is considered that countries Governments should be responsible for providing needed infrastructure for PROSIMOS, covering CAPEX costs (which in the Spanish case tot up to 48 million-odd Euros), while network operators should take care of OPEX costs. A further step in this line of though considers the share of the OPEX costs among the different mobile operators on their market position. This first type of business model has been named Model OnlyOp, thus referring to the fact that mobile operators only have to cover OPEX costs.

In the second solution we consider what happens when the customer (First Responder agencies) actively takes part in the cost distribution. This means that both CAPEX and OPEX costs can be divided in different ways and percentages between country Government, mobile operators and First Responders agencies. Also in this case all the mobile operators owning a private infrastructure are induced to implement PROSIMOS service. This second type of business model has been referred as Model 3Shared, implying that in this case three entities participate to the distribution of costs.

Finally, the third considered business model encompasses the complex procedures of Public Authorities, bringing up into discussion the issue of public open contests calls for service provision, with the objective of selecting which mobile operator would (on a sole/joint venture basis) implement PROSIMOS service. Only those mobile operators interested in deploying the service would apply to the call (needed appealing of the business model). Decision award criteria would have then to consider the distribution of the costs among the three parties and also the associated operational gain. This third business model has been called Model Exc, thus referring to the fact that in this case an exclusive agreement between a customer segment and a mobile operator according to free market practices is to be reached. As can be seen, each Business Model represents an evolution in complexity from previous ones.

The proposed models vary also from the point of view of the different revenue sources that can be applied (subscription fees, call per minute costs, flat rates, etc...) and they can be further differentiated in other variants that we will not describe here for brevity.

In order to validate the Business Model, a specific Simulator is being developed (in final stage at present moment) in the frame of the project, limited to the Spanish use case, as aforesaid mentioned: the simulator will perform an estimation of costs and incomes for the different business models thus allowing to better understand the most suitable one to be adopted.

It is not indeed straightforward the identification of the best business model for PROSIMOS service without the support of a simulator. This difficulty mainly arises from the fact that several actors take part on the business process. Rather than being a trivial customer/suppliers matter, where companies aim at reaching the maximum profit guaranteeing the satisfaction of the customers' needs, it is a public interest matter where also government and First Responder have to pay a key role in order to foster the implementation of the service. For this reason, we think that business models including a participation of government and emergency agencies in the distribution of costs will probably turn out to be the most suited one.

At this point, an important point must be raised. It is that PROSIMOS Business Models and associated Simulator are considering, at present moment, only voice communications. Although the network simulator (SPHERE) is able of providing information about data traffic behavior, the complexity of already performed work and the foreseen load associated to defining the corresponding BM for data traffic and holistic (voice and traffic) ones have strongly suggested to limit research at this stage only to voice capabilities, providing then the uppermost quality results.

PROSIMOS BMS will help future entities involved in PROSIMOS service to evaluate the performance of the service as well as the implementation costs and the type of revenue sources that are most suitable to refund the investment.

Concerning the BMS, it is composed of three main parts, one committed to the web interface, that will provide a friendly user interface, another one to the specific MATLAB business model simulator development and a third one comprised by auxiliary elements (MySQL database and the SPHERE simulator previously presented).

Previous input parameters are fed to the BMS through PROSIMOS' Web Interface (certain simplification is applied). Then BMS processes the input variables extracted from the database, through the different Data Analysis Modules. The obtained results are passed to the Data Processing Module in order to calculate the final outcomes, as for example, call cost or CAPEX and OPEX distribution. Finally, all output variables stored in the database are shown in the PROSIMOS Web Portal in an aggregated and understandable way. Examples of output variables are Internal Rate of Return, Gross Profit, Net Profit, Incomes (for Mobile Operators); number and type of prioritized calls (First Responders) carried out along the incident, etc.

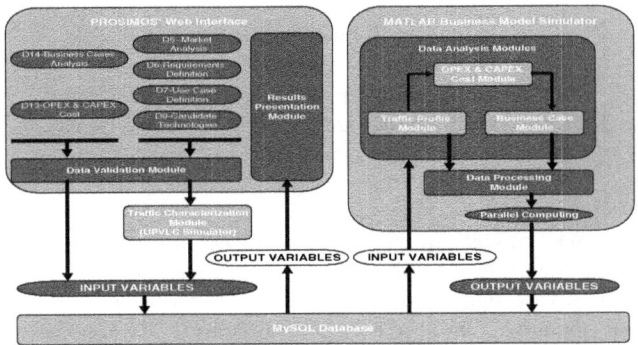

Fig. 4. Business Model Simulator Architecture

6   Conclusions and Current Progress of Work

Prioritization of First Responder communications in Public Mobile Networks will be an essential service in close future for some specific uses cases. PROSIMOS can be then regarded as an enabler "technology" for EMSOA. Conducted research has so far proposed both the technical business models approaches. Both of them will be validated in the simulation phase and are expected to provide important conclusions and recommendations for subsequent steps. At present moment the development of the BMS is in its final stage, and the simulation phase is expected to start in short time. It is expected that the BMS will be available through the project webpage (www.prosimos.eu) to authorized users and general public (under request).

Reference

PROSIMOS project public deliverables, http://www.prosimos.eu

Active Knowledge Modeling Supporting Emergency Mitigation

John Krogstie

Dept. of Computer and Information Science
Norwegian University of Science and Technology, 7491 Trondheim, Norway
krogstie@idi.ntnu.no

Abstract. We present in this paper a model-oriented approach, Active Knowledge Modeling (AKM) to provide flexible support to emergency mitigation. A case study has been performed on the approach. Although the case was performed in a restricted environment, the feedback from the participants was promising as for the expected needs of flexibility in the process that an AKM solution allows. Further work has to be done, both over a longer term following more of the emergency management process, and following other cases in other settings to support the utility of the approach.

1 Introduction

An emergency is "an unwanted and usually unexpected and sudden situation that threatens or damages humans, animals, property and/or the environment".

Emergency management is the sequence of decisions taken in order to limit the extent and damages of a crisis and, if possible, cease it.

An emergency typically suffers from uncertainty, shortage of time, lack of control, and lack of information. The regular decision process may have broken down and many different actors are involved. Emergency Management Information Systems (EMISs) provide a set of ICT tools for supporting the emergency management process during its entire lifecycle: mitigation, preparedness, response, and recovery phases. We will in this paper focus on the mitigation part, in particular the work needed to have a good information-basis to deal with likely emergencies. Although the main steps in building up information in an area can be modeled in a standard way on a high level, there is large variety of ways of performing this work, different ways that might fit the working style of different people differently. Thus putting too much emphasis on supporting a standardized information capturing and structuring process might be counterproductive. At the same time one want to ensure a certain level of coordination between the different people involved.

Active Knowledge Modeling [6] is an approach where one by using interactive process models can support processes that emerge through the usage pattern of the users [4]. We will in this paper illustrate how AKM can be used in supporting the information capturing aspects of emergency mitigation through a case study. In the next two sections we describe the emergency management process and AKM in more detail, including an application related to information management. Then a case study is presented, before we summarize the main results from the study.

M. Cezon and Y. Wolfsthal (Eds.): ServiceWave 2010 Workshops, LNCS 6569, pp. 82–89, 2011.

2 Overall Approach to Emergency Management

It is an ultimate objective to make all relevant *knowledge* accessible in an emergency. A wide range of preparation activities are necessary, such as planning, information gathering, training and documentation of experience and knowledge to prepare for the future. Making the information available in such a way that it may influence plans and future actions, involves a number of tasks:

- Retrieval and selection of relevant information.
- Organization of general and more specialized knowledge representations in a repository
- A representation language that is simple, flexible and user-oriented.

In addition to preparing the different actors for an emergency, planning, simulations and training can also be used to learn how the information system support should be customized and configured for different user roles, i.e., what information and services are needed by whom, and when. Fig. 1 illustrates how the emergency management phases of mitigation, preparedness, recovery and response can cooperate around a common emergency management repository. In this article, we concentrate on the information management in mitigation phase.

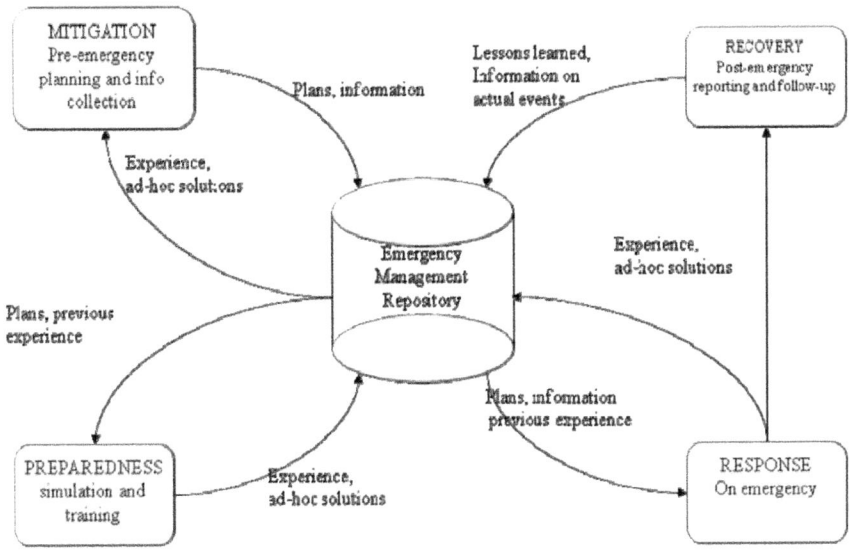

Fig. 1. Main parts of an emergency management system

3 Introduction of AKM

The Active Knowledge Modeling (AKM) [5, 6] approach is about discovering, externalizing, expressing, representing, sharing, exploring, configuring, activating, growing and managing enterprise knowledge. Active and work-centric knowledge has some very important intrinsic properties found in mental models of the human mind, such as reflective views, repetitive flows, recursive tasks and replicable knowledge architecture elements. One approach to benefit from these intrinsic properties is by enabling users to perform enterprise modeling using the AKM platform services to model methods, and execute work using role-specific, model-generated and configured workplaces (MGWP). Visual knowledge modeling should be as easy for users as scribbling in order for them to express their knowledge while performing work, learning and excelling in their roles. This will also enable users to capture contextual dependencies between roles, tasks, information elements and the views required for performing work.

To be active [1], a visual model must be available to the users of the underlying information system at execution time. Second, the model must influence the behavior of the computerized work support system. Third, the model must be dynamically extended and adapted, users must be supported in changing the model to fit their local needs, enabling tailoring of the system's behavior. Normal users should therefore be able to manipulate and use knowledge models as part of their day-to-day work [2].

In this case we used as starting point the Extended Enterprise Modeling Language (EEML) [3]. The kernel concepts are shown in Fig. 2 as a simplified logical meta-model. The process logic is mainly expressed through nested structures of *tasks* and *decision points*. The sequencing of the tasks is expressed by the *flow* relation. *Roles* are used to connect resources of various kinds (people, organisations, information, and tools) to the tasks.

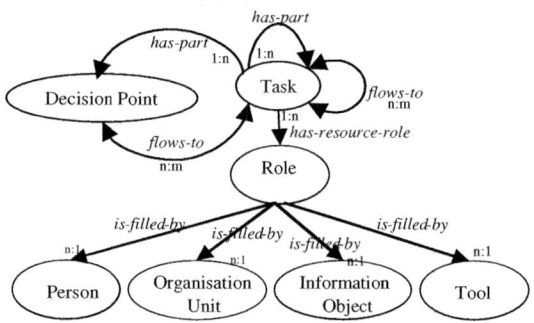

Fig. 2. Simplified meta-model of EEML

Moreover, the interactive nature of the models, meaning that the users are free to refine them during execution, increases their potential as sources of experience and knowledge. As such they *document* details on how the work was actually done, not only how it was once planned.

A prototype process-support environment, supporting this language (and other languages) was used in the case study below.

Based on the input from domain experts from several parts of the case organization, a generic process for Information management has been developed as illustrated in Fig. 3. The figure illustrate the top level of the model, the individual tasks are further decomposed in the model (not shown here).

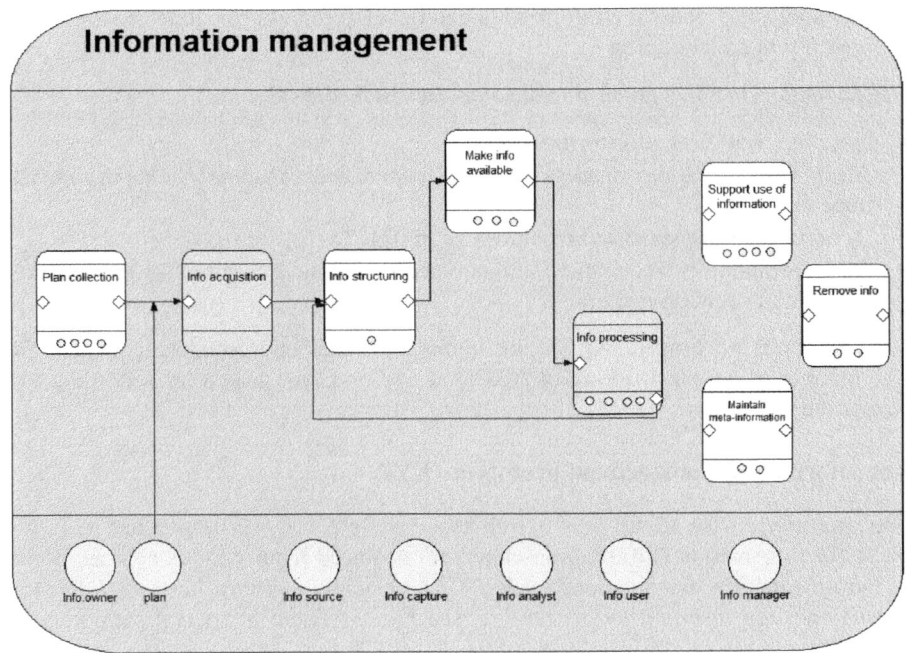

Fig. 3. Generic information management process

In its present state the model is primarily for human inspection, - no process execution engine is available for executing the model. However, tool support for *fragments* of the process was tested out in the case study, highlighted in yellow in Fig. 3, see below for further description.

4 Case Study

In this section we report a test performed with users for supporting part of the information gathering process. The idea was to get input on a model-based prototype system supporting part of the information management model in the ABCD-unit.

The main task of ABCD is to support the emergency management by retrieving information from various sources and process it into reports. ABCD handles information from any kind of information source, from various types of monitoring equipment to people. The work in the unit roughly proceeds as follows:

- The main questions to get answered are formulated in collaboration with the customer. Each main question is broken down into a set of more detailed question, each of which is detailed into several elements of information.
- Information/data from each type of source are collected into a temporary, source-specific storage.
- The information from each storage is distributed to the various analysts according to the domain of expertise of each analyst

- The analysts process the information and develop reports based on the information, possibly in collaboration.

  The main principles governing the activities in ABCD are:

- Only one way flow of information
- All information at any processing level (from raw data to analysis reports) must be traceable
- Definite roles are specified for the work in ABCD
- All information is to be stored at one place, which is accessible for the analysts as well as the decision makers.

The people working in ABCD are highly educated and competent in their field. The number of people working in ABCD at any one time may vary according to the size of the operation.

The information management prototype (XYZ)

The prototype to be tested was a web-based system for *registering* and *classifying* pieces of information (information elements) acquired from various sources. Related to the Information management model, XYZ basically support the tasks *information acquisition and information processing,* see Fig. 3. There is no real support for the actual planning.

The solution was based on a generic infrastructure for AKM-solutions. The prototype was configured by visual modeling (no programming), based on input from the case organization concerning which fields should be available for registering the relevant information. Due to time limitation, there was no time for tuning the solution before the trial. Nor did we get the opportunity for training the participants. Hence, the first day of the trial was also the first encounter the users had with the solution.

The model based configuration made the solution flexible, as most of the user interface elements (form, field, links) could be altered on the fly.

Key concepts in XYZ

The key concept in the system is that of 'Information element', referring to any piece of information that the user may wish to record. The information elements are to be "classified" by linking it to elements from the classification structures available and in normal use in the organization. The elements of the classification structure are updated continuously in parallel with registering information elements. Hence, whenever any of the incoming information adds to what is known about a registered person, organization, etc, this information is to be filled into the appropriate field. This way, one will not only provide a classification structure for Information elements, but this structure will constitute a comprehensive knowledge base in itself. It also implies the classification structure is under continuous change.

The XYZ test

The main objective of the test was to investigate if the approach taken in XYZ is appropriate for supporting information gathering and structuring.

The XYZ test was performed during two days in a single room at the premises of the case organization, using computers linked to a server over dedicated net. Hence, the trial was purely experimental and off-field – no real-life testing was attempted.

The test setting was an example of preparing for a operation. The information to be used as information sources was a number of text files retrieved by one of the test participants from relevant archives. The text files were loaded into the test server prior to the test. The subjects/participants of the trial were 10 people from ABCD. In addition two facilitators/observers were present. The overall process of the test was as follows:

1. Initially a brief introduction to the system was given.
2. Two of the participants decomposed the main question, while the others tried to familiarize themselves with the system and the corresponding approach.
3. Then the tasks were distributed among the participants. Using the provided text files, the participants then tried to answer their tasks by
   - searching for and reading potentially relevant text
   - registering new information elements in the system
   - updating the classification structure
4. When some amount of information had been registered, visualization of this information in a graphical enterprise modeling tool was provided.

Results and experiences from the trial

The trial was performed without logging; the results of the test was obtained by observation (the facilitators were present all the time during the test) and feedback forms. Instead of filling in the feedback-form individually, the participants decided to do it in cooperation. This approach resulted in a useful discussion, and provided a uniform feedback. A brief summary of the feedback is listed below

Conceptualization

'Information element' is a key concept in XYZ. As it turned out, this did not coincide with the participants' way of thinking. Their normal approach being to fill out the classification structure directly as completely as possible, using XYZ it was not always easy to decide whether the incoming information should be registered as an information element and linked to the classification structure, or some field in some part of the classification structure should be filled out. Often, both were necessary. However, the participants quickly got the idea of the "information element" concept, and came up with relevant requirements concerning how to update several affected parts of the classification structure directly from one information element.

Functionality

- Traceability must be preserved all the way from source documents to reports; it is not enough to be able to link information elements to the classification structure.
- XYZ did not offer any support for processing source documents, leaving the user with a lot of detailed reading to do.

- A seamless registration interface, independent of object type, is needed. During registration of new information, it is crucial that the need for navigating/clicking back and forth be minimized, and it should of course not be necessary to insert a piece of information more than once. Hence, one uniform page for registering new objects of any type is wanted, with functions to indicate which type and field should be updated with the new information.

User interface

- The user interface should be configurable, so as to be adapted to each single operation, client, role, etc in question. Minor things should also be configurable by the individual user.
- One should be able to apply color coding in the user interface, to promote good overview and instant awareness of the important changes in elements. This is especially relevant for planning, where color may be used to visualize completion status.
- Sort order in lists must be flexible and configurable. Ideally, any field in an element type could be used as sorting criteria. Which fields to actually apply should be configurable by the individual user.
- Graphical visualization (in the enterprise modeling tool) is a nice facility, especially as support for presenting the information to clients and others.

5 Conclusions

We have in this paper presented a case of using an AKM-solution to support the information management task of mitigation in emergency management.

The experience from the test described in the previous section indicates that in an environment specializing in information handling, the following services and features would be useful:

- Tailorable user interface: Operations vary greatly in many respects, and it is crucial that the supporting system can be configured to accommodate for and adapt to any variant. Moreover, within a single operation it is often so that separate roles have different needs for support and that also different people acting in the same role might prefer different ways of working, meaning that the system should also facilitate configuration on an individual level.
- Process support: This involves systems supporting the overall workflow of the operation, rather than supporting only specific tasks within the operation. In the kind of work focused on by ABCD, it specifically would mean to support both planning and following up the mission.
- Flexible linking between information elements of any kind: In the kind of enterprises we are talking about here, information forms the main product, and the key activities focus on combining known or believed facts to infer new hypotheses or facts.
- Information presentation and visualization: To present information in a way that facilitates understanding in an audience mostly means to construct some simplified view on to a complex web of information.

Model-generated workplaces based on Active Knowledge Models seem like a promising approach in this area, but we need to provide more long-term cases studies where one support also the other parts of the emergency management process and studies in other environments to investigate this more fully.

References

1. Jørgensen, H.D.: Interaction as a Framework for Flexible Workflow Modelling. In: Proceedings of GROUP 2001, Boulder, USA (2001)
2. Krogstie, J.: Modelling of the People, by the People, for the People. In: Conceptual Modelling in Information Systems Engineering. Springer, Berlin (2007)
3. Krogstie, J.: Combined Goal and Process Oriented Modeling: A Case Study. In: EMMSAD 2008 (2008)
4. Krogstie, J., Jørgensen, H.D.: Interactive models for supporting networked organisations. In: Persson, A., Stirna, J. (eds.) CAiSE 2004. LNCS, vol. 3084, pp. 550–563. Springer, Heidelberg (2004)
5. Lillehagen, F.: The foundation of the AKM Technology. In: Jardim-Goncalves, R., Cha, H., Steiger-Garcao, A. (eds.) Proceedings of the 10th International Conference on Concurrent Engineering, CE 2003, Madeira, Portugal. A.A. Balkema Publishers, Rotterdam (2003)
6. Lillehagen, F., Krogstie, J.: Active Knowledge Modeling of Enterprises. Springer, Heidelberg

A JXTA-Based Peer Architecture for Enhanced Service Discovery in SOA-Based P2P Applications

Paolo Bocciarelli, Andrea D'Ambrogio, and Michele Angelaccio

Dept. of Computer Science Systems and Production
University of Roma TorVergata, Roma, Italy
{bocciarelli,dambro,angelaccio}@disp.uniroma2.it

Abstract. The adoption of a P2P paradigm for implementing software applications based on service oriented architectures (SOA) is gaining momentum as a valid alternative to the classic client-server paradigm. In this context, service providers are strategically interested to describe and manage the quality of service (QoS) characteristics of offered services. The ability to carry out QoS-oriented service discovery activities is an essential issue for effectively managing the QoS of SOA-based P2P applications and as consequence to guarantee an good quality level among collaborating services. To this purpose, this paper introduces a JXTA-based peer architecture for enhanced service discovery in SOA-based P2P applications. The proposed approach builds upon a model-driven framework for predicting, at composition time, and managing, at execution time, the QoS of SOA-based P2P applications.

1 Introduction

The adoption of service oriented architectures (SOA)[12] is becoming mainstream in the design and implementation of large-scale distributed applications. SOAs are based on the concept of service, that is an atomic, self-contained and network reachable software unit that offers a specific and well-defined set of operations. In this scenario, a distributed application can be seen as a composition of a set of services in execution onto networked server hosts. The SOA provides the necessary support for the consolidation of multiple services into the overall application process. Web services [1] are the preferred technology for implementing the service concept. The Web services specification provides the mechanisms for the description, the publication, the discovery and the invocation of services. A service provider describes the service by creating a WSDL document, and then publishes it to one or more remote registries, such as UDDI. The service consumer retrieves the service description by enquiring the UDDI registries, and then uses such description to develop an application that interacts with the remote service via the SOAP protocol. One of the major weaknesses of the traditional SOA-based infrastructures, is that UDDI is a centralized repository that represents a single point of failure. The Peer-to-Peer (P2P) paradigm is emerging as a valid alternative to the classic client-server paradigm, and P2P overlay

M. Cezon and Y. Wolfsthal (Eds.): ServiceWave 2010 Workshops, LNCS 6569, pp. 90–100, 2011.

networks are becoming a promising, efficient, scalable and fault-resilient infrastructure for the implementation of SOA-based applications. In a P2P network the discovery can be implemented through decentralized approaches, maximizing the benefits deriving by the use of a distributed environment. In this context, the quality of service (QoS) management of composite services is a challenging issue. The availability of a wide number of peers joined to the network implies that several services, covering the same functional requirements, but with different QoS attributes, may be available. Services providers are strategically interested in the QoS management of the offered services, both at design and at execution time. At design time providers are interested to select the services that satisfy the QoS-oriented user requirements. At execution time they are instead interested to monitor the offered services in order to dynamically re-deploy or re-configure the composite service in case the agreed QoS level is no more satisfied. Our past work [7] proposes a model-driven approach for predicting at composition time, and managing at execution time, the QoS of composite services. In such an approach, a composite service is initially described in terms of its abstract model, i.e. a BPEL description representing the abstract workflow of the process. An extension of UML model, based on UML Profile for Scheduling, Performance and Time (SPT Profile)[11] is used to annotate performance data onto UML representations of BPEL processes. The automatic annotation of performance data onto BPEL-extended UML models is carried out by use of P-WSDL (Performance-enabled WSDL) [5] a lightweight extension of WSDL[15] based on the SPT Profile.

The UML performance-enabled description of the resulting composite service is finally translated into a LQN (Layered Queueing Network) performance model. In [2] we have extended and applied such a model-driven approach in a P2P environment. To this purpose, we have introduced Q-WSDL [6], a WSDL extention that takes into consideration a wide description of the QoS characteristics of a web services, thus not limited to the performance-related characteristics. In such a contribution we have proposed QSHARE, a novel peer architecture that

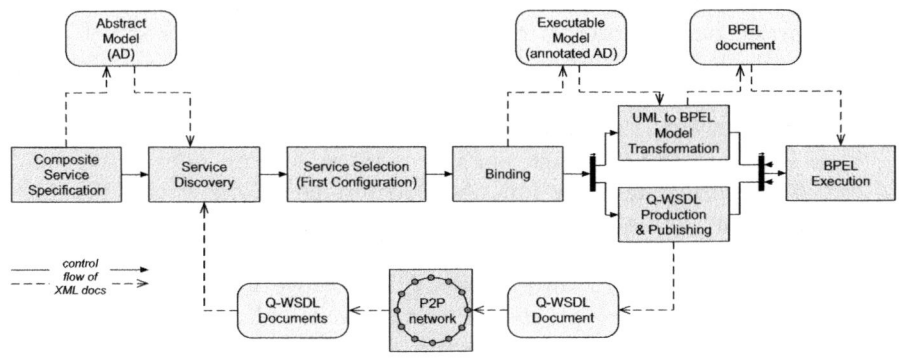

Fig. 1. Framework for the QoS management at design time

enables the QoS-based description and discovery of services in SOA-based P2P applications. QSHARE focuses specifically on the definition of an architecture for the keyword-based and QoS-enabled discovery of services in a SOA-based P2P application. It is easy to be convinced that such an extended service discovery can be considered as an essential feature of the framework for the QoS management. In this paper we proposes a first step towards the implementation of keyword-based and QoS-enabled discovery of services. Several challenging issues have been faced in the concrete application of the proposed approach. First of all the P2P infrastructures do not support natively a QoS-related description of available resources. Furthermore, the widely used structured and distributed P2P networks, such as CAN, Pastry or JXTA do not support a keyword-based discovery. In this paper we specifically focus on the JXTA-based implementation of the QSHARE architecture. The rest of paper is organized as follows: in Section 2 the model-driven framework for the QoS management of SOA-based P2P applications is briefly recalled. Section 3 summarizes the basic concepts of the JXTA P2P platform, while in Section 4 the JXTA-based QSHARE architecture is proposed. Finally, Section 5 gives an example application.

2 Model-Driven QoS Management Framework

In [3] we have proposed a model driven framework for managing the QoS of a SOA-based P2P application. In [2] such framework has been enriched by introducing the QSHARE peer architecture, which specifies how QoS attributes can be added to the service specification and how a QoS-enabled discovery step can be carried out. In this section we briefly recall the concepts behind the model-driven framework, in order to emphasize the differences between QoS management activities at design time, and at execution time. At design time, as shown in Figure 1, the distributed application is initially specified in terms of its *abstract model*,

that is a workflow of abstract services, described by means of an UML Activity Diagram (AD). Beside the functional requirements, specified by the abstract model, at this step the offered level of QoS has to be specified. A service discovery is then carried out in order to bind the abstract services to a set of concrete services available in the P2P network. Two main issues are to be addressed:

- in a P2P network a centralized UDDI registry is not generally available;
- in a P2P network, for each abstract service, a large number of concrete services covering the same functional requirements, but with different QoS characteristic, will be generally available.

To face this issues, a keyword-based service discovery that also considers the QoS characteristics of services should be made available. In section 4 a JXTA-based peer architecture that attempts to solve these problems is proposed.

Once a set of candidate services has been gathered for each abstract service, a service selection activity is carried out to identify the first configuration of the composite service: each abstract service in the abstract model is mapped to a specific concrete service, in order to satisfy both the functional and non-functional requirements of the overall distributed application. At this step, the abstract model is transformed into an *executable model,* consisting of an AD annotated with binding and performance data obtained from the Q-WSDL descriptions of concrete services. Finally, once the executable model is available, a BPEL engine is used to actually execute the application. At the same time, due to the fact that the composite service can be considered itself a new web service, the Q-WSDL description is derived and advertised within the P2P network. In order to better evaluate all the candidate configurations for the composite service, a *QoS analysis model* that takes into account the scalability issues related to the resource contention of software/hardware elements is to be built and evaluated for each configuration. Unfortunately, the first configuration of the composite service cannot be investigated by use of such techniques, due to the fact the the number of different models that are to be built and evaluated can be considerably high. To this purpose, a heuristic approach is to be preferred. As mentioned above, at execution time the QoS of the application is constantly monitored, as shown in Figure 2, that represents the framework for QoS management at execution time. Whether the operational conditions of the P2P network change (i.e., new nodes enter the network, one or more nodes fail, the QoS of a concrete service degrades, etc.) a QoS monitor, as proposed in the architecture presented in [4], enables the reconfiguration step. Starting from the abstract model and the executable model generated at the previous step, a keyword-based discovery is carried out in order to retrieve the candidate services that can replace the service (or the services) responsible for the QoS downgrade. A model-driven transformation is carried out to obtain the QoS analysis model that, once solved, allows to check if the evaluated configuration is able to satisfy the QoS requirements. The advantages of our methodology is that results obtained in first configuration will be enforced at execution time, where efficient evaluation techniques are used to adjust the configuration of the distributed application, in case of unavailability of a concrete service or of an unsatisfactory level of offered QoS.

3   JXTA Basic Concepts

JTXA [8] is a research project that defines a set of open protocols that enables peer-to-peer (P2P) computing. JXTA is not an API, and the specified protocols are totally independent of any program language. Several implementations, known as bindings, are available for specific languages such as Java or C++; In this paper we focuses specifically on the JAVA 2 binding (JXTA-JXSE ver 2.5) [9].

   A peer is the basic entity (e.g., a PC, a laptop, a PDA) connected to P2P network and it is univocally identified by a PeerId. Each peer provide a set of services that other peers in the P2P network can discover and use. All the peers must implement a set of core services and may also provide a set of additional services.

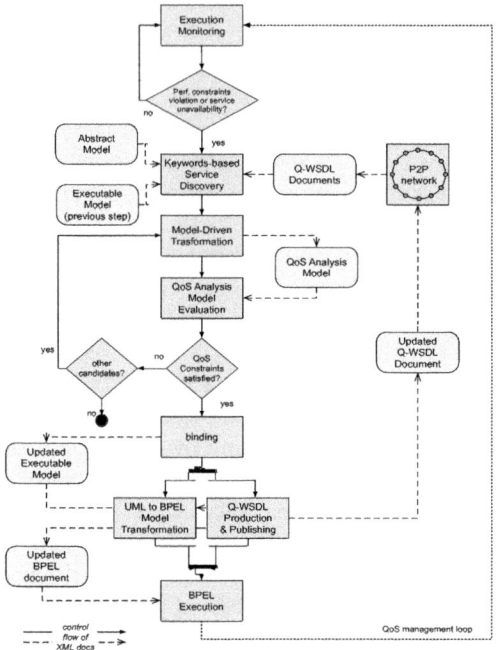

Fig. 2. Framework for the QoS management at execution time

In JXTA two types of peer can be found:

- *Edge Peer*: a node that implements all the core services; in a P2P interaction an edge peer behaves either as a client or as a server, depending on wheter it is a provider or a consumer of a service in the specific interaction.
- *Rendezvous Peer*: a node that supports edge peers in the retrieving of resources in the P2P network. The rendezvous peers maintain a repository of all the peers, services and other resources available in the network and are specifically involved in the indexing and discovering of those resources.

In JXTA all of the resources (i.e., peers, groups, services) are generically represented by an advertisement. An advertisement is a structured XML document describing the associated resource. Peers publish advertisements to publish the provided resources and to make them available to other peers. Other peers should search for advertisements in order to discover the resources available in the P2P network. The use of advertisements enables a powerful method that unifies the problem of finding resources within the network. Each peer, instead of facing each time a different problem for a specific kind of resources, has only to consider the general problem. Regardless the type of the specific resources, peers that aim to advise (or search) resources within the network, should:

- build an advertisement for the provided resource and publish it;
- discover advertisements describing the needed resources.

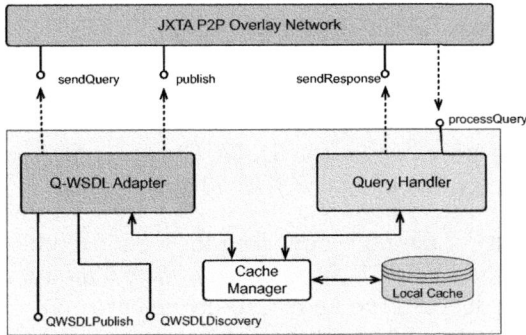

Fig. 3. JXTA-based Peer Architecture

The routing and the indexing in JXTA are based on a novel approach, that uses a loosely-consistent DHT with a limited-range rendezvous walker, defined Shared Resource Distributed Index (SDRI). A complete description about the SRDI and the routing mechanism is out of the scope of this paper. For a detailed description about SRDI the reader is sent to [13], an extensive explanation of the JXTA routing and discovery features can be found in [14] while a complete description about the JXTA protocols can be found in [10].

4   JXTA-Based Peer Architecture

Figure 3 illustrates the proposed peer architecture. It is based upon the QSHARE architecture, already discussed in [2] , and it is specialized taking into account the capabilities provided by the JXTA overlay network. The JXTA-based peer architecture is composed of the following elements:

- *Q-WSDL Adapter*: component that provides the methods:
  - QWSDLPublish(String QWSDLDoc)
  - QWSDLDiscovery(String[] keywords)

  Such methods realize an interface for publishing and discovering Q-WSDL documents, by hiding the low-level and implementation-specific primitives provided by the overlay network.
- *Query Handler*: a component that implements the JXTA interface Such methods realize an interface for publishing and discovering Q-WSDL documents, by hiding the low-level and implementation-specific primitives provided by the overlay network.
- *Query Handler*: a component that implements the JXTA interface *net.jxta.resolver. QueryHandler*, responsible for the processing of incoming query messages. It also interacts with the overlay network in order to send the response messages.
- *Local Cache*: local repository that stores the JXTA advertisements. In our scope, the local cache is used to store the advertisements associated to the Q-WSDL documents

- *Cache Manager* component responsible for the storing and the retrieving of Q-WSDL documetns in the local repository.
- `sendQuery` and `sendResponse` methods provided by the JXTA Resolver Protocol, which implement a routing mechanisms for query and response messages within the network.
- `publish` method provided by the JXTA Discovery Protocol, used to advertise and to make available a Q-WSDL advertisement.

The `QWSDPublish()` method is invoked in order to publish a Q-WSDL advertisement, while the *QWSDL Adapter* component interacts with the JXTA overlay network to advertise the Q-WSDL document to all of the peers participating to the P2P network. On the other hand, a peer that aims to retrieve a specific service, invokes the `QWSDLDiscovery()` method, in order to start a keyword-based discovery. The `QWSDPublish()` method is invoked in order to publish a Q-WSDL advertisement, while the *QWSDL Adapter* component interacts with the JXTA overlay network to advertise the Q-WSDL document to all of the peers participating to the P2P network. On the other hand, a peer that aims to retrieve a specific service, invokes the `QWSDLDiscovery()` method, in order to start a keyword-based discovery. The adapter creates a query message and invokes the JXTA method `sendQuery()`, to route the query towards the destination peer(s).

The *QueryHandler* component is instead in charge of managing the incoming query request messages. The next section gives the description of the keyword-based discovery.

4.1   Keyword-Based Service Discovery

The sequence diagrams of Figures 4 and 5 show how a peer interacts with the objects provided by the JXTA reference implementation during the discovery of an advertisement. The main ideas behind the shown interaction are the following: the `QWSDLDiscovery()` method, bypassing the JXTA discovery protocol, first uses the `QWSDLQueryMessage()` method to create directly a Q-WSDL query and then asks the Resolver Protocol to route it within the network. An edge peer that receives that message looks whether an advertisement matching the keywords exists in its is local cache. In the positive case the peer creates the response message, otherwise the query is discarded.

5   QSHARE Example Application

Let us consider the case of an adaptive workflow for nomadic operators connected through a wireless MANET infrastructure. The need of adapting the task process graph to existing contexts in an efficient way might require an adaptive service architecture that cannot be realized by use of a centralized approach but rather by use of a p2p approach like the one considered by QSHARE. As an example, let us consider an emergency scenario in which, in case of an earthquake, a search and rescue team is in charge of assuming the control of the situation. The

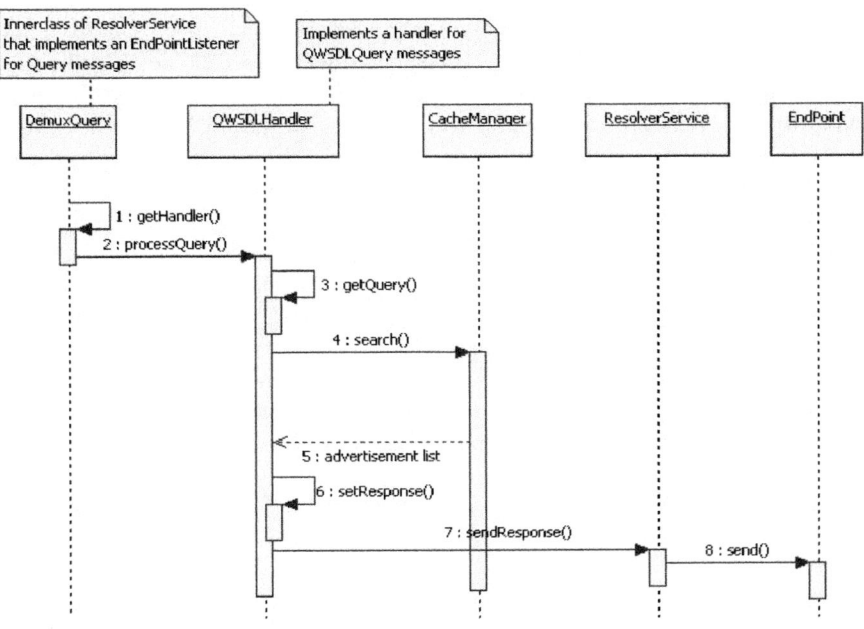

Fig. 4. Keyword-based discovery of Q-WSDL Advertisement at requestor side

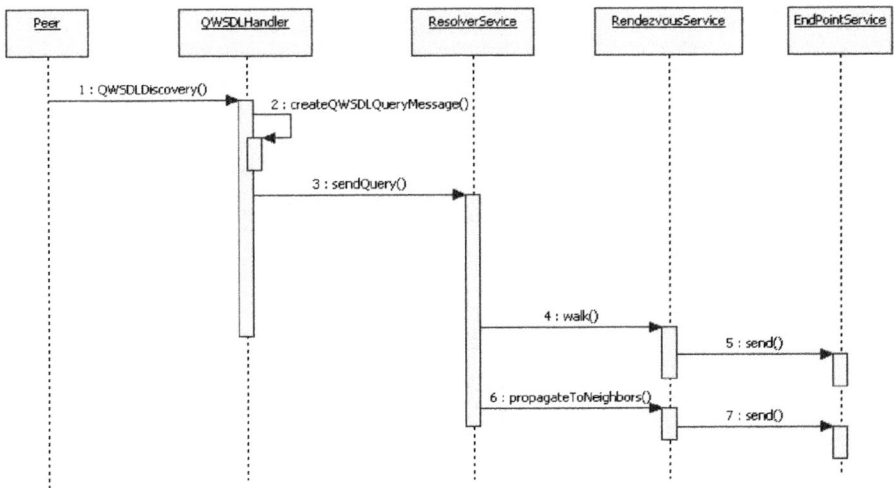

Fig. 5. Keyword-based discovery of Q-WSDL Advertisement at requestor side

Team Member 1 (TM1) is sent to the emergency site for taking pictures of the damaged buildings using his mobile device equipped with a digital camera and enabled for wireless connection. Once the pictures have been taken, TM1, by means of a keyword-based service discovery, query the P2P network to identify a service for sharing the pictures with the other members and uses the provided UploadImage operation to transfer the pictures. Finally TM1 notifies the other members about the availability of new images, that will be processed to plan the emergency operations on the damaged site. The behavior of TM1 is shown in Figure 6. In such a case, the QoS evaluation is a crucial issue. The selection of the concrete service for image sharing is heavily influenced by the provided bandwidth: the more bandwidth is guaranteed by the provider, the faster will be the intervention of the search and rescue team.

Once gathered the Q-WSDL descriptions (and consequently the associated QoS characteristics), is able to evaluate which is the most convenient service that provides the needed operation and is thus enabled to bind such a concrete service to the abstract service in the workflow.

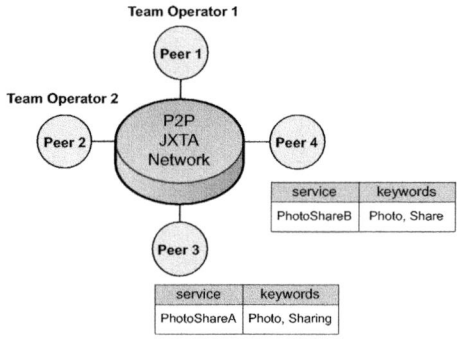

Fig. 6. Behaviour of TM1

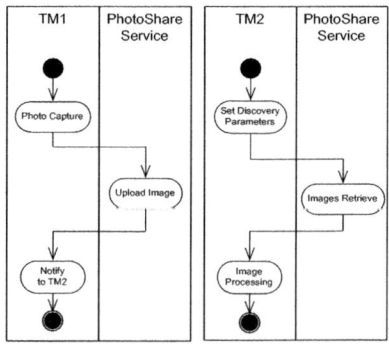

Fig. 7. Network topologys

Table 1. QoS for the photo share services

Peer	Service Operation	Network BitRate	Network De-lay	Service Time
3	PhotoShareA that makes uploadImage	25 Mbit/s	190 ms	500ms
4	PhotoShareB that makes uploadImage	10 Mbit/s	190 ms	650 ms

6   Conclusions

P2P overlay networks are emerging as a valid infrastructure for building efficient and scalable SOA-based applications with high level of QoS. The ability to efficiently carry out service discovery activities is a key issue for effectively managing the QoS of SOA-based P2P applications. In this respect, this paper has introduced a JXTA-based peer architecture, based on the QSHARE, to enable the QoS-aware keyword-based discovery of services in SOA-based P2P applications. Our approach, based on the JXTA Resolver Protocol, aims to extend the discovery capabilities of the native Discovery Services, providing a new keyword-based search criterion for advertisements. This work can be considered as a first step towards the application of the proposed model-driven framework for QoS management to JXTA-based P2P overlay networks. Further work includes the implementation of a peer prototype in order to evaluate the feasibility and the scalability of the proposed approach, as well its integration into the model-driven QoS management framework.

References

1. Alonso, G., Casati, F., Kuno, H., Machiraju, V.: Web Services. Springer, Heidelberg (2004)
2. Bocciarelli, P., D'Ambrogio, A., Angelaccio, M.: QShare: QoS-Enabled Description and Discovery of Services in SOA-Based P2P Applications. In: Proceedings of the 3rd International Workshop on Collaborative P2P Information Systems (COPS 2007), Part of the 16th IEEE International Workshops on Enabling Technologies: Infrastructures for Collaborative Enterprises (WETICE 2007), Paris, France, June 18-20 (2007)
3. Angelaccio, M., DAmbrogio, A.: A Model-driven Framework for Managing the QoS of Collaborative P2P Service-based Applications. In: Proccedings of the 2nd International Workshop on Collaborative P2P Information Systems (COPS 2006), Part of the 15th IEEE International Workshops on Enabling Technologies: Infrastructures for Collaborative Enterprises (WETICE 2006), Manchester (UK), June 26-28 (2006)
4. Canfora, G., Di Penta, M., Esposito, R., Villani, M.L.: QoS-Aware Replanning of Composite Web Services. In: Proceedings of 2005 IEEE International Conference on Web Services (ICWS 2005), July 12-15. IEEE Comp. Soc. Press, Orlando (2005)
5. DAmbrogio, A.: A WSDL extension for performance-enabled description of web services. In: Yolum, p., Güngör, T., Gürgen, F., Özturan, C. (eds.) ISCIS 2005. LNCS, vol. 3733, pp. 371–381. Springer, Heidelberg (2005)

6. DAmbrogio, A.: A Model-driven WSDL Extension for Describing the QoS ofWeb Services. In: Proceedings of the IEEE International Conference on Web Services (ICWS 2006), Chicago, USA, pp. 789–796 (September 2006)
7. DAmbrogio, A., Bocciarelli, P.: A Model-driven Approach to Describe and Predict the Performance of Composite Services. In: Proceedings of the 6th Int. Workshop on Software and Performance (WOSP 2007), Buenos Aires, Argentina, February 5-8 (2007)
8. JXTA project, https://jxta.dev.java.net/
9. JXTA Java Standard Edition v2.5: Programmers Guide (September 2007)
10. JXTA v2.0 Protocols Specification
11. Object Management Group, UML Profile for Scheduling, Performance and Time, version 1.1 (January 2005)
12. Papazoglou, M.P., Georgakopoulos, D.: Service-oriented computing. Communications of the ACM 46(10), 25–28 (2003)
13. Stoica, R., Morris, R., Karger, D., Kaashoek, M., Balakrishnan, H.: Chord: A scalable peer-to-peer lookup service for internet applications. In: Proceedings of the Annual Conference of the Special Interest Group on Data Communication, SIGCOMM 2001, San Deigo, CA (2001)
14. Traversat, B., Abdelaziz, M., Pouyoul, E.: Project JXTA: A Loosely-Consistent DHT Rendezvous Walker, Tech. report, Sun Microsystems (March 2003)
15. WWW Consortium, Web Services Description language (WSDL) Version 2.0, W3C Working Draft (January 2006), http://www.w3.org/TR/wsdl20

A Service Portfolio Model for Value Creation in Networked Enterprise Systems

Konstadinos Kutsikos[1] and Gregoris Mentzas[2]

[1] Business School, University of the Aegean, Chios, Greece
kutsikos@aegean.gr
[2] Institute of Communications and Computer Systems,
National Technical University of Athens, Athens, Greece
gmentzas@mail.ntua.gr

Abstract. Service science research is increasingly focusing on modeling value co-creation. However, there are concerns about the practical use of service systems-driven approaches to value creation in actual business settings. In this paper, we focus on the provision of knowledge services by a service system, and present an innovative model for clustering and profiling the value co-creation capabilities of such a service system. We then describe how this model drives the development of a new service management framework for managing the development of knowledge services. Finally, we present our early experiences from a practical deployment of our research findings in the development of a service system that offers knowledge services to enterprises for enhancing their collaboration quotient when participating in virtual organizations.

Keywords: service systems, service science, S-D logic, value co-creation model, business service management, virtual organizations.

1 Introduction

Service is a widely used term, with different definitions in different contexts. According to [13], service is the application of competences (knowledge and skills) by one entity for the benefit of another. The implied interaction between entities is the vehicle for value creation for all participants.

Value, however, is a concept that is hard to define and measure. In this paper, we adopt a simple definition [5]: value for an entity means that after acquiring a service, the entity is or feels better off, as measured by quantitative factors (e.g. revenues, costs) and qualitative factors (e.g. ease of use, trust). Two basic challenges then emerge: to understand how, when and where service value is created; and to manage the development, provision and operation of services, so that "better off" outcomes are maximized (i.e. service value is realized).

To address these challenges, two schools of thought on value creation have emerged. In the traditional goods-dominant (G-D) logic [14], value is created by service providers, is embedded in the service and is exchanged in the marketplace, usually for money ("value-in-exchange"). In the service-dominant (S-D) logic [15],

M. Cezon and Y. Wolfsthal (Eds.): ServiceWave 2010 Workshops, LNCS 6569, pp. 101–109, 2011.

value is created by services users, when they combine acquired services with own resources (skills, information, infrastructure, etc.) for achieving own goals in their operational context ("value-in-use").

Based on S-D logic, Service Science studies the creation of value within complex constellations of integrated resources, termed service systems [16]. The latter access, adapt and integrate resources in order to co-create value through exchanges of knowledge (knowledge-based services, knowledge objects).

In order to provide a service systems-based approach for resolving the two aforementioned challenges, [2] identify three key success factors: the instilling of the value co-creation concept in the service system; the balancing of innovation and commoditization dynamics; and the configuration of core resources in the service system. Managing these factors is then a matter of understanding the lifecycle of a service system.

However, this and similar research efforts in service systems tend to leave aside established practices in business service management, such as those described in [4]. This, in turn, may raise concerns about the practical use of service systems-driven approaches to value creation in actual business settings.

Addressing these concerns is the focus of our current research. Since every service business can be defined as a service system, we explore how certain key service system principles on value co-creation can be built into established service management frameworks, used by service businesses to develop and manage service offerings. These principles are: the three aforementioned key success factors for managing value co-creation in service systems; and the strong emphasis on knowledge flows as the core source of all value exchanges between service systems [16].

In this paper, we focus on the provision of knowledge services by a service system. Providing knowledge services is an approach to commercially exploit enterprise knowledge assets, offer competitive advantage and extend market reach. Knowledge service provision is a business trend which has been attributed to reasons such as the preference of managers from knowledge seeking companies for outsider knowledge [18] and is especially true in cases when knowledge can be packaged and hence become portable and migrant [11].

We present an innovative model for clustering and profiling the value co-creation capabilities of such a service system. We then describe how this model drives the development of a new service management framework for managing the development of knowledge services. Finally, we present our early experiences from a practical deployment of our research findings in the development of a service system that offers knowledge services to enterprises for enhancing their collaboration quotient when participating in virtual organizations.

2 Related Work

Focusing on value creation in service systems, [16] argue that in service systems, the "producer-consumer" distinction is inappropriate as value is created through chains of interactions between service system structures. [15] take this statement a step further by defining service system-based value in terms of a system's adaptiveness or ability to collaborate through value propositions. In other words, value creation in service systems is a co-creation process characterized by recursion and collaboration.

The first characteristic is exhibited by the following activities:

- A service system develops and offers services (i.e. value propositions)
- Value propositions are acquired by other service systems, defined as service users (value-in-exchange)
- Service users consume these external, acquired resources and combine them with internal resources for use in their own value creation processes (value-in-use).

The role of collaboration in value creation within service systems is exemplified by business types of service systems, such as networked organizations - highly knowledge-intensive organizational structures stemming from advances in information technology (e.g. virtual organizations). The ECOLEAD project [3] developed a generic model for measuring value co-creation within virtual organizations. The model is comprised of Value Generation Objects (i.e. tangible and intangible resources), a Performance Management System (for evaluating the value creation process) and Ethical Values (for capturing external involvement, at a macro level).

Beyond understanding the concept of value co-creation, the challenge is how to best manage the value co-creation process. [2] identify and analyze three factors that are critical to managing this process: the instilling of the value co-creation concept in the service system; the balancing of innovation and commoditization dynamics; and the configuration of core resources in the service system (i.e. people, technology, organization and shared information). Managing value co-creation then becomes a task of accounting for these factors through a service lifecycle model that is comprised of three phases: the infancy phase; the maturity phase; and the reincarnation phase.

For the purposes of our research, we wanted to explore how the aforementioned critical factors can be accounted for within traditional service lifecycle models, such as those described by [4], [6] and [7]. These models are generic, widely accepted for their theoretical and practical merit and are geared towards managing service development through discrete steps of a service's lifecycle: from service inception to service operation through to service retirement. Integrating the three value co-creation management factors into these models should provide new perspectives (and challenges) on the practical implementation of value co-creation in service systems.

3 A Value Co-creation Model for Knowledge Services

As described earlier, one of the key elements of value co-creation in any service system is the exchange of knowledge flows (knowledge-based services, knowledge objects).

Based on this fact, our research is focused on exploring value co-creation in a service system that owns knowledge-intensive assets (as a key internal resource) and provides access to them through service offerings. These assets may seem to be relevant only to organizations (service systems) that base their business models on information and/or knowledge-centric activities, such as publishing, software, education, research, or consulting activities. However, even manufacturing firms have a wealth of knowledge assets to expose to other organizations.

In such a service system, much like in any other service system, integration of internal and external resources is the essence of value co-creation, as expressed by e-services (value propositions) offered to other service systems. Value co-creation is then a function of: a) the participation of other service systems in the enhancement of developed services, or the development of new ones. This participation may range from no participation to full-scale involvement; b) knowledge assets, which may range from current best practices already validated by the service system to new knowledge acquired from (or co-produced with) other service systems.

Synthesizing the above concepts led to the development of a service value co-creation model, called Service Portfolio Model (SPM), shown in Fig. 1.

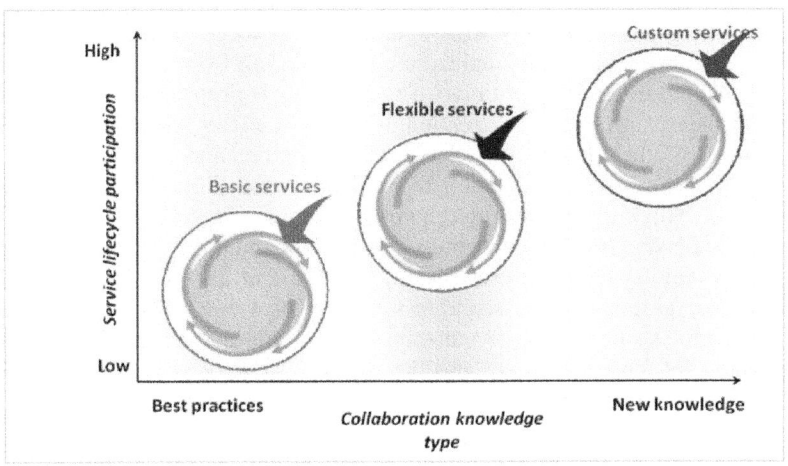

Fig. 1. Our Service Portfolio Model (SPM)

This model allows us to create rich value propositions for the chosen type of service system ("the provider"), by defining the following classes of offered services:

- Basic services – these are standardized services that encapsulate best-practices (generic or industry-specific) owned by the service system. External service systems' participation in the service development lifecycle is limited and is provided on an ad-hoc basis. Knowledge assets handled by this service class are expanded through updates generated internally, by the provider's own value creation process.
- Flexible services – these are configurable services that are based on a wide menu of options offered by the provider. External service systems participate in the service development lifecycle to co-develop new service configurations or new service configuration options, assisted by the provider's resources (human, technical, etc.). Services of this class expand stored knowledge by providing new syntheses.
- Custom services – these are highly customizable and user-driven services. External service systems' involvement in the service development lifecycle is high and should require an equally significant investment of the provider's resources (human, technical, financial, etc.). Services of this class may significantly expand stored knowledge - for example, with industry-specific practices

Based on these service classes, a service system can decide on the desired mix of innovative (but costly) and commoditized (but easily copied) e-services that it will offer. Balancing the mix then becomes a business decision on the desired profile of the offered services, potentially leading to reclassifying a service (upwards or downwards), breaking it into "service packages" belonging to different service classes, redeveloping it, terminating it or developing new services.

4   Managing Value Co-creation

The SPM model provides certain new insights on how value can be co-created in a service system. Equally important is to understand how the value co-creation process can be managed within a service system.

To that extent, we are currently developing a service management framework driven by the three factors described in [2]: the instilling of the value co-creation concept in the service system; the balancing of innovation and commoditization dynamics; and the configuration of core resources in the service system (i.e. people, technology, organization and shared information). The resulting Service Management Framework is driven by the SPM model and is depicted in Fig. 2.

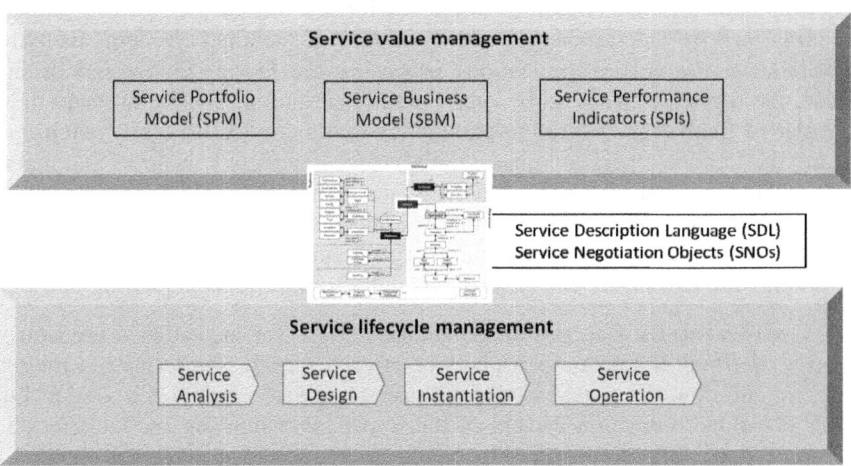

Fig. 2. Our Service Management Framework

The *Service Value Management* layer is comprised of:

- The Service Portfolio Model (SPM), a service classification model for profiling offered services (value propositions) and for balancing innovation and commoditization dynamics in a service system.
- The Service Business Model (SBM), for defining the business parameters that will drive the balancing of innovation and commoditization dynamics in the SPM. These parameters include key resources, cost structure, revenue model, and customer relationship model. Different configurations of these parameters will then drive the decision about breaking a service into "service

packages" that belong to two or more SPM service classes. The result is multiple value propositions out of a single service, thus increasing the service system's quotient for value co-creation.

- The Service Performance Indicators (SPIs), a set of value co-creation metrics for SPM-modeled services. Their goal is two-fold: to monitor service execution and to measure overall value creation. Hence, SPIs are linked to and/or extracted from SBM parameters. We have introduced two main categories (financial value SPIs, innovation value SPIs), which comprise metrics relevant to all co-creation participants. For example, revenue sharing is a key SPI for SPM Custom services. The latter, by definition, lead to development of new knowledge assets which can be then offered to others through existing or new services. In that case, additional revenue streams should be shared with the original co-creators of these knowledge assets.

The *Service Lifecycle Management* layer defines a service lifecycle model (based on [7]), depicting the key phases of service development – from service analysis to service operation. In this layer, the service system resources are configured for value co-creation. The Service Analysis phase captures all activities required to identify and contextualize a service, leading to the development of ontology for cataloguing service parameters. This ontology is the key input to the Service Design phase, which captures service requirements and produces a detailed design, including the specification of involved applications, processes, etc. During the Service Instantiation phase, the service is ready to become operational and all contracting activities occur in order to finalize the operating parameters that a service user will require. Finally, during the Service Operation phase, the service is actively consumed and maintained. Related runtime metrics (defined as SPIs) are monitored for the purposes of contract management and billing. The data that is collected is then fed into the Service Value Management Framework for informing its components.

Linking the two layers and ensuring their coordination, the model includes:

- The Service Description Language (SDL), for providing a uniform way of defining the business aspects of offered services, in terms of ontologies. In addition, the SDL-based definition of services provides a way to build the value co-creation drivers of the upper layer into the service lifecycle, thus contributing to instilling the value co-creation concept across services. In this preliminary phase, we are developing SDL based on USDL v3.0 (Universal Service Description Language), which was developed as part of the SAP-led Theseus/TEXO research program for describing business services [1].
- The Service Negotiation Objects (SNOs), based on the SPIs and SDL, for use in service contracting during the Service Instantiation stage of the lifecycle.

5   The Framework in Action

As part of our research within the SYNERGY project (an EU, FP7 project) [8],[10], we applied our service management framework in the realm of virtual organizations (VOs) – a good proxy for service systems [13].

The aim of the project is to support networked enterprises in their successful participation in VOs. A SYNERGY service system is developed, comprised of knowledge assets relevant to collaboration creation and operation, along with services to discover, capture, deliver and apply such knowledge [10].

A key part of SYNERGY service system's knowledge infrastructure is collaboration patterns (CPats), defined as a prescription which addresses a collaborative problem that may occur repeatedly in a business setting. It describes the forms of collaboration and the proven solutions to a collaboration problem, and appears as a recurring group of actions that enable efficiency in both the communication and the implementation of a successful solution. The CPat can be used as is in its application domain or it can be abstracted and used as a primitive building block beyond its original domain [9][17].

CPat services offered by a SYNERGY service system enable other service systems (enterprises) to access the CPats repository. These services provide recommendations for actions and tools to be used, awareness of the state of collaborators and the state of the collaboration work, as well as statistical analysis based on previous and ongoing VO collaborations.

As a scenario of our framework in action within the SYNERGY project, consider the case of a SYNERGY service system ("the Provider") that participates in a VO comprised of pharmaceuticals (other service systems) that want to develop and test a series of new drugs [17]. One of the collaboration activities within this VO is the design of a joint laboratory experiment, which includes planning and scheduling of pre-experiment tasks (e.g. defining and agreeing on the experiment's objectives). An existing CPat called 'OrganizeExperiment' already encapsulates best practices for similar tasks, accumulated over time through this CPat's uses in other VOs. At run time, two types of CPat services can be invoked: CPat Recommender service, which recommends actions to continue collaboration, as well as tools related to the CPat's collaboration tasks; and CPat Awareness service, which provides awareness of the state of collaboration tasks. Both these services are Basic Services, as per our SPM model. The CPat itself will be updated by the Provider, if new best practices arise.

At a different point in time, an external event may lead to changes in existing CPats or even dictate creation of new ones. For example, new rules imposed by public health authorities may require new lab experiments through the participation of new partners in the VO. New CPats may need to be co-created in order to capture new collaboration tasks, which may be specific to this case or may be generic enough to become available to future service users. A CPat Design service will enable VO participants and the Provider to co-create any new CPats. This is not necessarily a fully automated service. VO representatives may need to consult with the Provider's human experts and collaborate offline, e.g. on defining a commercial exploitation plan for the new CPats. As this is co-creation of new knowledge assets, all participants should agree on SBM parameters, e.g. for revenue sharing or joint equity. These will then be translated into relevant SPIs (e.g. share revenue %) which will be recorded in SDL and taken into account during the Service Operation phase of the CPat Design service's lifecycle. It is important to note that although this is a Custom Service, as per our SPM model, it may depend on other SYNERGY services, such as the SYNERGY Basic Services described above.

6 Conclusions and Further Work

There is no doubt that there is a tremendous need for service innovations or new ways of creating value with intangible and dynamic resources, to fuel economic growth and to raise the quality and effectiveness of services, especially for knowledge-intensive industries.

To that extent, our research work aims to provide a framework for profiling and managing value co-creation in service systems. We are currently developing this framework around three basic pillars: our Service Portfolio Model (SPM); established service lifecycle management processes, that are enhanced to account for SPM-driven value co-creation parameters; and the USDL v3.0 service description language, as a way of instilling SPM-driven parameters in the end-to-end development of a service (value proposition).

Initial results from applying the above in a business setting of collaborating SMEs are encouraging. A next step in this research direction will extend SPM to account for more internal resources of a service system, beyond knowledge assets. In addition, we will be seeking other practical deployments of the framework, in order to test and improve its practicality.

Acknowledgments. Work presented in this paper has been partially supported by the European Commission under the 7th Framework Programme on ICT in support of the networked enterprise through contract No 216089.

References

1. Cardoso, J., Winkler, M., Voigt, K.: A service description language for the Internet of services. In: Alt, R., Fähnrich, K.-P., Franczyk, B. (eds.) First International Symposium on Services Science (ISSS 2009). Logos-Verlag, Berlin (2009)
2. Chen, Y., Lelescu, A., Spohrer, J.: Three factors to sustainable service system excellence: A case study of service systems. In: 2008 IEEE International Conference on Services Computing, vol. 2, pp. 119–126 (2008)
3. Galeano, N., Romero, D.: D21.4a – Characterization of VBE value systems and metrics. ECOLEAD Project (2007)
4. Gangadharan, G.R., Luttighuis, P.O.: BHive: A reference framework for business-driven service design and management. Journal of Service Science 2, 81–110 (2010)
5. Gronroos, C.: Service logic revisited: who creates value? And who co-creates? European Business Review 20(4), 298–314 (2008)
6. Kohlborn, T., Fielt, E., Korthaus, A., Rosemann, M.: Towards a service portfolio management framework. In: 20th Australasian Conference on Information Systems, Melbourne, pp. 861–870 (2009)
7. Kohlborn, T., Korthaus, A., Rosemann, M.: Business and software lifecycle management. In: 2009 Enterprise Distributed Object Computing Conference (EDOC 2009), Auckland, pp. 87–96 (2009)
8. Mentzas, G., Popplewell, K.: Knowledge-Based Collaboration Patterns in Future Internet Enterprise Systems. ERCIM News 77 (2009)
9. Papageorgiou, N., Verginadis, Y., Apostolou, D., Mentzas, G.: Semantic Interoperability of E-Services in Collaborative Networked Organizations. In: ICE-B 2010 - The International Conference on e-Business, Athens (2010)

10. Popplewell, K., Stojanovic, N., Abecker, A., Apostolou, D., Mentzas, G.: Supporting Adaptive Enterprise Collaboration through Semantic Knowledge Services. In: 4th International Conference Interoperability for Enterprise Software and Applications (I-ESA 2008), Berlin (2008)
11. Smyth, H., Longbottom, R.: External Provision of Knowledge Management Information Services: The Case of the Concrete and Cement Industries. European Management Journal 23(2), 247–259 (2005)
12. Spohrer, J., Anderson, L.C., Pass, N.J., Ager, T., Gruhl, D.: Service Science. Journal of Grid Computing 6(3), 313–324 (2008)
13. Vargo, S.L., Lusch, R.F.: Service-dominant logic: What It Is, What It Is Not, What It Might Be. In: Lusch, R.F., Vargo, S.L. (eds.) The Service-Dominant Logic of Marketing: Dialog, Debate and Directions, pp. 43–56. M.E. Sharpe Inc., New York (2006a)
14. Vargo, S.L., Lusch, R.F., Morgan, F.W.: Historical perspectives on service-dominant logic. In: Lusch, R.F., Vargo, S.L. (eds.) The Service-Dominant Logic of Marketing: Dialog, Debate and Directions, pp. 29–42. M.E. Sharpe Inc., New York (2006b)
15. Vargo, S.L., Maglio, P.P., Akaka, M.A.: On value and value co-creation: A service systems and service logic perspective. European Management Journal 26, 145–152 (2008a)
16. Vargo, S.L., Lusch, R.F.: From products to service: Divergences and convergences of logics. Industrial Marketing Management 37, 254–259 (2008b)
17. Verginadis, Y., Apostolou, A., Papageorgiou, N., Mentzas, G.: Collaboration Patterns in event-driven environments for Virtual Organizations. In: AAAI 2009 Spring Symposium on Intelligent Event Processing, Palo Alto (2009)
18. Zucker, L., Darby, M.R., Armstrong, J.S.: Commercializing Knowledge: University Science, Knowledge Capture, and Firm Performance in Biotechnology. Management Science 48(1), 138–153 (2002)

On the Use of Feature Models for Service Design: The Case of Value Representation

Erik Wittern and Christian Zirpins

Karlsruhe Institute of Technology (KIT),
Institute of Applied Informatics and Formal Description Methods (AIFB),
Englerstr. 11, 76131 Karlsruhe, Germany
{erik.wittern,christian.zirpins}@kit.edu
http://www.aifb.kit.edu/

Abstract. Current findings in the field of service science have revealed many specific characteristics of service systems, but these results have not yet been fully adopted by the service engineering discipline. In particular we are now aware that the value proposition of a service is not only vital for its success but also deeply depending on context and co-creation. So far, there is only limited work on considering this fact for the design of service systems. In this paper, we discuss the utilization of feature modeling, which is known from the software engineering domain, for service design. We argue that feature modeling offers considerable potential to not only represent value from diverse perspectives but also to involve service customers in participatory service design.

Keywords: Service Science, Feature Modeling, Participatory Design.

1 Introduction

As the trend towards service economies is widely recognized and well documented [21] service science establishes as a new transdiscipline of academic as well as industrial research [15]. Corresponding to this movement, literature has proposed a shift from a goods-dominant logic to a service-dominant logic (S-D logic) [17]. In S-D logic, peculiarities of services, such as co-creation of value or operant resources, are addressed [18]. S-D logic assumes that a firm providing a service cannot determine its value in isolation. Rather, value results from the co-creation process in which the customer of the service is greatly integrated [14]. The service provider can only offer a *value proposition* to the customer. Competitive advantage results from the degree to which the value proposition meets the needs of customers [17]. Therefore, service science regards research and enhancement of value propositions as a major goal [15].

From an engineering perspective, an important activity that needs to consider value aspects is the design of a new or enhanced service offering. Such activities require adequate models and methods to support a structured methodology. However, while a number of existing modeling approaches allow to represent value aspects, there are only a few ones that consider specific service characteristics. In this paper, we propose to consider *feature modeling* as a tool to

M. Cezon and Y. Wolfsthal (Eds.): ServiceWave 2010 Workshops, LNCS 6569, pp. 110–118, 2011.

represent value from multiple stakeholder perspectives. Feature modeling allows capturing aspects of services that matter to different stakeholders in form of features. Features correspond to processes or resources of services. They can thus capture the physical and logical aspects of a service, including for example its enabling technology. Through annotations, the value of features for different stakeholders can be expressed. Feature modeling thus allows to combine diverse views on a service design in one model. As a result, reasoning over service feature models enables, among other things, taking value aspects into account when choosing enabling technologies.

The contribution of this paper is a critical discussion of the utilization of feature modeling for service design, i.e. to model a service's value proposition. Furthermore, we sketch a mapping of feature modeling concepts to service aspects which provides a fundamental step towards feature modeling of services. Finally, we discuss methodical options for the utilization of service feature models throughout a typical service lifecycle in a beneficial way. Subsequently, the remaining of this paper is structured as follows: In section (2) we introduce feature modeling. In section (3) we present our proposed mapping of feature modeling and service aspects that results in a *service feature model*. We also discuss how service feature modeling can be utilized throughout a service lifecycle. In section (4) we present an example of a service feature model. Section (5) surveys related work. Finally, we summarize the paper and give an outlook on our future work in section (6).

2   Feature Modeling

Feature Modeling originates from the software engineering discipline. It was developed to discover and represent the commonalities among software systems from a shared domain [10]. Features are user-visible aspects or characteristics of a domain. In feature modeling, features are typically arranged in tree structures, so-called feature diagrams. Branches can be defined to be mandatory, optional as well as inclusive or exclusive alternatives. Furthermore, cross-tree dependencies of features, such as *requires* or *excludes*, can be modeled, called feature dependencies.

Since its introduction, feature modeling has been intensely studied [3]. Several extensions of the original model have been proposed [3]. These include for example the notion of feature attributes [9] or cardinalities of features and feature groups [6]. Beyond expressive power, the appeal of feature modeling results to a large extend from the fact that it enables automated reasoning. Various reasoning approaches have been introduced that are mainly based on Propositional Logic, Constraint Programming or Description Logic [3].

3   Feature-Based Service Design

Feature modeling offers various beneficial characteristics for the task of designing a service's value proposition. Because service feature modeling will most likely be utilized by service providers, its applicability for service design needs to be considered having in mind the service provider's potential benefits. For example, the modeling and optimization of value propositions for stakeholders other than the service provider aims to make the service more compelling, which will ultimately benefit the service provider as well.

As feature modeling is meant for representing features of a system from a user-perspective and in the context of a given domain, it is exactly on the right level of granularity and abstraction for representing the particularities of a service system, which determine its value for the customer. Because the feature concept is close to the value proposition of a service, its abstraction-level is also likely to be meaningful to customers. Thus, there is an opportunity to involve customers in various forms of participatory design.

On the other hand, feature models focus on static system properties and do not explicitly represent the interactions of involved stakeholders. Services however are characterized by the interaction processes between their providers and clients, during which value is generated and exchanged. Another typical service systems characteristic that is not per se represented in generic feature modeling approaches is the role of ICT in service provision, which effects interaction channels and co-creation processes and thereby – again – the value proposition.

For the above reasons, feature modeling is in fact an opportunity for service design but can not be simply utilized as-is. The approach needs to be adapted to the needs of representing service systems. In particular, an appropriate mapping of feature concepts to service system aspects appears fundamental. In the following we will present such a mapping strategy for *service feature modeling* and discuss its characteristics concerning value representation. Furthermore, we will outline options for the application of service feature modeling in a typical service lifecycle.

3.1   Mapping Feature Concepts to Service Aspects

The mapping we propose is illustrated in figure 1. The overarching idea is to map features to two main aspects of services, namely processes and resources. This approach follows the common process-oriented view of services. To further underpin this, we structure processes based on the fundamental service-blueprinting concept of Bitner et al. [4]. By doing so we explicitly differentiate a service's processes regarding the stakeholders that are mostly concerned.

Resources are considered to enable the processes on behalf of different stakeholders. We propose to structure resources corresponding to the four primary resources identified in service science, namely technology, people, organizations and shared information [16]. Because of the strong role of ICT in general and Web technologies in particular for service delivery, we further define technology as ICT architecture. Correspondingly, technology / ICT architecture can be refined into the three layers infrastructure, platforms and applications [2].

An important aspect to be represented in a service feature model is the relationship between processes and their enabling resources. In feature modeling,

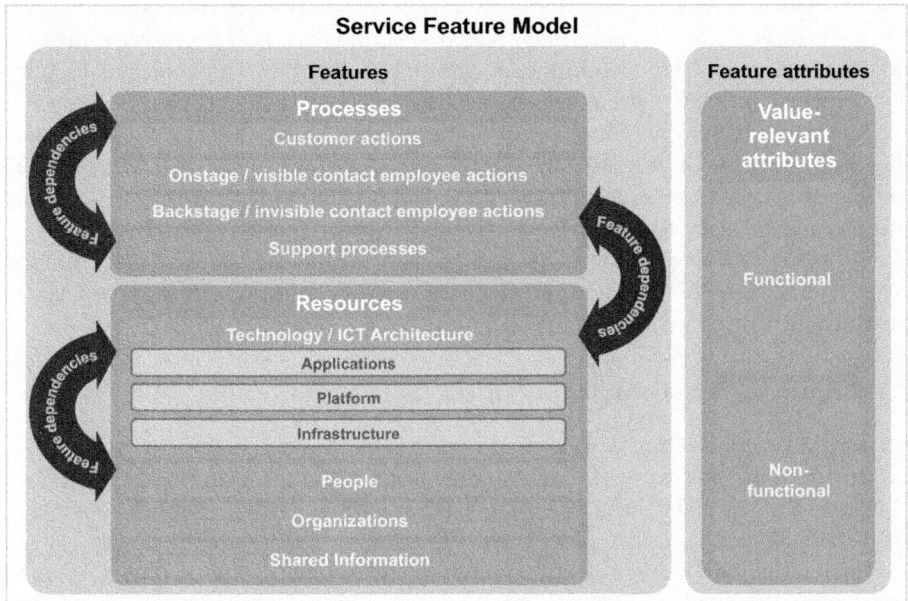

Fig. 1. Proposed mapping of feature modeling to services

feature dependencies can be used to model the dependencies between processes and resources, as well as the dependencies between processes or resources themselves.

3.2   Feature-Based Value Representation

A major capability of our service feature modeling approach is the representation of value. To represent a value aspect in the model, it fundamentally needs to be defined and quantified. However, we believe that the approach of capturing value in a model is somewhat utopian: As agreed in S-D logic, value results from the co-creation process between service provider and customer. As customers can have highly diverse perceptions and requirements, value cannot be defined for a service per se. Still, we believe that it is possible to capture those service aspects that are likely to influence a service's value proposition in a certain context. Customers perceive the value of services and products in terms of attributes and their performances [22]. The selection and evaluation of attributes depends on the customers desired consequences. Desired consequences themselves depend on the customers goals and purposes. Based on this notion, through adapting a service's attributes and their performances, the value perception of the customer can be influenced.

We believe that a service's value-relevant attributes consist of functionalities and non-functionalities. Features in service feature modeling represent the service's functionalities. We propose that value aspects should be analyzed and represented for both process- and resource-features. Value should be represented for process-features as the customers evaluation of a service highly depends on the service processes [4]. Because resources determine how well the service processes can be performed, they also influence value. For example, the choice of IT infrastructure will influence the resulting QoS attributes of the service processes. To express value in service feature modeling, *feature attributes* can be used, which classically express only non-functional properties of a feature. Feature attributes consist of a name, a domain and a value [3]. Using feature attributes, features can be annotated with the value they cause for certain stakeholders.

Additionally, features attributes can be used to model a feature's non-functional properties as they classically do in feature modeling. For example, a process feature can be annotated with its *processing time* or *cost*.

3.3   Feature-Based Methods in the Service Lifecycle

Service feature modeling can be used in different stages of a typical service lifecycle. In the following we will discuss some options building upon the established ITIL service lifecycle model [13] that includes the three main phases *Service Design*, *Service Operation* and *Service Transition*.

During the *Service Design*, service feature modeling can be used to model alternative designs on a rather abstract level. Through annotating features with value-relevant aspects, the service feature model can be used to choose among competing service designs in an early design phase. The choosing can be automated by transferring the feature model to an applicable representation (e.g. constraint logic programs) and processing it using constraint solvers [11]. More detailed models, that describe for example technical or process-oriented details of a service, can be referenced from the service feature model. The detailed models can eventually provide more precise figures to be integrated in the service feature model. Thus, the service feature model obtains its validity in further design stages. Feature models are easy to understand. Thus, they can be utilized to communicate service designs to different and potentially diverse stakeholders. Doing so allows for example the integration of otherwise non-integrated stakeholders into the design of a service already during the design phase. We currently follow this approach in the COCKPIT EU-Project in which we try to enable citizens' participation in the design of new public services [5].

During the *Service Operations* phase, the service feature model can be used to assess the service provisioning. Customers' preferences are likely to change over time. Mapping updated preferences with the service feature model allows to determine how well the value proposition of the current service design is. Eventually, such assessments can even trigger the adaptation of the service to an alternative set of features in order to enhance the service's value proposition.

Finally, service feature modeling might be utilized during the *Service Transition* phase. The service feature model states the dependencies between features. Thus, the service feature model supports the service transition by making the implications of changes explicit. Here again, the inclusion of processes, resources

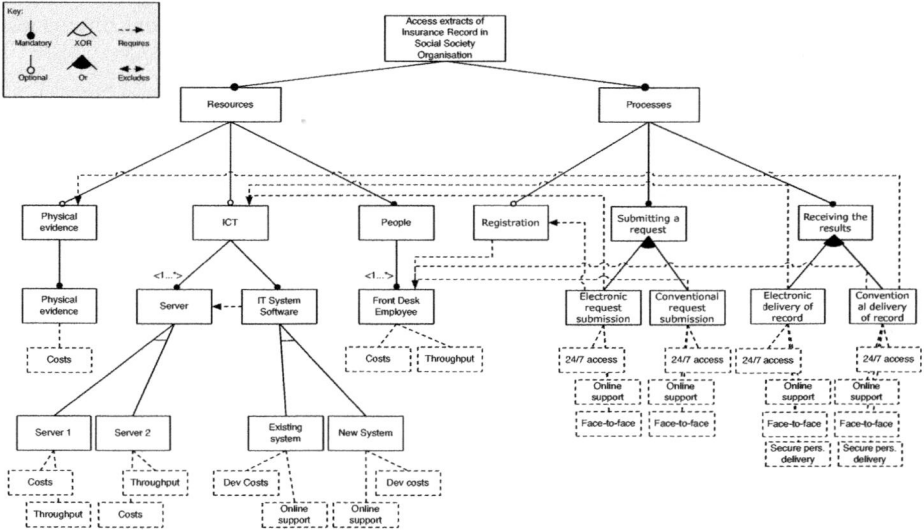

Fig. 2. Exemplary service feature model from COCKPIT scenario

and value aspects in the model provides a basis for educated decisions under consideration of diverse factors. The usage of feature modeling to support the adaptability of service systems has already been proposed [12].

4   Example of a Service Feature Model

To show how service feature modeling can be used, figure (2) illustrates a service feature model based on a scenario from the COCKPIT project [5]. The Citizens Collaboration and Co-creation in public Service Delivery project aims to foster the participation of citizens in the design of new public services. The service modeled in figure (2) originates from the Greek Ministry of Interior Decentralisation & E-government. The service allows citizens to access their insurance record in order to verify that their employers have paid their contribution to the Social Security institute.

In capturing the value-relevant features, the example follows our proposed mapping to processes and resources (see section [3.1]). There are two processes describing the request and the delivery of an insurance record. Both can either be performed electronically or conventionally. The feature attributes, marked by the boxes with dashed lines, express value-relevant properties of the features. Feature dependencies indicate relationships between features. For example the electronic request of an insurance record requires the registration process to be included in the service. Overall, the service feature model contains various possible configurations of the service. In COCKPIT, by letting citizens evaluate the value-relevant attributes of features, we aim to determine the most-valued configuration. For example, depending on how citizens value 24/7-access, online support or face-to-face contact with an employee, electronic or conventional service requesting should be provided.

5   Related Work

In [20], the usage of e³-value [8] to model value in service systems is proposed. In this approach, the design of a service starts with a value model that does abstract from IT services and processes. The authors argue that the value model thus depicts a stable reference point throughout the service lifecycle and that the model addresses business evolution at the appropriate level (i.e. strategic decisions can be addressed in the value model while technological decisions are addressed elsewhere). In contrast, our approach considers that the generation of value is closely related to decisions on technological, organizational or process level. Thus, a complete separation of the value model seems unfavorable. For example, in case that technological change is required, the impacts on value need to be understood and considered.

Feature modeling has used in the service-oriented world to model and negotiate non-functional service aspects [7]. Feature models are used to represent QoS attributes. The latter establishment of e-contracts is based on feature model configurations, which includes QoS negotiation. In [19], similarly, feature modeling is used to specify non-functional constraints in service oriented architectures. Automated reasoning over the feature models is proposed to validate the fulfillment of desired properties. In contrast to these works, we propose to model the causes for non-functional properties (such as ICT architecture) rather than only the properties themselves. Instead of using feature modeling to represent and negotiate over given properties, our model aims to optimize these properties by design.

Despite the existing literature that addresses value modeling or the representation of non-functional properties with feature models, we believe that our approach is novel as it combines value aspects with their causes on technological, organizational and process level.

6   Conclusion and Future Work

Feature modeling is an elaborated approach to model commonalities and differences between modular variants – e.g. offerings of software product-lines. We believe that feature modeling is also a suitable approach to be used in a service context. In particular, we believe that feature modeling is a useful addition to previous service modeling approaches (see for example [1]) because it unites organizational, technological, process related and value aspects within one model. Thus, service feature models provide a solid basis for reasoning over service designs under consideration of value aspects. The formalization of feature models enables the reasoning to be performed automatically. Especially if potential service design decisions are complex, automation of reasoning can be beneficial.

We believe that feature modeling can be expanded to further enhance its applicability in the service world. These extensions will focus on modeling conditions (such as benefits and expenses) for the adaption of features during runtime. Also, annotations should be introduced to indicate the stakeholders that are influenced by features. This would allow to perform automated reasoning over service feature models dedicated to certain stakeholders (i.e. maximizing the value proposition for a customer or minimizing the costs of the service delivery for the provider).

Acknowledgement. This work was supported by the COCKPIT project (Citizens Collaboration and Co-Creation in Public Sector Service; European Seventh Framework Programme, FP7-248222).

References

1. Banavar, G., Hartman, A., Ramaswamy, L., Zherebtsov, A.: A Formal Model of Service Delivery. In: Maglio, P.P., Kieliszewski, C.A., Spohrer, J.C. (eds.) Handbook of Service Science. Service Science: Research and Innovations in the Service Economy, pp. 481–507. Springer, US (2010)
2. Baun, C., Kunze, M., Nimis, J., Tai, S.: Cloud Computing: Web-basierte dynamische IT-Services. Informatik im Fokus. Springer, Heidelberg (2010)
3. Benavides, D., Segura, S., Ruiz-Cortés, A.: Automated analysis of feature models 20 years later: A literature review. Information Systems 35(6), 615–636 (2010)
4. Bitner, M.J., Ostrom, A.L., Morgan, F.N.: Service Blueprinting: A Practical Technique for Service Innovation. California Management Review 50(3), 66–94 (2008)
5. COCKPIT Project: Citizens Collaboration and Co-creation in public Service Delivery (2010), http://www.cockpit-project.eu
6. Czarnecki, K., Helsen, S., Eisenecker, U.: Staged Configuration Using Feature Models. In: Nord, R.L. (ed.) SPLC 2004. LNCS, vol. 3154, pp. 162–164. Springer, Heidelberg (2004)
7. Fantinato, M., de Gimenes, S.I., de Toledo, M.B.F.: Supporting QoS Negotiation with Feature Modeling. In: Krämer, B.J., Lin, K.-J., Narasimhan, P. (eds.) ICSOC 2007. LNCS, vol. 4749, pp. 429–434. Springer, Heidelberg (2007)
8. Gordijn, J., Akkermans, H., van Vliet, H.: Business modelling is not process modelling. In: Mayr, H.C., Liddle, S.W., Thalheim, B. (eds.) ER Workshops 2000. LNCS, vol. 1921, pp. 40–51. Springer, Heidelberg (2000)
9. Kang, K., Kim, S., Lee, J., Kim, K., Shin, E., Huh, M.: FORM: A feature-oriented reuse method with domain-specific reference architectures. Annals of Software Engineering 5, 143–168 (1998)
10. Kang, K.C., Cohen, S.G., Hess, J.A., Novak, W.E., Peterson, A.S.: Feature-Oriented Domain Analysis (FODA) Feasibility Study. Tech. rep., Carnegie Mellon University, Pittsburgh, Pennsylvania (November 1990)
11. Karataş, A.S., Oğuztüzün, H., Doğru, A.: Mapping extended feature models to constraint logic programming over finite domains. In: Bosch, J., Lee, J. (eds.) SPLC 2010. LNCS, vol. 6287, pp. 286–299. Springer, Heidelberg (2010)
12. Morin, B., Barais, O., Jezequel, J.M., Fleurey, F., Solberg, A.: Models@ Run.time to Support Dynamic Adaptation. Computer 42, 44–51 (2009)

13. Office of Government Commerce: ITIL Service Design. The Stationary Office, UK (2007)
14. Prahalad, C., Ramaswamy, V.: Co-opting Customer Competence. Harvard Business Review 78(1), 79–87 (2000)
15. Spohrer, J.C., Maglio, P.P.: Toward a Science of Service Systems. In: Maglio, P.P., Kieliszewski, C.A., Spohrer, J.C. (eds.) Handbook of Service Science. Service Science: Research and Innovations in the Service Economy, pp. 157–194. Springer, US (2010)
16. Spohrer, J., Maglio, P.P., Bailey, J., Gruhl, D.: Steps Toward a Service Systems. Computer 40(1), 71–77 (2007)
17. Vargo, S.L., Lusch, R.F.: Evolving to a New Dominant Logic for Marketing. Journal of Marketing 68(1), 1–17 (2004)
18. Vargo, S.L., Lusch, R.F., Akaka, M.A.: Advancing Service Science with Service-Dominant Logic. In: Maglio, P.P., Kieliszewski, C.A., Spohrer, J.C. (eds.) Handbook of Service Science. Service Science: Research and Innovations in the Service Economy, pp. 133–156. Springer, US (2010)
19. Wada, H., Suzuki, J., Oba, K.: A feature modeling support for non-functional constraints in service oriented architecture. In: IEEE International Conference on Services Computing, SCC 2007, pp. 187–195 (2007)
20. Weigand, H., Johannesson, P., Andersson, B., Bergholtz, M.: Value-based service modeling and design: Toward a unified view of services. In: van Eck, P., Gordijn, J., Wieringa, R. (eds.) CAiSE 2009. LNCS, vol. 5565, pp. 410–424. Springer, Heidelberg (2009)
21. Wölfl, A.: The Service Economy in OECD Countries. STI Working Paper DSTI/DOC(2005)3, Organisation for Economic Co-operation and Development (2005)
22. Woodruff, R.B.: Customer Value: The Next Source for Competitive Advantage. Journal of the Academy of Marketing Science 25(2), 139–153 (1997)

Towards a Hybrid Simulation Modelling Framework for Service Networks⋆

Yan Wang and Willem-Jan van den Heuvel

European Research Institute in Service Science
Tilburg University, The Netherlands
{Y.Wang13,W.J.A.M.vdnHeuvel}@uvt.nl

Abstract. The increasingly globalized service-centric economy has brought much attention on the concept of service networks. Scientific disciplines, such as management and service oriented computing, have commenced studying on how to design, develop, manage, and govern service networks. What is really needed for service networks to be developed, provisioned and managed in practice, however, are disciplined methods and tools that are able to take into account, tune and reconcile both technical and business considerations. This paper may be seen as a first, yet critical step in realizing the above vision. In particular, this paper explores a hybrid service network simulation approach that is able to analyze, optimize and tune the performance of service networks and their resources, including software services and human operated services. Our holistic, hybrid simulation framework will be firmly grounded on pre-existing simulation techniques that have been widely used in process modelling and simulation.

Keywords: Service network, Hybrid simulation, System dynamics, Agent based modelling, Discrete event simulation.

1 Motivation

The service sector is an important contributor to modern economies, accounting for more than 50 percent of the gross national product in countries such as Brazil, Germany, Japan, Russia, and the UK, and, making up 80 percent of the US economy [1]. Clearly, the face of the global economy is rapidly being transformed into a global, services-centric economy with networked enterprises transacting and co-creating value on digital infrastructures with a global reach, giving rise to the concept of service networks. Service networks may be defined as systems of service systems that are open, complex and fluid, accommodating the co-production of new knowledge and services through organic peer-to-peer interactions [2]. Resources in service systems may include people, software systems, computing devices and sensor networks, organizations and shared information,

---

⋆ The research leading to these results has received funding from the European Community Seventh Framework Program under the STREP Cockpit and the Network of Excellence S-Cube grant agreements.

M. Cezon and Y. Wolfsthal (Eds.): ServiceWave 2010 Workshops, LNCS 6569, pp. 119–128, 2011.

such as business rules, regulations, measures and methods. By now, industry has adopted service-oriented computing in conjunction with cloud computing as the de-facto distributed enterprise-computing paradigm for implementing and interconnecting resources in service networks through software (cloud) services.

The design, development, management and governance of service networks have gained much attention in two, largely isolated scientific disciplines. Firstly, service networks have been intensively studied in the discipline of management and business, improving our understanding of their key attributes and classification, their business case, and the operation and management of (integrated) supply chains [3]. Secondly, the engineering of service networks has been recently been picked up by the discipline of service (cloud) computing [4], considering how to design, program, test, deploy and provision software services into aggregated software services.

Clearly, what is needed for service networks to be developed, provisioned and managed in practice, are disciplined methods and tools that are able to take into account, tune and reconcile both technical and business considerations. This paper may be seen as a first, yet critical step in realizing the above vision. In particular, we aim to develop and explore a hybrid service network simulation approach that is able to analyze, optimize and tune the performance of service networks and their resources, including software services and human operated services. Our holistic, hybrid simulation framework will be firmly grounded on pre-existing simulation techniques that have been widely used in process modelling and simulation.

In this paper, we will firstly review process simulation techniques in section 2. Section 3 then studies existing hybrid process simulation methods that have been suggested to create synergy and overcome weaknesses of individual simulation methods. In section 4 we introduce a hybrid simulation model and technique for the service networks assist in analyzing and predicting the impact of process changes, resource re-allocations and network re-configurations on the performance of service networks. The proposed hybrid modelling framework is further illustrated with an exploratory case study in section 5, and concluded in section 6.

2   Business Process Simulation

Developing and managing service networks may benefit tremendously from previous research in business processes engineering that -like the engineering of service networks- is about dealing with the changes either internally within the organization or in the business environment, and may cascade into a cocktail of effects on the human resources (e.g. type and skills), in their involvement (e.g. working hours and schedule), in the process activities (e.g. steps and sequence), and in the supporting technology (e.g. software services) [5]. In service networks, changes originate from multiple interactions among the involved network partners and their resources, their clients and the context in which they live.

Simulation can improve our understanding of the dynamic behavior of business process. In particular, simulation is a useful tool to predict and understand the impact of changes to resource allocations (e.g., a human actor is replaced by a software services) and network configuration (e.g., a network partner outsources part of its work to external partners) to the performance of a service network, considering qualitative and quantitative aspects. In addition, it helps to reach common understanding and consensus amongst various network partners (e.g., public administrators, citizens and service designers) and educate them, without disrupting operational processes. In doing so simulation allows us to iteratively discover, define, refine and improve our knowledge of the principles and laws of service networks, and make more informed and accountable decisions. For this purpose, simulations rely on formal, often mathematical, abstractions of a service system, where specific parameters can be altered so experimenters can study their effects over time.

Over the years, simulation has been extensively studied and applied in various domains including chemistry, physics, sociology, business and management, computer science, and, information systems. There are three mainstream paradigms in simulation modelling, viz. System Dynamics (SD), Discrete Event (DE) simulation, and Agent Based (AB) simulation. They are different in terms of level of abstraction, as they capture and imitate the dynamics of the system at either operation level or context level [6].

SD analyzes feedback loops and the emerging behavioral effects, such as exponential growth or decline, that result from them. It models populations as discrete actors and conceptualizes processes in terms of aggregated stock and flows and constraint information. Stocks are the accumulation of resources at different states in the processes, which can be material, people, money and so on. The flows connect the stocks and provide the backbone for transporting objects from one stock to another one. The moving rates are determined by the constraint information which comes from the system capacity and business strategy.

DE modelling analyzes system changes after a specific time interval or incoming event where between any two events/time intervals the service system remains stable. DE models are defined in terms of entities, resources and block charts describing entity flow and resource sharing. In DE models, entities (e.g. people, tasks or messages) passively travel through the block of flowcharts, where they could be delayed, stopped, processed, etc.

AB modelling simulates the operation and collocations between autonomous agents. While each agent has its own individual perception and incomplete information of an end-to-end process, they are able to communicate and share information with other agents. The behavior of an agent is defined by its internal state, which is a cognitive structure that determines what action the agent takes at time t, give its perception of the environment.

3   Hybrid Simulation

From 1997, papers on comparing or integrating SD and AB modelling have surfaced, commencing with Kim and Juhn [7] who analyzed the main features of

AB and SD, focusing on different perspectives on the population of homogeneous actors such as producers, transporters and consumers. The most common two approaches of unifying SD and AB are either using SD to model the global environment while having individual agents inside, or modelling an agent's internal structure with the help of SD. For example, Akkermans [8] explores the decentralized co-ordination between multiple agents in supply chain management by modelling multiple convergent supply networks with SD. Every actor in the networks captures a mental model of the performance of the actor it is interacting with. The actors' behavior is adapted based on their mental models and influenced by their past behaviors. Such combined simulation model provides the complexity of the behavior of the involved supply chain agents, and the feedback perspective that drives most of the decisions and actions of them. Also in a supply chain setting, Schieritz and Grler's approach [9] contrasts with Akkermans' choice. They model the supply chain schemata in AB terms, and agents' mental models in SD terms. The decisions made from the agents' internal structures influence the agents interactions, and based on the agents' interactions the supply chain structure is formed.

Hybrid SD-DES modelling approaches started to appear around the late 1990s and early 2000s in software industry. More recently, researchers from other disciplines, such as manufacturing and construction, also started working on hybrid SD-DES simulation. There are three basic structure types for hybrid SD-DES modelling [10], namely SD dominant, DES dominant and parallel SD-DES structures. In SD dominant hybrid modelling, the top-level feedback interactions are modeled in SD, and DES is used to simulate the internal sequential interactions of several effective variables in the SD model. The direction of interactions is from the DES part to the SD part. In DES dominant hybrid modelling, the top-level system structure is modeled with DES, and the SD is applied to model the feedback interactions inside several variables of the DES model. Contrary to the previous type, the direction of interactions here is from the SD part to the DES part. Parallel hybrid SD-DES modelling is preferred when there are mutual effects between sequentially inter-acting components and the components interacting through feedback loops.

4   Towards a Hybrid Simulation Approach for Service Networks

Service networks have expanded business reach and range with global partner collaborations while service provision and management is decentralized. This makes the end-to-end processes that live within them much more dynamic and complex than ever before. We strongly believe that using a hybrid simulation modelling approach would enable us to predict, analyze and visualize the impact of changes in service networks over time, and trace back to the root-cause of performance anomalies and errors. Unfortunately however, existing hybrid simulation approaches for business processes typically assume that the environment in which those processes live are rather stable and limited in terms of the nature and number of actors and interactions.

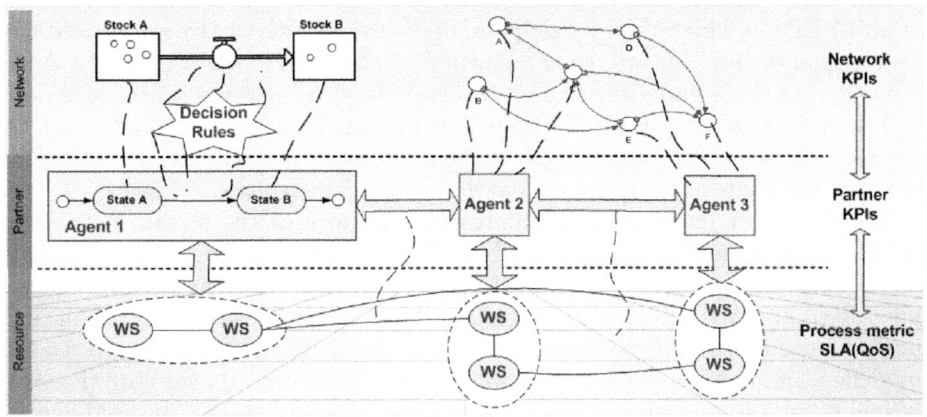

Fig. 1. Towards a hybrid simulation approach for service networks

Figure 1 graphically depicts our hybrid simulation model that comprises: network, partner and resource dimension. The bottom layer of Figure 1 makes up the resource layer of service networks, constituting two types of processes, viz. software service-enabled process orchestrations that are under the control of single network actors (cf. the white spheres), and end-to-end service enabled process choreographies (cf. arrows connecting the spheres).

Each software service-enabled process orchestration (SEPO) defines the logical sequencing and timing of software service invocations, e.g. Web Service (WS) orchestration, from a local/single system point of view. Their performance is typically expressed with Quality of Services (QoSs) metrics, such as web service response time, web service availability, security, and, reliability. SEPOs are scripted into choreographed service-enabled processes (CSEPs) that support end-to-end process interactions between network partners in a service network. CSEPs are governed by Service Level Agreements (SLAs) that meticulously stipulate the QoS that may be expected from each network partner, as well as penalties in case of non-conformance. Analysis and evaluation of end-to-end performance in service networks thus implies simulating aggregated (or global) SLAs in order to find the set of SLAs that leads to the desired performance, e.g., in terms of lead time or response time. We will rely on discrete event simulation to simulate SLA performance of SEPOs and CSEP at this level of our framework, since it has been a proven its effectiveness in evaluating QoS of software applications [11].

The middle layer in Figure 1 is called the partner layer, and models the SEPOs and CSEPs from the perspective of service network partners. We rely on Agent-based modelling for this purpose. Each agent has its own perception of itself participating in CSEPs and collaborating with other involved agents. Part of the agent's behavior is modeled as state automata, for instance for Agent 1, it shows the changes of its state from State A to State B. The bidirectional arrows between Agent 1 and Agent 2, and between Agent 2 and Agent 3 denote the interactions among them.

In particular, this level aggregates the QoS of partner SEPOs in the context of all CSEPs in which they participate, and subsequently maps aggregated QoS over a span of time (mostly some months) to partner KPIs. For example, Agent 1 in Figure 1 aggregated the QoS of the Web Services at the resource layer such as response times to partner KPIs such as average throughput. In addition, the interactions among the agents reflect the aggregated performance of all CSEPs, and are also influenced by the global SLAs in resource layer.

The top layer models and evaluates performance of the service network at large. This thus means not only aggregating the performance of all CSEPs over all participating partners, but also the KPIs of all network partners, and subsequently tuning performance at the resource and partner level so that the optimal performance is reached at the service network level. The service network layer is modelled, simulated and visualized with system dynamics. By running the simulation, we aim to quantify, predict and visualize network-level KPIs, and analyze the impact of changes on the network performance over time by posing what-if scenario. In jargon of system dynamics, this involves tweaking corresponding stocks, flows and variables.

5   Exploratory Case Study

The hybrid simulation model that has been introduced in section 4 will now be further illustrated and explored. Instead of making it long and tedious, we restrict ourselves to giving a high-level overview and revealing the cross-layer connections of this case study.

Figure 2 models a service network comprised of three SEPOs, viz. Place order (marked in blue), Request payment (marked in orange) and Dispatch order (marked in green). Two participants are involved, namely Customer A and Supplier B. The Place order is initiated by Customer A with order information, and completed by Supplier B who handles the pending orders. Regarding the information of those accepted orders, Supplier B requests Customer A to do the payment. The Dispatch order starts with Supplier B sending the ordered products to Customer A, and ends with Customer A receiving the products. Collectively, these three SEPOs make up the CSEP Order Management.

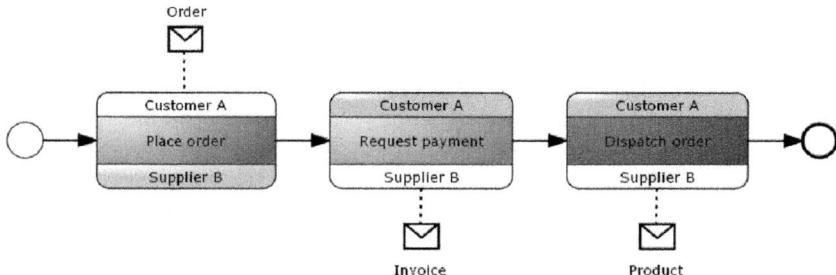

Fig. 2. Order Management Choreography

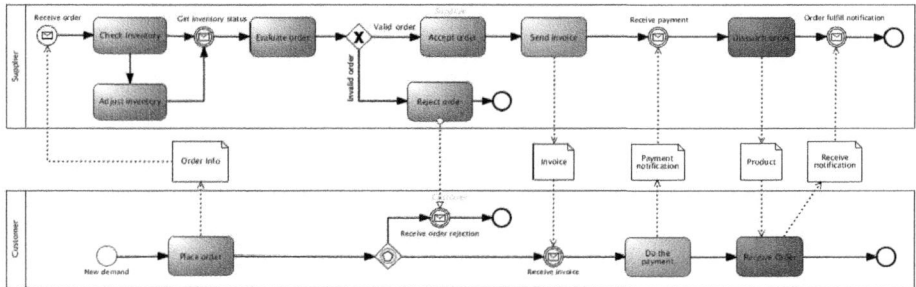

Fig. 3. Order Management Process

Figure 3 depicts the conceptual process model of the CSEP Order Management from technical perspective, in which the activities are colored in compliance with their corresponding SEPOs shown in Figure 2. The execution of these activities is supported by various software services, which performances are governed respectively by local SLAs and reflected in the QoS metrics. The end-to-end performance is rendered with global SLAs associated with CSEP Order Management, that aggregate the local SLAs attached to SEPOs. For instance, the global SLAs should specify the time allowance that starts from placing orders until the order being accomplished, whilst the local SLAs should restrict the processing time of each SEPOs. The sum of average time needed for processing Place Order, Request Payment and Dispatch Order is no longer than the processing time of Order Management specified in global SLAs. These activities are operated at the resource level, and the process model can be further fed into discrete-event simulation for capturing the KPIs of those software services.

In addition, this end-to-end process model (Figure 3) is described from an agent-based viewpoint, that all the activities are modeled within the boundaries of the process participants, either Customer A or Supplier B, by whom the activities are performed. Each SEPO is completed depending on the collaboration of the participants. The interactions between these two evolve the process by exchanging tangible or intangible resources, such as the order information, payment notification and the products etc.. Thus the performance of participant interactions are linked with the SLAs associated with CSEP.

At the network level, the CSEP Order Management is represented by means of system dynamics simulation in order to accommodate business managers (Figure 4). The inflow New order arrival rate is perceived as the number of orders sent every time unit, which is determined by the Actual order rates. The arrived orders are pending in the stock Order backlog. Once an order has been fulfilled, it leaves the backlog through the outflow Order fulfill rate. If the order is not valid, it is eliminated from the backlog through the outflow Order reject rate. In order to be fulfilled, a valid order firstly has to be accepted, enters the stock Accepted Orders and waits for being dispatched. The rate for dispatching the orders depends on whether the payment process has been done, meaning that it has to wait for the accomplishment of sending New requests for

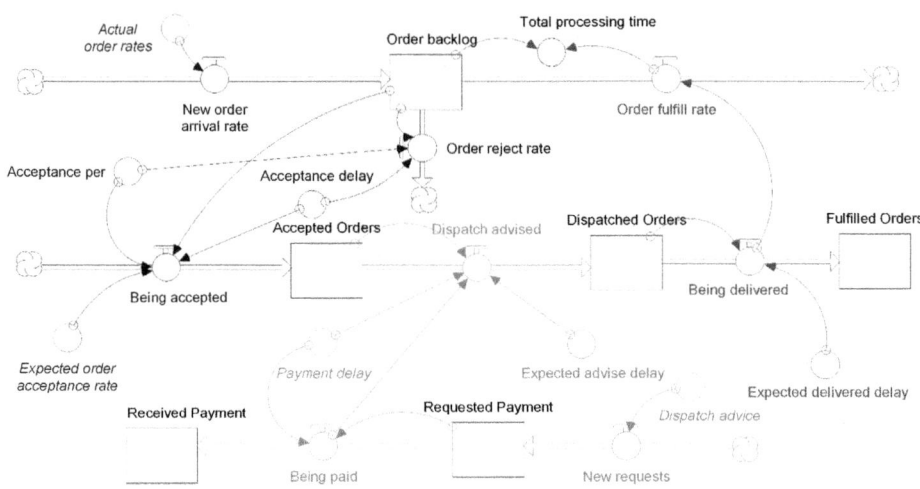

Fig. 4. System Dynamics Model of Order Management Process

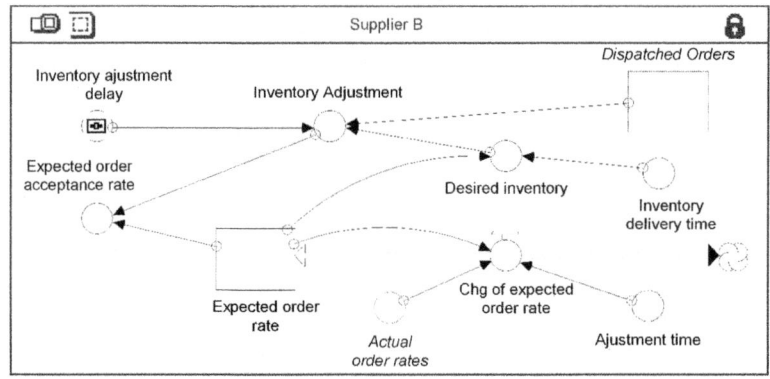

Fig. 5. System Dynamics Model of partial Supplier B's domestic management

payment and `Being paid`. Once the order enters the stock `Dispatched Orders`, it is ready to be delivered. The rate of orders `Being delivered` equals to the `Order fulfill rate`.

The flow rates in the business process are constrained and influenced by multiple delays and the participants' perceptions of the service network. For example in Figure 4, the flow rate `Being accepted` is determined by the capacity of Supplier B. If there is sufficient capacity, all the valid pending orders can be accepted every time unit. Otherwise, the number of orders that can be accepted equals to the expected order acceptance rate. The `Expected order acceptance rate` is Supplier B's estimation of their own capacity allocated in SEPO `Place Order`. It can be found in Figure 5 that the `Expected order acceptance rate` depends on Supplier B's ability of `Inventory Adjustment` and their Expected order arrival rate. The amount of inventory that needs to be adjusted is determined by the Dispatched Orders subtracted from the Desired inventory, and how much time it needs for the adjustment. The Desired inventory comes from Supplier B's estimation for the arriving order rate, and how much time it needs for delivering the goods to the inventory. In system dynamics, the above mentioned causal relations are defined in the following way:

$$Being\_accepted = MIN(Order\_backlog * Acceptance\_per/Acceptance$$
$$\_delay, Expected\_order\_acceptance\_rate) \qquad (1)$$
$$Expected\_order\_acceptance\_rate = Expected\_order\_rate + Inventory\_Adjustment \qquad (2)$$
$$Inventory\_Adjustment = (Desired\_inventory - Dispatched\_Orders)/$$
$$Inventory\_ajustment\_delay \qquad (3)$$
$$Desired\_inventory = Expected\_order\_rate * Inventory\_delivery\_time \qquad (4)$$

All of these causal relations are made according to Supplier B's business rules regarding their perceptions on their role in the service network and the collaboration with the other participant. Therefore the network performance is linked with the KPIs of participant interactions.

Note that there are three colored parts in this system dynamics model (Figure 4), which are corresponding to the SEPOs in the process model (Figure 3) respectively. Here the system dynamics simulation is used for capturing the behavior and capacity of the overall service network, finding the network bottleneck and forecasting the performance of service network regarding tactical or strategic modifications, by accumulating the performance of the network participants' behaviors and operations on software services over time. Thus it implies that the network KPIs aggregate the CSEP SLAs and the KPIs of partner interactions. For example, regarding the network KPI Total processing time, which is defined as Order backlog divided by Order fulfill rate in Figure 4, it relies on the performances of all the software services (e.g. checking inventory, etc.), together with human operations (e.g. decision makings on accepting the orders, etc.). The capacity measured at network level considers the combined behavior of software services and human operations. With system dynamics simulation, we can adjust the capacity allocation and observe the corresponding impact on network performance.

6   Conclusion

Having conducted several exemplary case studies, one of which we have presented herein, we have carefully concluded that there are multiple perspectives capturing particular dimensions on a service network. The layered hybrid modelling framework entails a structured approach to model and correlate these dimensions.The models on each layer zoom into particular concerns, e.g. the quality of service-enabled processes, the partner interactions and the network performance. Besides the separation of concerns, these models are also interconnected in this framework by means of multiple aggregations of SLAs and KPIs. Thus the service networks can be viewed in a more comprehensive and holistic way, and some hidden connections within the network that have been neglected are revealed.

Based on our initial case studies and experiments, we have now gained some preliminary proof that hybrid simulation models of a service network allow us to predict the potential performance regarding modifications from both technical and business perspectives. We are able to tune the network performance from various dimensions, including resource, participant and network level. The aggregation of SLAs and KPIs in the service network provides the means for tracing the changes and the impact of changes.

Our future work will concentrate on further experimenting with and refining the hybrid service network, working toward a common and unified metamodel underpinning the approach as well as an integrated prototypical toolset.

References

1. Paulson, L.D.: Services science: A new field for today's economy. Computer 39, 18–21 (2006)
2. van den Heuvel, W.J.: Changing the face of the global digital economy. Inaugural Address (November 2009)
3. Papazoglou, M., Ribbers, P.: e-Business: Organizational and Technical Foundation. John Wiley, Chichester (2007)
4. Greasley, A.: Using process mapping and business process simulation to support a process-based approach to change in a public sector organisation. Technovation 26(1), 95–103 (2006)
5. Hlupic, V., Vreede, G.J.D., Orsoni, A.: Modelling and simulation techniques for business process analysis and re-engineering. International Journal of Simulation 7(4), 1–8 (2006)
6. Lee, S., Han, S., Pena-Mora, F.: Hybrid system dynamics and discrete event simulation for construction management. In: ASCE International Workshop on Computing in Civil Engineering, Pittsburgh, PA (2007)
7. Kim, D.h., Juhn, J.h.: System dynamics as a modeling platform for multi-agent systems. In: The 15th International Conference of The System Dynamics Society, pp. 1–7 (1997)
8. Akkermans, H.: Emergent supply networks: System dynamics simulation of adaptive supply agents. In: Hawaii International Conference on System Sciences, vol. 3 (2001)
9. Schieritz, N., Grossler, A.: Emergent structures in supply chains - a study integrating agent-based and system dynamics modeling. In: Proceedings of the 36th Hawaii International Conference on System Sciences, pp. 94–102. IEEE, Los Alamitos (2003)
10. Alvanchi, A., Lee, S., AbouRizk, S.: Modeling framework and architecture of hybrid system dynamics and discrete event simulation for construction. In: Computer-Aided Civil and Infrastructure Engineering, pp. 1–15 (February 2010)
11. Jamoussi, Y., Driss, M., Jezequel, J.M., Ghezala, H.H.B.: Qos assurance for service-based applications using discrete-event simulation. International Journal of Computer Science Issues 7, 1–11 (2010)

Empowering Citizens in Public Service Design and Delivery: A Reference Model and Methodology

Y. Taher[1], Willem-Jan van den Heuvel[1], S. Koussouris[2], and C. Georgousopoulos[3]

[1] ERISS – Tilburg University, The Netherlands
{Y.Taher,W.J.A.M.vdnHeuvel}@uvt.nl
[2] DSSLab – National Technical University of Athens, Greece
[3] Intrasoft International S.A

Abstract. The importance of public service delivery for improving the relationship between governments and their citizens has been recently recognized as a major challenge for e-Government research. In this paper, we propose a new reference model and an associated governance methodology where citizens' opinions directly impact the service delivery decision-making process. Our proposal supports iterative development of public services; starting from abstract citizen needs, and subsequently aligning them with the strategy of public bodies, laws and regulations through a stepwise process of reconciliation and refinement until they can be modeled, simulated, and evaluated.

Keywords: Public service, service Design, Modelling, Representation.

1 Introduction

Governments, including local municipalities, provinces and national public bodies, deliver public services to their citizens. Public services can range from simple services such as publishing information to services as complicated as issuing passports, civil acts certificates, and building/commercial activity permissions.

All of us depend on public services for many aspects of our existence, and they unmistakably make up a part of everyday life. However, too often our interactions with public service organisations are characterised by deep dissatisfaction, hanging on the end of a phone, arguing over our consumer rights, feeling ignored and misunderstood.

Two main problems lie at the heart of the fundamental disconnect between people and public services. First, 'public service' is still seen as a commodity rather than something more profound, a form of human interaction. Public organisations still seek to deliver services for the lowest cost and maximum profit, without explicitly consulting their citizens while designing their service offerings. This, we argue, eats away at the fundamental purpose of public service: to provide support and to help people live their lives to their full potential.

The second problem is that there is –so we argue herein – that still no common representation or reference model for public service design and delivery. Today, public services are created in a rather ad-hoc manner. This results in the lack of

M. Cezon and Y. Wolfsthal (Eds.): ServiceWave 2010 Workshops, LNCS 6569, pp. 129–136, 2011.
© Springer-Verlag Berlin Heidelberg 2011

common understanding of, or even misunderstanding about, public service concepts. Each public service designer uses its own representation and as a result they produce fragmented and proprietary pieces of services that have limited value outside their own organisation, hindering the integration, reuse and assembly of services provided by external public organisations. In particular, the lack of a common reference model makes it very hard – if not impossible - to assemble and evolve services from various sources and to provide aggregated services that meet complex citizens' requirements. Moreover, the lack of a common reference model inhibits the creation of machine-readable public service descriptions that could enable functionalities like automated service discovery and composition.

To overcome the problems mentioned above, public organisations should look for new ways of gaining more and deeper insights about their citizens' actual problems and opinions, which can be used to improve public services offerings and delivery. Public organisations need to experience public services as citizens do. Moreover, public organisations should agree on a standard public service formal representation – a common reference model – supporting citizens' requirements analysis, service conceptualisation, modelling, deployment and delivery, in a way that the whole public service system is understood and expressed as an integrated design before implementing and changing.

In this work, we present a novel reference model – acting as a modelling guideline – for public service design and delivery process. Grounded on this reference model, we introduce a generic methodology for designing public services so that it contributes to the homogenisation of public services descriptions while promoting their sharing and reuse. It is the aim of this methodology to make the service design and delivery traceable, transparent and comparable to both service providers and clients while facilitating service process improvement and reengineering. In addition, the methodology supports a repeatable and disciplined evaluation of alternate designs and impact assessment. Both the reference model and the associated new governance methodology are distilled from actual cases which have been analyzed in the context of the EU STREP Cockpit project, In particular, we have studied cases at the municipalities of Tilburg and Venice, and the interior Greek ministry in Athens. Due to space restrictions we will limit ourselves to outlining the abstract workings of the governance methodology (section 2) and the key concepts populating the reference model (section 3) in the remainder of this article.

In particular, the reference model combines four layers, where each focuses on a particular phase proposed methodology. First, the service conceptualisation layer expresses the actions associated with the decision to conceptualise and implement a service by relying on laws, policies, and public requirements. Second, the service modelling layer expresses the actions associated with the modelling of the service modules and processes including functional and non functional service requirements. Finally, the service deployment and delivery layer not only defines the way an already implemented service will reach its target audience, but also evaluation metrics to analyse citizens' feedbacks. Due to reasons of scope, we will limit ourselves to the two design-time activities in the governance methodology, viz. Service conceptualization and modelling.

2 Empowering Citizens Role in Designing and Delivering Public Service Offerings

Public service delivery aims to satisfy citizens' needs. It can be considered almost unexplainable that citizens' engagement to all stages of public service delivery is, even nowadays, kept to a minimum. As postulated in the introduction, the current model used by governmental agencies for designing and providing services to the citizens is severely lacking citizen participation and involvement; a fact which generates a number of important issues, ranging from the deployment of unwanted or unusable services, to the lack of trust of governments, due to the lack of transparency of processes that take place during service creation. Moreover, as citizens' expectations are changing in high pace, citizens expect governments to become more transparent than they are at present and to provide services as effectively and efficiently as possible. The current model of public service delivery relies too much on government bureaucracy and on decision makers to deliver public services, without involving citizens, something that has proven to be generally unsatisfactory in most parts of the developing world and at the same time not as transparent as requested.

Having this in mind, in parallel with the efforts put together nowadays by governments to regain their citizens' trust and to reengage them in the decision making process, it is more than obvious that the current model for designing services is not sustainable any more. Not only does it lack effective ways for collecting citizens opinions and of exposing the internal decision to the public (a fact which will guarantee transparency), but in addition it has no standard mechanisms for integrating citizens contributions into the decision making process for the delivery of services. Moreover the current model does not have the concepts and mechanisms to support information provision and consultation for achieving the active participation of the citizens to the decision making process by shaping a dialogue, the outcome of which, would be one the main input in taking any final decisions concerning the delivery of a service.

In order to foster the engagement of citizens, we argue that novel technologies, typically based on Internet technology- may be used. Public administrations have to take advantage of modern tools in order not only to attract the direct input from active citizens, but also to exploit a huge amount of opinions that can be found mostly on the web (eg. Web-2.0 applications). Moreover, citizens should be provided with the ability to have a visual representation of the direct results that their involvement may induce. Thus, a new "governance model" is needed, which should compromise the existing successful tasks of the past (like business process modelling) with new features that allow the active interaction with citizens (like opinion mining and simulation), all based on the idea of infusing Web-2.0 characteristics to service conceptualization, design, deployments and operation phases, so that public bodies can have direct feedback and fine-tune their offered services accordingly.

Figure 1 illustrates the different stages of the new Governance model for public service delivery, alongside with the various actions that affect each stage. Features as opinion mining, cost and value modelling, simulation and visualisation, deliberation and profiling are the major additions to the existing ways of designing and deploying services, which leverage the old models to a higher level of citizens' participation and engagement. In more detail, the information flow of the new model can be summarized in the following steps:

1. Web 2.0 sources are monitored for opinions and needs on public services and the results forwarded to public service decision makers.
2. Once the decision making process for the delivery of identified services is initiated, public service decision makers start modelling the selected services. Citizens' opinions and wishes on the selected public services are in the disposal of the decision makers to be taken under consideration.
3. Modelled Services are simulated and visualized supporting decision makers on making adjustments that will reflect on budgetary and operational constraints of the organization.
4. Citizens are presented with the visual simulation of the services in appropriately developed deliberative platform.
5. Citizens' informed judgment on the simulated operation and related costs of the selected public services is expressed and returned to the decision makers for further consideration and final decisions.
6. Services are deployed and offered to citizens through context aware mechanisms and various delivery channels.
7. Evaluation of services is performed; mostly by opinion mining various Web-2.0 sources and feedback is presented to decision makers to further optimise the services.

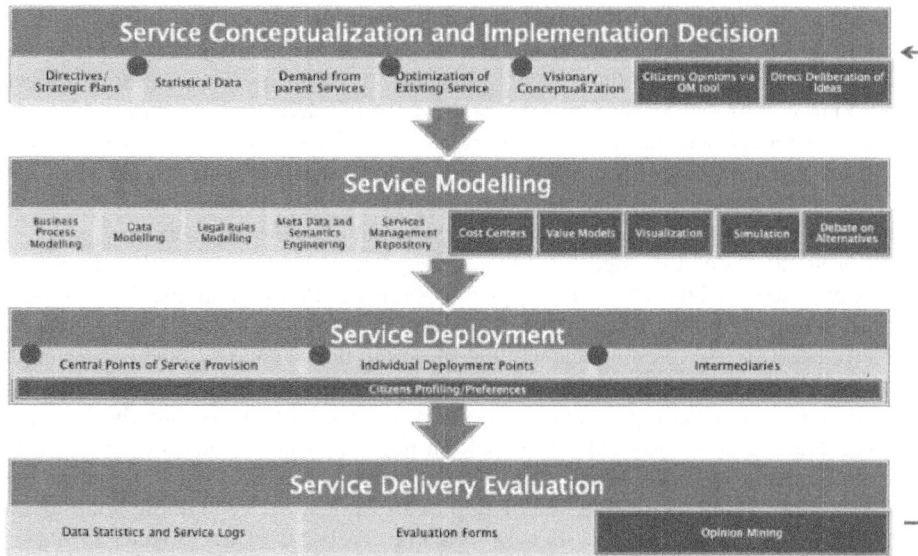

Fig. 1. New Governance Model

The adoption of such a model is expected to improve user experience regarding public services, as those services will be tailored to their needs based on their own selections. Moreover, such a model does not only serve the need of public administrations for service (re-)engineering or for porting human-operated services to electronic versions based on the demands of the citizens. Its true power lays in its ability to proactively design new services for uprising issues based on the analysis of public opinions that identify emerging problems and issues, which are not covered by existing services.

3   A Reference Model for Public Service Design and Delivery

The proposed reference model is intended to help public organisations to deliver higher quality public services. To do so, we treat the act of designing public services as a citizen-centric activity in relation to the role of the service providers. This section focuses on the key aspects of designing public services: the understanding of the requirements and preferences of citizens, the modelling concepts and relations, and the different way of structuring and visualising the services.

The reference model acts as a modelling guideline to ensure the conceptual integrity of a public service model. The reference model underpins the public service governance model supporting iterative development of public services; starting from abstract citizen requirements, and subsequently aligning them with the strategy of public bodies, laws and regulations through a stepwise process of reconciliation and refinement until they can be deployed monitored and evaluated.

As explained in the introduction, in this paper - due to space restrictions - we restrict ourselves to introducing the key concepts for each phase of the governance model. Taking into account these considerations, a four layer-of-abstraction reference model is proposed; where each layer is logically mapped to the phases of the governance model (see section 2). These four layers are explained hereafter.

The service conceptualisation layer

Improving the communication between the citizens and public administrations allows the latter to have better understanding about the citizen requirements and preferences, which is – without any doubt – a key prerequisite for delivering more adaptive public services to the citizen ever-increasing dynamic needs. This results in creating public services, which continue to have a significant positive impact on the citizen's life.

In this context, the service conceptualisation layer provides the public administrations with the key concepts and relations to achieve the aforementioned vision. Its main purpose is to allow for better alignment between the citizen requirements and associated legal resources and the strategic plans of public administration.

The service conceptualisation layer consists of a core conceptual model used in order to represent the different concepts, components, and stakeholders during the service conceptualisation phase. The key constituents of the service conceptualization layer are:

• **Legal resources.** Laws, policies, regulations, legislations etc. that govern the entire functioning of public administrations including the design of the public services they provide.
• **Strategic plan.** An authoritative guide or instruction set up by the governments to achieve a desired long-term outcome. For example, the *Socio-Economic Development Program* is one of the strategic plans set up by Tilburg municipality that stipulated

long-term outcomes to leverage social inclusion and increase of well-being of people at risk of exclusion (e.g., elderly, new migrants, etc.). The Werkplein service – a job intermediation service – is one of many public services provided by Tilburg municipality to realize this strategic plan.

- **Target Group.** A group of citizens that are missing a designated requirement.
- **Requirement.** Something vital, desirable, or deemed a basic necessity to an individual or group of citizens (Target Group). In order to be dealt with, a requirement should align with the Legal resources and recognized by a strategic plan. For example, the "Job Finding" public requirement which is need by a large group of citizens such as school leavers, old job seekers, young graduates, etc. aligns with the legal resources adopted by Tilburg municipalities and recognized by one of the municipally strategic plans, the Socio-Economic Development Program.
- **Action Plan.** A kind instruction set by a public administration following the recognition of a relevant public requirement. For instance, "Helping Citizen to Find a Job", is the action plan set by Tilburg municipality to carry out the recognized public requirement "Job Finding". An action plan results in the creation a relevant public service.
- **Public Service.** A pivot concept obtained as a result of profound understanding and analysing of public requirements. A public service can be seen as collaborative activity between a public administration and a target group of citizens to explicitly fulfilling their designated requirement. At this stage, the service is still seen as a high-level concept coming up with not only a clear definition of the function it should provide but also well defined direct, middle, and strategic outcomes.

Once a clear definition of the service concept and its outcomes is set up, the public organisation appoints a delivery organisation – which could be a particular department of the public organisation – to carry out the service modelling phase.

The service modelling layer

This layer's purpose is to transform the service concept into a concise administrative procedure with well defined inputs, outputs, and steps. The different elements of this layer are explained below:

- **Service Process.** A set of tasks, with a clear starting point while leading to clearly defined results. An aggregation of service processes constitutes a public service. For instance, *"Open job seeker case"* is one of many processes composing the Werkplein service. Such a process is responsible to achieve the following tasks: identifying a job seeker, opening a case, constructing a CV, setting up job interviews, following up interviews, and exiting the system. We associate to a *service process* descriptions about the service request initiating the process such as "Find me a job", the process stakeholders such as "job seeker, case manage, and IT system", the expected inputs such as "application form", and the requirements to be met by the process such as "Fast time to employment, Job match to Skills, salary meets expectations, etc.". A specific attribute "Priority" for service requirement is set by the associated stakeholders in order to ensure the balance between the different stakeholders' requirements.

- **Task**. The smallest level of decomposition of a process, responsible to fill out a specific activity, such as "set up a job interview". We associate to a *task* descriptions about the activity resources such as "IT system, telephone", the service time such as "X minutes", roles such as "Administrative assistant, Job seeker, and Job vacancy provider", and possible next tasks.

4 Discussions and Related Work

Service-oriented design and development incorporate a broad range of capabilities, technologies, tools, and skill sets, many of which have been initially explored in the domain of Service Oriented Architecture, and that include ([1],[2],[3]):

- Managing the entire services lifecycle, including: identifying, designing, developing, deploying, finding, applying, evolving, and maintaining software services.
- Delivering high quality workable service-oriented solutions that respect QoS requirements.

Existing service development lifecycle models from the industry include Service Lifecycle Process [13], Service-Oriented Modelling Framework [5], and Mainstream SOA Methodology (MSOAM) [7]. Service-Oriented Modelling and Architecture (SOMA) [1] is the IBM methodology for service-oriented analysis and design. Vendors such as SAP and BEA, and firms providing analysis and design consulting services, e.g., Cap Gemini [6], and Everwhere-CBDI [9] provide additional methodologies. Some of the existing assets from the industry are proprietary and for company internal use, or are only partially published. In academia, we have witnessed proposals such as Service Development Lifecycle Methodology (SDLM) [11], Service Centric System Engineering (SECSE) Methodology [12], and Architectural Framework for Service Definition and Realization (SOAF) [8]. These methodologies are domain independent in nature, and lack the ability to faithfully render public services in such a way that it is understandable by non-IT experts.

In future work, we aim to define a formal model that mainly considers the logical part of the public services development life cycle as well as the mapping to software services, and defines various viewpoints on it to address the specific needs of stakeholders involved. This will result in establishing a platform to engage citizens in the (re-) design of public services, and adopt best practices and tools for architecting public service solutions in repeatable, predictable ways which deal with changing citizen needs. This formal model will be based on existing works such as [11], [14], [15], and [16].

5 Conclusion

Following recent developments in the public sector reform agenda, public service developers are in critical need of guidance in the area of public service design and delivery. In this article, we have proposed a reference model and methodology to assist public service engineers in designing and delivering better quality public services. This has been ensured by incorporating the citizen needs as major inputs for the service design and delivery process. The public service engineering methodology and reference model are expected to become the cornerstone of a comprehensive governance model improving the quality of public services, creating significant service acceptance and satisfaction while still controlling public expenditure.

Acknowledgements. The work is sponsored by the EU FP7 as part of the COCKPIT project.

References

[1] Arsanjani, A.: Service-oriented Modeling and Architecture. IBM developerworks (Novemeber 2004), http://www-106.ibm.com/developerworks/library/ws-soa-design1/

[2] Brown, A., et al.: SOA Development Using the IBM Rational Software Development Platform: A Practical Guide. Rational Software (September 2005)

[3] Dhanesha, K.A., Hartman, A., Jain, A.N.: A Model for Designing Generic Services. In: IEEE SCC 2009, pp. 435–442 (2009)

[4] Arsanjani, A.: Service-Oriented Modeling and Architecture (SOMA), IBM developerWorks (2004), http://www.ibm.com/developerworks/webservices/library/ws-soa-design

[5] Bell, M.: Service-Oriented Modeling (SOA): Service Analysis, Design, and Architecture. Wiley, Chichester (2008)

[6] Engels, G., Hess, A., Humm, B., Juwig, O., Lohmann, M., Richter, J.P., Voß, M., Willkomm, J.: A Method for Engineering a True Service-Oriented Architecture. In: Proc. of ICEIS 2008 (2008)

[7] Erl, T.: Service-Oriented Architecture: Concepts, Technology & Design. Prentice Hall, Englewood Cliffs (2005)

[8] Erradi, A., Anand, S., Kulkarni, N.: SOAF: An Architectural Framework for Service Definition and Realization. In: Proc. of SCC 2006, pp. 151–158. IEEE Computer Society, Los Alamitos (2006)

[9] Everware-CBDI Inc., CBDI Service Architecture & Engineering: A Framework and Methodology for Service-Oriented Architecture (SOA). CBDI Report (2006)

[10] Kruchten, P.: The Rational Unified Process: An Introduction. Addison-Wesley, Reading (2003)

[11] Papazoglou, M., van den Heuvel, W.J.: Service-Oriented Design and Development Method. In: IJWET 2006, Inderscience Enterprises, vol. 2(4), pp. 412–444 (2006)

[12] SECSE, Service-Centric System Engineering (2004-2008), http://secse.eng.it/pls/secse/secse.home

[13] SOA Practitioners' Guide Part 3: Introduction to Service Lifecyle (2006), http://www.healthmgttech.com/editorial_whitepages/SOAPGPart3.pdf

[14] Dhanesha, K.A., Hartman, A., Jain, A.N.: A model for designing generic services. In: Proceedings of IEEE International Conference on Services Computing, pp. 435–442 (2009)

[15] Yang, D., Tong, L., Ye, Y., Wu, H.: Supporting Effective Operation of E-Governmental Services Through Workflow and Knowledge Management. In: Proceedings of the 7th International Conference on Web Information Systems Engineering, pp. 102–113 (2006)

[16] Apostolou, D., Stojanovic, L., Lobo, T.-P., Miró, J.-C., Papadakis, A.: Configuring E-Government Services Using Ontologies, vol. I3E, pp. 141–155 (2005)

A Description Framework for Digital Public Services

Yannis Charalabidis and Fenareti Lampathaki

National Technical University of Athens, 9 Iroon Polytechniou, Athens, Greece
{yannisx,flamp}@epu.ntua.gr

Abstract. Service description frameworks and relevant metadata appear as a key enabler that assists management of resources related to the provision of personalized, efficient and proactive services oriented towards the real citizens' needs. As different authorities typically use different terms to describe their resources and publish them in various Digital Service Registries that may enhance the access to and delivery of governmental knowledge, but also need to communicate seamlessly at a national and pan-European level, the need for a unified digital public service metadata standard emerges. This paper presents the creation of an ontology-based extended metadata set that embraces services, documents, XML Schemas, code lists, public bodies and information systems. Such a metadata set formalizes the exchange of information between portals and registries and assists the service transformation and simplification efforts, while it can be further taken into consideration when applying Web 2.0 techniques in governance.

Keywords: Service definition frameworks, service metadata, semantic interoperability, organizational interoperability.

1 Introduction

Over the years, several public and ICT initiatives across Europe have tried to describe services and other resources for use by systems and applications to serve citizens, business and administration agencies [5]. However, proposing a set of structural and syntactic metadata for digital public services and relevant resources is not adequate and effective to help services discovery and knowledge sharing [8], [13] leading to the conclusion that web-based resources and their mutual relationships can still be considered rather ungoverned [18].

The evolution of Internet, at the same time gives way towards building a Semantic Web that enables seamless communication between machines [3]. In this context, creating and populating rich semantic metadata on the Web has been commonly accepted as the route leading to the Government Semantic Web vision [8]. Metadata is a fundamental concept in building governmental digital collections or public information centres that describe and categorize e-government resources online [23].

In this direction, the present paper proposes a metadata set for describing e-Government resources gaining experience from relevant e-Government Metadata standardization efforts. Effectively applied in the context of the Greek e-Government Interoperability Framework [11], [15] and the Interoperability Registry Prototype implementation [21], the proposed metadata set is customized to the particular needs

M. Cezon and Y. Wolfsthal (Eds.): ServiceWave 2010 Workshops, LNCS 6569, pp. 137–144, 2011.

of the e-Government services, documents, XML Schemas, code lists, public bodies and information systems and formalizes their meaning. It further contributes to accelerate the exchange and retrieval of service-related information by governmental sites on the fly and to enhance the perspective over service provision guiding any transformation effort [8].

The structure of the present paper is as following: Section 2 describes the current state of the art in e-Government metadata schemas and standards, analyzing the main elements contained in most implementations worldwide. Section 3 presents an overview of the ontology that synthesizes the proposed metadata set creation, while the actual metadata sets for services, documents, XML schemas, and code lists are outlined in Section 4. Conclusions upon the merits and limitations of the approach, as well as next challenges to be tackled are provided in Section 5.

2   Relevant Work

Standardizing metadata sets for describing web resources has attracted great interest both from research and practical reality, as indicated in the following initiatives:

- *Dublin Core Metadata Initiative (DCMI)* [9] provides simple standards to facilitate the finding, sharing and management of information that extends over a broad range of purposes and business models.
- *United Kingdom's e-Government Metadata Standard (UK eGMS)* [16] lays down the elements, refinements and encoding schemes to be used by government officers when creating metadata for their information resources or designing search interfaces for information systems.
- *Australian Government Locator Service (AGLS)* Metadata Element Set [1] provides a set of metadata elements designed to improve the visibility, accessibility and interoperability of online information, organizations and services.
- *New Zealand Government Locator Service (NZGLS)* Metadata Element Set [22] originally designed for use by any governmental agency wishing to make information sources or services more readily discoverable is suitable for more general use.
- *Singapore Government Metadata Standard (SGMS)* [19] aims to help agencies achieve consistency when adhering to e-Government policies.
- *Canada Metadata Standards* [9] officially adopts Dublin Core as the core metadata standard for Web resource discovery since 2001.
- *IDABC Management Information Resources for e-Government (MIREG)* [12] came to supplement MOREQ (Model Requirements for the Management of Electronic Records) results and aimed to develop extensions to the Dublin Core for government information based primarily on the national metadata recommendations of the Member States' public administrations.
- *CEN/ISSS Workshop on Discovery of and Access to e-Government Resources (CEN/ISSS WS/eGov-Share)* [5] presents the ontology for the description of e-Government resources (Services, Process descriptions, Standards and interoperability frameworks, (Requirements) documents) and the metadata schema that is used in its work.

However, such metadata standards and schemes for network resources apply mainly to documents, electronic archives and public sites [1] or do not cover all the requirements for service-related modeling.

Research papers that have provided sets of metadata and ontologies for modeling services, such as [3], [6], [13], [17], [18], [24], as well as relevant initiatives for describing spatial information [13] and standards [14] have also been taken into account. However, despite the fact that a set of international standards and protocols, such as RDF (Resource Description Framework), OWL (Web Ontology Language), Atom Syndication Format, RSS (Really Simple Syndication), SKOS (Simple Knowledge Organization System) and XTM (XML Topic Maps), accompanies such metadata initiatives in order to formally depict e-Government metadata, a complete solution requires such a wide range of different technologies that to date have not rallied around a standard metadata representation [19].

The main emerging conclusions from studying the underlying state of the art thus include:

- Lack of a comprehensive, yet easy to use standardized metadata schema for e-Government resources that adopts a "follow-the-service" approach and captures the semantics of all the service-surrounding information, such as XML Schemas and code lists.
- Lack of orientation towards transforming services and real time service provision at web front-ends.
- Lack of easily accessible glossaries and predefined code lists for use in such metadata definitions, that resolve language issues as all the relevant metadata descriptions need to be in local language (for the government officials to understand, modify and approve) and at least in English (for ease of communication with other governments and practitioners).

3   The Service Description Framework Fundamentals

The definition of the proposed extended e-Government Metadata Standard is driven by the e-Government ontology and emphasizes on the formalization and the representation of the following basic entities – classes:

- *Services* provided in conventional or electronic means by the public authorities to the citizens and businesses.
- *Documents*, in electronic or printed format, that constitute the inputs or outputs of a service or are involved during their execution.
- *Information Systems*, which support the service provision and encompass the web portals as well as the back-office and the legacy systems.
- *Public Bodies* embracing all the service points and the authorities of the public sector that provide services, issue documents, create XML Schemas and code lists and own supporting information systems.
- *Web Services* for the interconnection and the interoperability among information systems during a service execution.
- *Legal Framework* that regulates the service provision, the documents issuance and the overall operation of the public bodies.

- *XML Schemas* and *Code Lists* with which the electronically exchanged documents comply and which are exploited in web services.

Figure 1 presents an abstract overview of the e-Government Ontology which is described in detail in [6] and [21]. The basic clusters of attributes are provided within each class, as well as the main relationships between them giving way to further analysis in Section 4. It needs to be noted that as far as the class Web Service is concerned, the proposed approach adopts the metadata definition prescribed in the OWL-S standard.

Additional classes of the ontology, completing the representation but not presented in further details in the present paper, are the following:

- Classes representing service types, document types, information system types, the (functionally oriented) service category list, and relevant categorization elements.
- Classes representing activity steps (start, finish, decisions, etc), giving the ability for in-depth description of the service flows.
- Classes for representing user-oriented elements, such as life events and business episodes.
- Classes holding information on various characteristics of services and documents, such as authentication methods, ways of service provision, levels of service sophistication, etc.

The majority of the above additional classes constitute an important addition to existing ontologies, such as the eGMS or the CEN/ISSS, providing for automated reconciliation and semantic matching of relevant annotations among systems of different organizations, directly contributing to semantic interoperability achievement. They have been modeled as Controlled Lists in the metadata sets that follow in the next section.

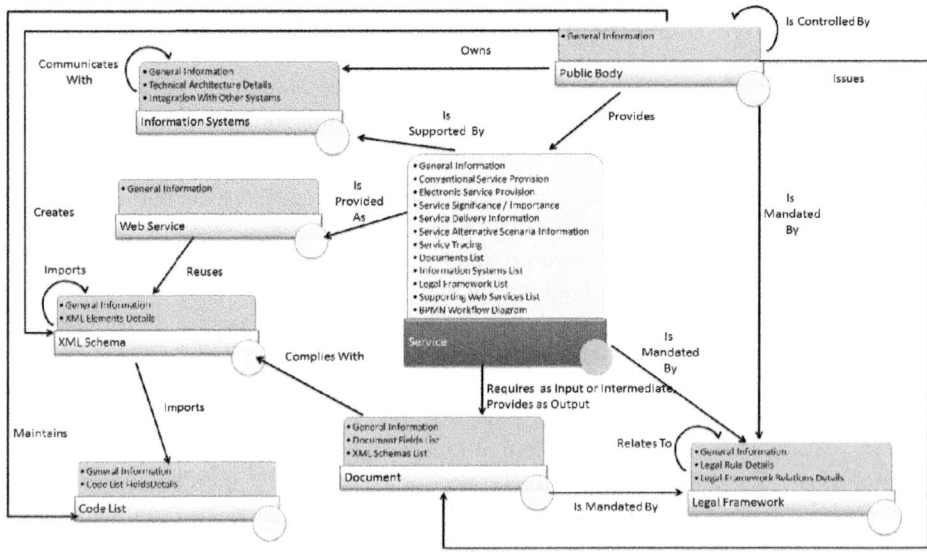

Fig. 1. The main entities of the framework

4 The Detailed Service and Resources Metadata

4.1 Services

The metadata set customized to the conventional and / or electronic services' requirements consists of 12 groups as following[1]:

- *General Information* including: Identifier, Title, Responsible Public Body, Final Service (*), Addressee (*), Type (*), Aggregation (3 level-GCL) (*), Life Event (*), Business Episode (*), Service In Abstract Level (*), Parent Service , Service Delivery Channels (*)
- *Conventional Service Provision* including: Demand On Physical Presence In Submission (*), Demand On Physical Presence In Receipt (*), Conventional Authentication Method (*)
- *Electronic Service Provision* with: Website, Electronic Service Delivery Method (*), Current Online Sophistication Level (*), Target Online Sophistication Level (*), Multilingual Content (*), Offline Operation (*), Progress Monitoring Support (*), Personal Data Level (*), Trust Level (*), Required Authentication Level (*), Current Authentication Mechanism (*), Registration Process (*).
- *Service Significance / Importance* including: Transactions Volume (per year), Frequency of Service Requests, Based On European Policies (*)
- *Service Delivery Information* including: Delivery Cost, Delivery Time, Responsible Department, Responsible Public Servant, Service Preconditions, Related Announcements, Related Attachments.
- *Service Alternative Scenaria Information*[2] with Identifier, Title, Conditions, Resources for Public Administration, Resources for Addressee, Total Resources, Cost for Public Administration, Cost for Addressee , Total Cost, Time for Public Administration, Time for Addressee, Total Time
- *Service Tracing* including Source, Date. Published, Date. Modified, Date. Valid (From-To), State (*), Language (*)
- *Documents List* with Identifier, Title, Position In Service (*), Mandatory (*), Replaces Document, Self-appointed Call (*)
- *Information Systems List*
- *Legal Framework List*
- *Supporting Web Services List*
- *BPMN (Business Process Modelling Notation) Workflow Diagram*

4.2 Documents

The metadata set that accompanies the documents claims novelty in incorporating the documents fields' definition that guides the XML Schema design and the code lists creation at later stages. In particular, the metadata set for documents consists of:

---

[1] The fields marked with (*) take values from appropriate predefined, controlled lists.
[2] It includes computed fields based on the step-by-step calculation of cost, time and resources, taking into account the possibility of faults.

- General Information with Identifier, Title, Creator, Publisher, Type (*), Subject, Coverage Format (*), Language (*), Addressee, Audience, Mandate. Authorizing Statute, Source, Date. Published, Date. Modified, Date. Valid (From-To), State (*).
- Document Fields List conposed of: Name, Description, Aggregation, Filled In By, Mandatory (*), Complex Type (*), Multiple Values (*), Predefined Values from Code List, Type (*), Length.
- XML Schemas List

The metadata set built around XML Schemas is further customized according to the type of the XML Schema [7] and has been based on the UN/CEFACT Core Components Technical Specification:

- *General Information* including Identifier, Title, Creator, Version, Type (*), Format (*), Date. Published, Date. Valid (From-To), State (*)
- *XML Elements Details* with Unique Identifier, Name, Dictionary Entry Name, Type (*), Version, Definition, Object Class Term Qualifier, Object Class Term, Property Term Qualifier, Property Term, Associated Object Class Term Qualifier, Associated Object Class Term, Representation Term (*), Date Type Qualifier, Primitive Type (*), Qualified Data Type, Cardinality Min, Cardinality Max, Facets (i.e. Pattern, Length, Min/Max Length, Enumeration, Total Digits, Fraction Digits, Min/Max Inclusive/Exclusive), Context: Business Process, Context: Organization, Context: Region (*), Business Term, Example, Remarks.

4.3 Controlled Lists

In order to avoid populating the metadata set with unstructured information, a set of controlled lists has been created. An indicative extract includes the Government Category List, the Service Type Controlled List and the Life Event Controlled List, as following:

- *Government Category List (1st Level out of 3)* [3] with the following values: City Planning and Land Registry; Civilization and Free Time; Education and Research; Environment and Natural Resources; Finance and Economy; Health and Social Care; Information and Communication; International Affairs and European Union; Justice, State and Public Administration; People, Communities and Way of Living; Public Order and Defence; Services for Companies; Transportation Means, Trips and Tourism   Work; Insurance and Pension
- *Service Type* including the following values: Request, Information Discovery, Declaration, Return, Registration, Participative Actions, Permit / Licence, Certificate Issuance, Payment
- *Life Event* identifying the following values: Birth, Marriage, Divorce, Death in Family, Sickness, Employment, Dismissal, Retirement, Property Acquisition, Property Loss, Residence Change, Education, Travel Abroad, Military Service, Other …, Not Applicable, Unknown

---

[3] Indicative list: more than 300 service categories included in the 3-level Government Category List.

5 Conclusions

The proposed service description framework brings the power of annotating services with commonly agreed metadata into the exchange and the retrieval of service-related information stored in Interoperability Registries by governmental sites on the fly. As the need for transforming services to obtain a more citizen-centric orientation based on their real needs and life events is more and more stressed, the proposed approach has already included metadata around service delivery scenaria that can guide any business process re-engineering effort in the public sector.

Problems faced during the adoption and application of the proposed metadata set were not trivial and have to be to be taken in mind during relevant attempts by government officials and practitioners. The adoption of a common "governance policy" over metadata appears as a worthwhile track towards this direction. Language issues also need to be taken care of early in the process, as the provision of pan-European e-Government Services is already on the way. Finally, adequate time and effort should be spent for educating and working together with government officials at various levels, for obtaining a common perspective over the metadata set.

As the proposed metadata set is incorporated into the Greek e-Government Interoperability Framework [11] and the Interoperability Registry Prototype implementation [21], future steps along our work mainly include exploration of how such a metadata set as the proposed one can: (a) be exploited in intelligent governmental service front-ends that enhance end users experience and have recently started to gain momentum at the international research scene [4], mainly when it comes to provided public services cataloguing and user groups profiling information, and (b) be further elicited in order to properly take into account service addressees' feedback when creating the service alternative scenaria.

References

1. Alasem, A.: An Overview of e-Government Metadata Standards and Initiatives based on Dublin Core. Electronic Journal of e-Government 7(1), 1–10 (2009)
2. Australian Government, National Archives of Australia, AGLS Metadata Standard, Version 1.3, http://www.naa.gov.au/records-management/publications/AGLS-Element.aspx
3. Barone, A., Di Pietro, P.: Semantic of e-Government Processes: a Formal Approach to Service Definition (Arianna). In: Proceedings of EGovINTEROP 2006, Bordeaux, France (2006)
4. Cantera, J.M., Reyes, M., Hierro, J., Tsouroulas, N.: White Paper on Service Front-Ends in the Future Internet of Services and Next Generation SOA, http://www.nexof-ra.eu/sites/default/files/nxt_gen_soa_workingdraft_21july2008.pdf
5. CEN/ISSS Workshop on Discovery of and Access to e-Government Resources (CEN/ISSS WS/eGov-Share): Sharing e-Government resources: a practical approach for designers and developers, http://www.cen.eu/cenorm/businessdomains/businessdomains/isss/workshops/wsegovshare.asp
6. Charalabidis, Y., Askounis, D.: Interoperability Registries in e-Government: Developing a Semantically Rich Repository for Electronic Services and Documents of the new Public Administration. In: Proceedings of the 41st Hawaiian International Conference of System Sciences, HICCS 2008, Hawaii (2008)

7. Charalabidis, Y., Lampathaki, F., Askounis, D.: Unified Data Modeling and Document Standardization Using Core Components Technical Specification for Electronic Government Applications. Journal of Theoretical and Applied Electronic Commerce Research 3(3), 38–51 (2008)
8. Charalabidis, Y., Lampathaki, F., Psarras, J.: Combination of Interoperability Registries with Process and Data Management Tools for Governmental Services Transformation. In: Proceedings of the 42nd Hawaiian International Conference of System Sciences, HICCS 2009, Hawaii (2009)
9. Devey, M., Cote, M.-C., Bain, L., McAvoy, L.: Celebrating 10 Years of Government of Canada Metadata Standards. In: Proceedings of International Conference on Dublin Core and Metadata Applications (2010)
10. Dublin Core Metadata Element Set, Version 1.1, http://dublincore.org/documents/dces/
11. Greek Ministry of Interior, Greek e-Government Interoperability Framework, http://www.e-gif.gov.gr/
12. IDABC Management Information Resources for e-Government, http://ec.europa.eu/idabc/en/document/3615/5585
13. INSPIRE (Infrastructure for Spatial Information in Europe) Draft Implementing Rules for Metadata (Version 2), http://inspire.jrc.ec.europa.eu/reports/ImplementingRules/draftINSPIREMetadataIRv2_20070202.pdf
14. ISO/IEC WD 24706 Information technology – Metadata for technical standards and specifications documents, http://jtc1sc32.org/doc/N1251-1300/32N1257-WD24706.pdf
15. Lampathaki, F., Charalabidis, Y., Sarantis, D., Koussouris, S., Askounis, D.: E-Government Services Composition Using Multi-faceted Metadata Classification Structures. In: Wimmer, M.A., Scholl, J., Grönlund, Å. (eds.) EGOV. LNCS, vol. 4656, pp. 116–126. Springer, Heidelberg (2007)
16. Office of the e-Envoy, e-Government Metadata Standard, Version 3.1, http://www.govtalk.gov.uk/documents/eGMS%20version%203_1.pdf
17. Palmonari, M., Viscusi, G., Batini, C.: A semantic repository approach to improve the government to business relationship. Data & Knowledge Engineering 65, 485–511 (2008)
18. Peristeras, V., Tarabanis, K.: Governance Enterprise Architecture (GEA): Domain Models for E-Governance. In: Rauterberg, M. (ed.) ICEC 2004. LNCS, vol. 3166. Springer, Heidelberg (2004)
19. Singapore Government Metadata Standard (SGMS), http://www.igov.gov.sg/NR/rdonlyres/B90E7579-E494-477A-86B7-E532F3FBC1B4/18178/2010ReportonSingaporeeGovernment.pdf
20. Smith, J.R.: The Search for Interoperability. IEEE Multimedia 15(3), 84–87 (2008)
21. Sourouni, A.-M., Lampathaki, F., Mouzakitis, S., Charalabidis, Y., Askounis, D.: Paving the way to eGovernment transformation: Interoperability registry infrastructure development. In: Wimmer, M.A., Scholl, H.J., Ferro, E. (eds.) EGOV 2008. LNCS, vol. 5184, pp. 340–351. Springer, Heidelberg (2008)
22. State Services Commission, NZGLS Metadata Element Set, Version 2.1, http://www.e.govt.nz/standards/nzgls/standard/element-set-21/nzgls-element-set-2-1.pdf
23. Tambouris, E., Manouselis, N., Costopoulou, C.: Metadata for digital collections of e-government resources. The Electronic Library 25(2), 176–192 (2007)
24. Vassilakis, C., Lepouras, G.: An Ontology for e-Government Public Services. Encyclopedia of E-Commerce, E-Government and Mobile Commerce, 865–870 (2006)

The Business Service Representation Language: A Preliminary Report*

A.K. Ghose, L.S. Lê, K. Hoesch-Klohe, and E. Morrison

Decision Systems Lab
School of Computer Science and Software Engineering
University of Wollongong
NSW 2522, Australia
{aditya,lle,khk789,edm92}@uow.edu.au

1 Introduction

The recent interest in services science has led to research in *business service management*, using a multi-disciplinary synthesis of thinking from the disciplines of computing, management, marketing and potentially several others. Business services can be of many different kinds. The notion includes within in its ambit business process outsourcing services, clinical services, customer contact services as well as IT-enabled services, to name a few representative examples. A key component of any business service management framework is a service modeling language.

The development of such a language poses several challenges. Unlike web service modeling, business service modeling requires that we view human activity and human-mediated functionality through the lens of computing and systems engineering (and building a framework that is general enough to include both notions of services within its ambit). This clearly requires an enhanced set of modeling constructs that go beyond those that have been used for web service modeling. This also requires a modeling notation at higher level of abstraction - one that supports the description of complex business functionality using abstract modeling constructs that offer a natural fit with concepts used to describe these services in everyday discourse. In the course of our research, we have found a close correlation between the notions of *services* and *contracts* (although the two notions are by no means identical). Our study of real-life business service descriptions, in domains as diverse as government services, IT services and consulting services, suggests that some contractual concerns appear routinely in service descriptions, and are part of the discourse on service design and redesign. Our survey of existing service modeling frameworks also suggests that while these are interesting and worthwhile, none come with the complete set of required features. The development of the Business Service Representation Language (BSRL) described in this paper was motivated by these concerns.

BSRL was developed as part of a project to develop a framework and supporting toolkit for strategic service alignment. The Strategy Modeling Language

---

* This work has been funded by the Australian Cooperative Research Centre for Smart Services http://www.smartservicescrc.com.au/

M. Cezon and Y. Wolfsthal (Eds.): ServiceWave 2010 Workshops, LNCS 6569, pp. 145–152, 2011.
© Springer-Verlag Berlin Heidelberg 2011

(SML) developed in this project provides the value modeling component to BSRL service models (discussed in detail later in the paper).

2   The BSRL Meta-model

A service model in BSRL consists of the following components:

Service ID

Preconditions

Post-conditions

Inputs

Outputs

Goals: These are the *intended effects/postconditions* of a service (note that not all postconditions are intended - e.g., it might not be my goal to debit my account with a certain amount of money, but that might be the effect of seeking to achieve the goal of purchasing an airline ticket using an online ticket booking service).

Assumptions: These are conditions on whose validity the execution of a service is contingent, but whose validity might not be verifiable when a service is invoked or during its execution. Assumptions need to be monitored during the execution of a service - if a violation is detected (once the truth status of the condition is revealed), the service may have to be aborted. Assumptions are common in informal service descriptions, but might not be identified as such. In our work modeling business services offered by government agencies, we have found references (in textual service descriptions) to lists of "'client responsibilities"'. These are statements of what service clients are responsible for doing, in order to enable the provider to fulfill the relevant service. These are clearly not pre-conditions, since they cannot be evaluated when a service is invoked. Indeed, checking to ensure that a client has fulfilled all client responsibilities is impractical in general. Instead, one can use the non-fulfillment of these responsibilities as a trigger for aborting the execution of a service, or for abrogating the contractual obligations of the service provider. "Force Majeure" clauses in contracts are also examples of assumptions (i.e., the provider commits to delivering a service provided no natural disaster intervenes etc.)

QoS specifications: Quality-of-Service (QoS) factors are described as a set of ⟨QoS-factor, range⟩ pairs, where the range provides the upper and lower bounds of QoS factors with quantitative evaluations (note that upper and lower bounds might be equal), or is a qualitative value.

Delivery schedules: These are specified as a set of ⟨functionality, deadline⟩ pairs. Arguably, a delivery schedule is part of a QoS specification, but these require special handling during service decomposition - hence the special status accorded to them.

Payment schedules: These are represented in a manner similar to delivery schedules. These are not ontologically part of a service QoS specification, but are arguably part of the set of assumptions. Like delivery schedules, these require special handling during service decomposition - hence the special status accorded to them.

Penalties: These are specified as a set of ⟨ condition, amount ⟩ pairs, such that *amount* is the penalty paid if *condition* becomes true. Arguably, penalties are part of the QoS specification, but these require special handling.

Value model: For each stakeholder in the service, a distinct value model is included in the service description. A value model represents how a service delivers value to a given stakeholder. A value model can serve as the basis for service design, and for re-design in the face of change (where the impact on value models of alternative re-designs provides the basis for deliberation on how best to implement change).

Resource model: The ability to understand how a service needs to be provisioned is a critical component of service design. This understanding also underpins any attempt at service optmization. A resource model describes available resources in a manner as expressive as a UML class diagram, with the usual part-whole and generalization-specialization relationships. In addition, a special *uses* relationship is required to describe how a given resource might use another. In general, a set of BSRL service models might share a common *resource ontology* - the resource model for a service is then a reference to a set of resource classes/instances in this ontology. These might be at different levels of abstraction. For instance, a service might be described as using a "printer" resource, or more specifically an "inkjet printer" resource or even more specifically an "HP inkjet printer resource". Note that the notion of a resource is general, and might include in its ambit people, tools, energy, other operating inputs and so on.

We note that not all service models will populate every component of the template described above. We do not commit to a specific language for representing pre- and post-conditions, goals and assumptions. These could be described informally in natural language, or formally (such as in temporal logic, as used in goal-oriented requirements engineering [11] [9]). Our current tool support for BSRL (not described in this paper due to space restrictions) offers a controlled natural language interface [10] for specifying these, and then uses ontology-mediated techniques to obtain formal representations. Figure 1 provides the diagrammatic meta-model.

3   The Service Value Model

A value model, as mentioned earlier, is a critical component of a service model. It provides the basis for service design (in very much the same way that a requirements model provides the basis for system design - arguably, requirements modeling is a special kind of value modeling). Value models support service re-design, with alternative re-deisgn assessed in terms of their impact on the value model. Traditionally, value modeling has been considered in economics and decision theory, with *utilities* being used as value measures. Utilities are inadequate for our purposes for many well-understood reasons (which we shall not elaborate here for brevity) including the difficulties associated with obtaining numeric measures of the utility to a given stakeholder from a service. More recently, Gordijn et al have proposed the e^3 Value framework [3] which provides conceptual modeling constructs to describe how actors exchange *value objects*. We believe that

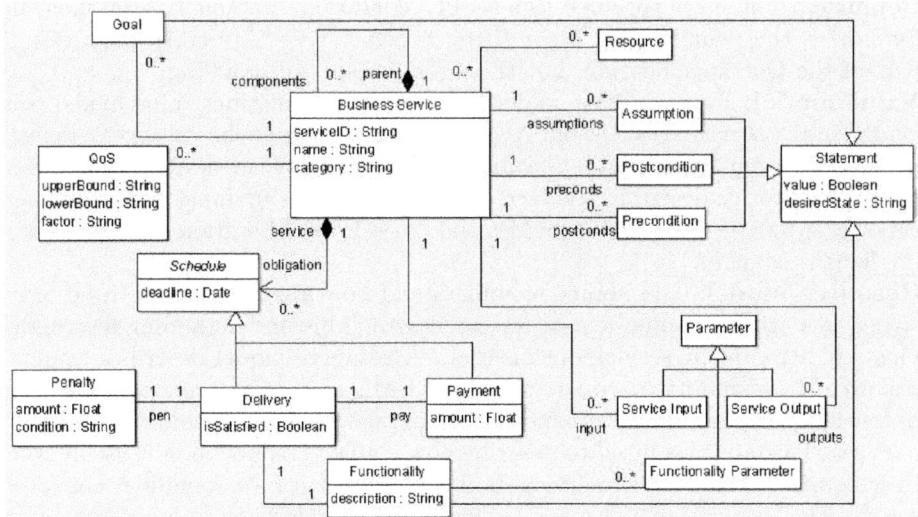

Fig. 1. BSRL meta-model

the notion of value objects can be generalized, and that ultimately a service
or system delivers value to a stakeholder by helping achieve the goals or objectives of the stakeholder. In an enterprise setting, *enterprise strategies* provide the
goals/objectives of the enterprise stakeholder. We have developed the *Strategy
Modeling Language (SML)* to provide a formal basis for representing enterprise
strategy, and have evaluated its expressive adequacy over a range of real-life
organizational strategy documents (SML turns out be adequate). SML provides
a useful value modeling framework and is outlined below.

An SML *strategy model* is a set of *strategy statements* of the following three
kinds:

– A *goal*: Goals are descriptions of conditions that an organization seeks to
  achieve. Goals admit boolean evaluation, i.e., an organization is able to
  clearly determine whether it has achieved a goal or not (consider the following example: *"Our corporate strategy is to be the market leader in mobile
  handsets"*). This notion of a goal closely corresponds to that used in goal-
  oriented requirements engineering.
– An *objective function*: An objective function is a construct used in operations research techniques to define what the *preferred* or *optimal* solution
  to an optimization problem might be. These are typically articulated as
  maximize f or *minimize f*, where *f* is a function defined on the *decision
  variables* (using which the constraints that *feasible solutions* are required
  to satisfy are also written). Our analysis of a large number of actual corporate strategy documents, as well as the management literature, suggests that
  startegies involving *corporate performance measures* or *key performance indicators (KPIs)* are articulated in the form of maximization or minimzation

objectives. Consider the following statements of strategy: *Our strategy is to minimize order lead times, or, "Our strategy is to maximize customer satisfaction"*. In the first of these, the intent is to minimize a function encoding order lead time while in the second, a funcion encoding some definition of customer satisfaction (for instance, using average customer wait times at the customer contact centre, the number of escalations, the number of product returns etc.) is maximized.

– A *plan*: A plan is a set of goals together with a set of sequencing and related coordination constraints. In the most general sense, a plan can be as complex as a process model. In this paper, we will view plans only as linear sequences of goals. This is because SML is designed to be used by senior management, i.e., individuals within an organization who might be involved in strategy formulation. Also, our analysis of a large number of actual corporate strategy documents suggests that strategies are typically articulated at a very high level of abstraction, where control structures more complex than linear sequencing is never required. A typical example is the following anonymized but actual strategy statement: *Our strategy is to first gain market acceptance in NZ, then position ourselves in the UK market, then use the UK market credibility to enter the Australian market*. There are three steps (goals) in this strategy, connected via a linear sequencing relation.

In the following, we will use the terms *strategy model* and *value model* interchangeably.

Value models underpin the analysis required for *service evolution*. We shall use the notion of service evolution to denote situations in which service models need to be modified. Drivers for such modifications might be:

– Service re-purposing, necessitated by altered requirements/goals/strategies that the service was designed to realize.
– Service improvement, i.e., improving the performance of the service relative to one or more QoS factors
– Operational drivers, such as changes to service delivery platforms.
– Compliance, i.e., service re-design triggered by a finding of non-compliance.

We are interested in two different kinds of analysis to support service evolution: impact analysis and trade-off analysis. In impact analysis, we aim to understand the impact of a proposed change on the value model of a service. For instance, which strategies in a given stakeholder's value model will become unrealized as a consequence of the change? Which stakeholders' value models will be impacted by the proposed change? In trade-off analysis, we seek to identify the best amongst alternative service designs (in terms of their impact on the value model) implementing the required change.

The impact of a candidate change to service model can be represented by $(\bigoplus_{i=1...n} V_i - V_i')$, where V_i is the value model for stakeholder i associated with the original service design, V_i' is the value model for stakeholder i associated with the changed service design, $-$ is an abstract difference operator (thus $V_i - V_i'$ represents elements of V_i that are not in V_i'), and $\bigoplus$ is an abstract combination operator (thus, if the value models were represented as sets, then this would be the set union operator). These abstract notions can be further elaborated in a formal fashion to obtain an algebraic generalization of a set of useful instances, but this is not presented here due to space constraints. Note that this captures one of possibly many intuitions on how to assess the value impact of a change - others (such as ones that accord importance to the new value proposition in V_i') could also be of interest.

A given change constraint (e.g., re-purpose the service in a given manner, make a service design compliant, or improve a QoS factor to meet a given threshold) can be implemented in multiple different ways. Trade-off analysis will be required to identify which of these alternative realizations of the change request we would choose to adopt. One way this could be done is to seek the alternative which minimizes impact (either with respect to set inclusion or with respect to set cardinality).

4   Related Work

Web Service Description Language (WSDL) [2] provides an implementable technical language that describes how a service can be accessed and invoked over the web. Semantic web services (WSMO, OWL-S, WSDL-S etc.) [6] allow for semantic markup of service description, and support pre- and post-conditions. SAWSDL [4] is another such language. In [7], O'Sullivan has examined both the functional non-functional properties of business services. Most of these features have been incorporated in the Universal Service Description Language (USDL) [1] which aims to provide a general framework for generic services (i.e. either technical or business). This language features three service perspectives namely business, operational, and technical.

Table 1 compares existing service modeling frameworks with BSRL in terms of the modeling constructs of interest.

The following observations supplement the comparison in Table 1:

– WSDL provides support for specifying low-level technical details that are not of interest in business service modeling.

Table 1. Comparison of Service Description Languages

	WSDL	WSDL-S	SAWSDL	OWL-S	USDL	BSRL	WSMO
Input/Ouput	✓	✓	✓	✓	✓	✓	✓
Pre-Condition	×	✓	×	✓	✓	✓	✓
Post-Condition	×	✓	×	✓	✓	✓	✓
Goals	×	×	×	×	×	✓	✓×
Value Model	×	×	×	×	×	✓	×
Assumptions	×	×	×	×	×	✓	✓×
QoS Specifications	×	×	×	×	×	✓	?
Delivery Schedule	×	×	×	×	×	✓	×
Payment and Penalties	×	×	×	×	×	✓	×

- Web Service Modeling Ontology (WSMO)[1] provides for assumptions but our notion of assumption differs in several ways. WSMO assumptions are only meant to be checked at service invocation time, while BSRL assumptions are constantly monitored. BRSL assumptions are intended to also model the contractual obligations of parties outside of the service provider. As well, BSRL assumptions play a role in service decomposition.
- BSRL does not make explicit provision for ontologies but these could clearly be used in conjunction with BSRL to provide semantic markup of *all* constructs.
- BSRL does not provide support for process modeling as OWL-S does. This is a deliberate choice to provide a sufficiently abstract notation for business service modeling.

Pijpers et. al. have presented a framework and methodology for modeling business services called the e^3 Family [8] that examines three perspectives of an organization one of which is focused on business service modeling. The use of separation of concerns in [8] aids in clarifying discussions by relevant stakeholders. The i* agent-oriented conceptual modeling language [11] has also been used for service modeling. Neither of these approaches provide support for the contractual aspects of BSRL. i* supports QoS modeling only in very general terms, as diagrammatic *softgoals*, related to other i* constructs via positive and negative *contribution links*. Neither i* nor the e3value framework support assumptions, penalties or schedules. i* is arguably better suited as value modeling framework and has been proposed as a diagrammatic front-end to the Strategy Modeling Language [5].

5   Conclusion

BSRL has been evaluated by modeling a range of government, IT and consulting services, and has been found to be adequate. The most detailed evaluation was carried out with government services, where a substantial service catalogue of a state government agency was modeled in BSRL. Our experience also suggests that BSRL can provide guidance to analysts in terms of what needs to be included in service descriptions - without such guidance, some service descriptions end up incomplete and inadequately structured.

BSRL deliberately ommits any support for process modeling. This is based both on observation of actual business service documentation practice and on the obligation to offer a sufficiently abstract set of modeling constructs. However, it is easy to see how BSRL service descriptions can be refined into process descriptions with the goals, post-conditions and QoS specifications providing guidance to the process designer.

This preliminary report ommits considerable detail. It also omits a detailed framework for service decomposition and service-contract interplay. These, plus detailed experience reports, will be made available in the full version of the paper.

---

[1] WSMO homepage http://www.wsmo.org

References

1. Cardoso, J., Winkler, M., Voigt, K.: A service description language for the internet of services. In: Proceedings of First International Symposium on Services Science, Berlin, Germany, vol. (1), pp. 1–10 (March 2009)
2. Curbera, F., Duftler, M., Khalaf, R., Nagy, W., Mukhi, N., Weerawarana, S.: Unraveling the Web services web: an introduction to SOAP, WSDL, and UDDI. IEEE Internet Computing 6(2), 86–93 (2002)
3. Gordijn, J., Yu, E., Raadt, B.: E-service design using i^* and e^3 value modeling. IEEE Software 23(3), 26–33 (2006)
4. Kopecky, J., Vitvar, T., Bournez, C., Farrell, J.: Sawsdl: Semantic annotations for wsdl and xml schema. IEEE Internet Computing 11, 60–67 (2007)
5. Le, L.-S., Zhang, B., Ghose, A.K.: Representation of strategy using an i*-like notation. In: Pernici, B. (ed.) CAiSE 2010. LNCS, vol. 6051, pp. 113–117. Springer, Heidelberg (2010)
6. Lara, R., Roman, D., Polleres, A., Fensel, D.: A conceptual comparison of WSMO and OWL-S. In: (LJ) Zhang, L.-J., Jeckle, M. (eds.) ECOWS 2004. LNCS, vol. 3250, pp. 254–269. Springer, Heidelberg (2004)
7. O'Sullivan, J.J.: Towards a precise understanding of service properties. Ph.D. thesis, Queensland University of Technology (2006)
8. Pijpers, V., Gordijn, J., Akkermans, H.: Business strategy-IT alignment in a multi-actor setting: a mobile e-service case. In: Proceedings of the 10th International Conference on Electronic Commerce. ACM, New York (2008)
9. Regev, G., Wegmann, A.: Defining Early IT System Requirements with Regulation Principles: The Lightswitch Approach. In: 12th IEEE International Conference on Requirements Engineering, Los Alamitos, CA, USA, pp. 144–153 (2004)
10. Schwitter, R.: Controlled natural languages for knowledge representation. In: Proceedings of 23rd International Conference on Computational Linguistics, Beijing, China, pp. 1113–1121 (2010)
11. Yu, E.: Towards modelling and reasoning support for early-phase requirements engineering. In: Proceedings of RE-97 - 3rd Int. Symp. on Requirements Engineering, pp. 226–235 (1997)

Analysis of Complex Events in Memory Evolutive Systems

Andrée C. Ehresmann and Jean-Paul Vanbremeersch

Faculté des Sciences Mathématiques,
33 rue Saint-Leu, 80039 Amiens, France
ehres@u-picardie.fr
http://pagesperso-orange.fr/ehres

Abstract. Complex Event Processing is studied in the frame of Memory Evolutive Systems, a mathematical model, based on category theory, for evolutionary self-organized hierarchical systems such as biological, social or cognitive systems. Their self-organization depends on the interactions between a net of internal functional subsystems, each operating at its own rhythm. We show how the cooperation/competition between these 'coregulators' is at the root of ubiquitous complex events. The property leading to the emergence of higher order complex events is characterized: it is the "Multiplicity Principle" (a kind of 'degeneracy' property) satisfied in particular by neuro-cognitive systems where it allows for the development of higher order cognitive processes, up to consciousness.

Keywords: Complex system, Emergence, Event, Category theory, Colimit.

1 Introduction

Though any phenomenon (in Pierce's sense) can be called an 'event', the usual meaning is rather a noteworthy occurrence; but 'noteworthy' depends on the context where it is observed: in which system? through which viewpoint and at which timescale?

Complex event processing is generally studied in a social system (e.g., a large enterprise, a society, a nation, ...), a biological system (a cell, an organism,...) or a cognitive system. Such a system is evolutionary, with a tangled hierarchy of components of various complexity levels, self-organized thanks to a multiplicity of mutually entailed functional regulatory subsystems, each operating at its own rhythm; an event corresponds to a sudden detection of an expected or unexpected change of state, either by one of them or by an external observer.

Here we analyze complex events in the frame of our theory of *Memory Evolutive Systems* (MES) developed for modeling this kind of systems, and based on a 'dynamic' category theory integrating multiple temporalities (cf. our book [5]).

2 Structure of the System

First we need to make sense of the structure and dynamics of the system, that will be illustrated by the example of a large business enterprise.

M. Cezon and Y. Wolfsthal (Eds.): ServiceWave 2010 Workshops, LNCS 6569, pp. 153–159, 2011.

2.1 Configuration of the System around a Given Time

The configuration of the system at a given time t is modeled by a category H_t. Recall that a category [6] is an oriented (multi-)graph with an internal composition which maps a path (f, g) from A to B on an edge fg from A to B, is associative and such that each object has an identity; a vertex is called an *object*, and an edge a *morphism* (or more simply a *link*). The objects of the category represent the state at t of the components of the system existing at this date, the links the interactions between them around t. A link operates with a propagation delay and more or less strength, depending on the available energy resources.

The components are distributed in several complexity levels, organized in a 'tangled' hierarchy in which an object A of level $n+1$ binds together and functionally represents at least one pattern Q of linked components of levels $\leq n$ (mathematically: it is the colimit of Q, cf. Section 4).

For an enterprise, the objects of H_t correspond to the (states at t) of the members of staff, the more and more complex services or departments they form; and also the resources and material necessary for the activities. The links represent channels through which information or material can be transmitted.

2.2 Change of State

The change of states from t to $t' > t$ is modeled by a *'transition'* functor from a subcategory of H_t to $H_{t'}$. If a component A existing at t still exists at t', the transition associates to A its new state at t'. Thus a component of the system is modeled by a maximal sequence of objects of the categories H_t connected by the transitions (representing its successive states). The transitions verify a transitivity condition, and the family of categories H_t (indexed by the timescale of the system) and the transition functors between them form what we have called a *Hierarchical Evolutive System* [2]. The *stability span* of a component of level $n+1$ is the longest period during which it persists and admits a lower order decomposition which maintains its working conditions.

While a transition preserves some components, it may also lead to events of the following kinds: addition of new components, formation (or preservation, if it exists) of a component binding some given pattern of linked components, suppression or decomposition of some components (cf. the four "archetypal changes" of Thom [7]: birth, fusion, death, scission). These changes are modeled by the *complexification* process with respect to a procedure having objectives of these kinds, and the complexification can be explicitly constructed [2].

For an enterprise, such events correspond for instance to the hiring of new employees, the formation of a higher service regrouping some lower ones, departure of an employee.... The stability span of a complex component, say a service, is related to the period during which it persists with little turnover (same employees realizing the same function).

2.3 Self-organization

The system has a multi-scale self-organization. Its dynamic (reflected by the transitions) depends on the cooperative and/or competitive interactions between a net of mutually entailed specialized functional subsystems called *Coregulators*. Each coregulator has its own complexity level, some admissible procedures in relation with its function, and its own discrete timescale possibly changing in time; this timescale is extracted from the continuous timescale of the system which allows coordinating the whole system.

The coregulators can take profit of previous events and experiences thanks to the development of an evolutionary subsystem, the *Memory*, whose components flexibly record the knowledge of the system of any kind: past noteworthy events and experiences, behaviors and procedures, internal states.... Each coregulator has a differential access to this memory, in particular to retrieve the admissible procedures characterizing its function.

In an enterprise, the coregulators correspond to various services and departments modulating the dynamic, their rhythm varying from one day for workshops to some years at the manager level. The constantly revised memory collects the knowledge necessary for a correct functioning (different procedures, production strategies, values, past experiences, supplies on hand, ...), as well as past important events and archives of any nature.

3 Dynamic of the System and Associated Events

The dynamic of the system is modulated by the interactions between the dynamics imprinted by the various coregulators, each operating independently as a hybrid system at its own rhythm.

3.1 Dynamic of a Particular Coregulator

Each coregulator operates stepwise. A step extends between two successive instants t and $t+d$ of its discrete timescale, and it is divided in 3 phases:

(i) Analysis: formation of the coregulator *landscape* (modeled by a category) L_t at t which gathers the partial incoming or remembered information.
(ii) Decision: choice, on the landscape L_t, of an admissible procedure Pr with the help of the memory.
(iii) Command: the objectives of Pr are sent to effectors to be executed.

The command phase extends during the continuous duration of the present step; its dynamic is generally described by differential equations implicating the propagation delays and strengths of the links, and it should move the dynamic of the landscape toward an attractor. The result is evaluated at the beginning of the next step (by comparing the new landscape L_{t+d} with the anticipated landscape modelled by the complexification of L_t with respect to Pr). If the anticipated result is not reached, we say that there is a *fracture* for the coregulator.

For example, in an enterprise the step of a given service is divided into a phase of analysis and preparation, leading to the formation of the current landscape; a phase of design and decision, where a strategy is chosen, and a command phase, for the execution followed by its evaluation. In a secretariat: looking for newly delivered mail, sorting the letters by order of urging and answering the most important ones; at the next step, the results of the strategy are evaluated. There will be a fracture if some pressing chores have not been realized.

3.2 Main Events at the Root of Fractures

Ubiquitous events may cause errors in the receiving of information, and the selection or carrying out of commands. Particularly important are those arising from the competition with other coregulators. Indeed, at a given time, the procedures of the various coregulators are selected on their own landscapes, but the commands are executed by effectors operating on the system itself. To avoid fractures, these commands should fit together, that is not always the case, for instance when two coregulators need a same non-shareable resource (e.g. two services of an enterprise simultaneously need the same repairman).

The global procedure actually carried out on the system comes from an equilibration process between their different procedures, called the *interplay among the* coregulators, possibly by-passing the procedures of some of them and causing fractures.

In particular each coregulator has *structural temporal constraint*s due to the temporal and material constraints imposed by the propagation delays of the inks and the stability spans of the components. At each step they are expressed by the inequalities

$$p << d << z$$

where p is the coregulator *time-lag* (= mean propagation delay of the links in the landscape), d is its *period* (= mean duration of the step, possibly changing over time), and z is the minimum stability span of the intervening components. They must be respected for a step beginning at t to be achieved in time.

Whence the following events may cause a fracture for the coregulator, or even prematurely interrupt the step:

(i) increase of the time lag so that information is not received in due time, or no admissible procedure is found, or the commands of the procedure cannot be sent in time to effectors;
(ii) decrease of the stability spans: the information is no more valid, the landscape is unreliable, or the procedure cannot be executed by lack of adequate effectors.

4 Complex Event Processing in Memory Evolutive Systems Satisfying the Multiplicity Principle

In systems able to develop processes of higher complexity (such as higher cognitive processes for cognitive systems), there occur complex events, generated by an accumulation of lower level events implicating several coregulators and only observable by an external observer with a global view of the system, or perhaps by some higher 'intentional' coregulators. We have proved that such systems are characterized by a kind of degeneracy property (in the sense of Edelman [1]), which we call the *Multiplicity Principle* [4], [5].

4.1 The Multiplicity Principle, Key to Higher Complexity

We have said that a component A of level $n+1$ admits at least one decomposition into a pattern Q of level $< n+1$ which it binds. Let us say more explicitly what it means. A *pattern* Q is a family of components Q_i with some distinguished links between them. A *collective link* (c_i) from Q to A is a family of links c_i from Q_i to A commuting with the distinguished links of Q.

The component A binds Q (or is its *colimit*) if there is such a collective link (c_i) through which any collective link (g_i) from Q to C factors. Then A has *ramifications* down to level 0, obtained by taking first a lower level decomposition Q of A, then a lower level decomposition of each component Q_i of Q, and so on, down to decompositions of level 0. We define the *complexity order* of A as the length of its shortest ramification (it is $< n+1$).

If A and C bind respectively patterns Q and P, a (Q, P)-*simple link,* called an *n-simple link* if Q and P are contained in the levels $\leq n$, is a link from A to C which binds a *cluster* G of links between components of Q and P well correlated by the distinguished links of Q and P. An n-simple link represents a cluster as an entity, thus just reflects properties of the lower components of A and C. A composite of n-simple links binding adjacent clusters is n-simple.

Besides the n-simple links, there may exist other links which emerge at level $n+1$. However for that the system must satisfy the following

Multiplicity Principle (MP): There are objects C, called *n-multiform*, which bind 2 patterns Q and P of levels $\leq n$ though the identity of C is not (Q, P)-simple.

This property is ubiquitous in living systems. Roughly it means that there are patterns Q and P which are functionally equivalent (since they have the same binding) though they are not connected by a cluster. It implies the existence of *n-complex links* from A to A' obtained by composing n-simple links binding non-adjacent clusters; their emergence constitutes a complex event at the level $n+1$ since they do not depend 'locally' on lower level links between components of A and A', but rely on the global structure of the levels $\leq n$.

4.2 Main Consequences of the MP

We have proved [4], [5] the following.

Complexity Theorem. The MP characterizes the systems in which there are components of complexity order strictly greater than 1.

If the MP is not satisfied, any component is 'reducible' to level 0 in only one step, meaning it binds a pattern contained in level 0 ('pure reductionism').

Corollary. The MP extends to a complexification, so that in a MES it allows for the emergence over time of an intertwined hierarchy of components of increasing complexity orders.

In particular the MP is satisfied in our model MENS for a neuro-cognitive system. MENS is obtained by successive complexifications of the evolutive system of neurons (whose components are the neurons and the links are the synaptic paths between them). Its higher order components represent mental objects or processes of increasing complexity.

We have shown [5] how the MP makes possible complex systemic events such as:

(i) Development of a *semantic memory* in which components of the memory are classified into intransitivity classes called *concepts*, with possible shifts between instances of a same concept.

(ii) Development over time of a subsystem of the memory, the *Archetypal Core* AC, which consists of well connected integrated key components, recalling the most significant complex events experienced by the system; their constant recall make their links stronger and faster, so that they autonomously propagate and maintain their activation. AC acts as a flexible internal model of the main characteristics of the system, maintaining its identity.

4.3   Role of the MP in the Generation of Complex Events

Switches between un-connected ramifications of a complex object and shifts among instances of a concept are complex events which give more freedom degrees to the dynamic, in particular to the interplay among the coregulators. Indeed, the interplay results from a dynamic modulation between the various procedures selected by the coregulators, to comply with the external and internal constraints (physical laws, energy requirements, temporal structural constraints, and so on), and can be compared to a kind of Darwinian selection, with its unforeseen complex events. Now the commands of a procedure lead to the unfolding of any one of the ramifications of their effectors, so that the possibility of complex switches give more possibilities for finding a compromise between conflicting commands. In presence of a semantic memory, there is added plasticity coming from shifts from a command to other instances of the same concept, which allow recalling the instance the most adapted to the context.

The development of an archetypal core triggers still more complex events at various levels. Indeed, an arousing event for a higher coregulator is propagated to part of AC, either automatically or as the result of procedures chosen by lower coregulators after a more detailed analysis of the present situation. Due to the properties of AC, this activation diffuses through archetypal links, is autonomously sustained for an extended period, and spreads to other parts of the system through processes of shifting among instances of concepts and switching among the ramifications of these instances.

4.4   Cascade of Complex Events

A fracture for a coregulator may remain unknown to another coregulator; in particular we may have 'epistemological events' coming from the uncovering by the coregulator of some features up to now not observable in its landscape though already existing in the system and possibly observable by some other coregulators. For example a more efficient instrument allows observing some new details which could not be observed before, though nothing is changed for the system itself.

However an accumulation of small events for a particular coregulator may later trigger some events, possibly a fracture, for another coregulator. This is the case if we consider two 'heterogeneous' coregulators, say a 'mini' coregulator with a short period, and a 'macro' coregulator of higher complexity and much longer period. Small changes at the mini-level are not observed in real time in the landscape of the macro coregulator (because of the propagation delays), but a succession of such events can later cause a fracture for the macro coregulator (for instance if they progressively suppress components which play a part in its landscape or its procedure). Now the repair of this fracture by the macro coregulator may backfire to the mini coregulator by imposing constraints and cause a fracture to it. We speak of a *dialectics between heterogeneous coregulators*.

For instance in an enterprise if some goods are not delivered to a lower level workshop, it can be unable to send in time the product it fabricates (say nuts) to a higher level assembly line. A short delay in the workshop will be easily made up, However if the situation cannot be remedied before the users have exhausted their reserves, the fracture is reflected to other units which will have to slow or even stop their production, so that commands are not satisfied. If the lack of nuts persists or recurs often, the intervention of higher coregulators (personnel department, or management), may decide to reorganize the enterprise, e.g. by automation with concurrent reduction of the workforce.

When a fracture for a coregulator represents a small enough event, it can be easily repaired at the next step. Otherwise if it persists for several steps or even blocks the action of the coregulator, we speak of a *dyschrony* for the coregulator. It is a temporal event observable by coregulators with much longer timescales; its repair may necessitate a higher level intervention, imposing a *re-synchronization* (i.e. change of period) of the coregulator. This process may backfire to coregulators of increasing levels, leading to a *cascade of re-synchronizations*. We have developed a *Theory of Aging* for an organism based on such a cascade of re-synchronizations of coregulators of higher and higher levels [3], [5].

References

1. Edelman, G.M.: The Remembered Present. Basic Books, New York (1989)
2. Ehresmann, A., Vanbremeersch, J.-P.: Hierarchical Evolutive Systems: A mathematical model for complex systems. Bull. of Math. Bio. 49(1), 13–50 (1987)
3. Ehresmann, A., Vanbremeersch, J.-P.: Evolutive Systems: An application to an aging theory. In: Cybernetics and Systems, pp. 190–192. Tata McGraw Hill Pub., New Delhi (1993)
4. Ehresmann, A., Vanbremeersch, J.-P.: Multiplicity Principle and emergence in MES. Journal of Systems Analysis, Modelling, Simulation 26, 81–117 (1996)
5. Ehresmann, A., Vanbremeersch, J.-P.: Memory Evolutive Systems: Hierarchy, Emergence, Cognition. Elsevier, Amsterdam (2007)
6. Eilenberg, S., Mac Lane, S.: General theory of natural equivalences. Trans. Am. Math. Soc. 58, 231–294 (1945)
7. Thom, R.: Esquisse d'une Sémiophysique, InterEditions, Paris (1988)

Business Process Modelling Notation
from the Methodical Perspective

Vaclav Repa

The Department of Information Technology, University of Economics, Prague,
W. Churchill sqr. 4, 130 67 Prague 3, Czech Republic
repa@vse.cz

Abstract. This paper evaluates some characteristics of the BPMN language from the perspective of the business system modelling methodology. Firstly the context of the business process management and the importance of standards are discussed. Then the Business System Modelling Methodology is introduced with special attention paid to the Business Process Meta-model as a basis for the evaluation of the language. In the special section particular basic concepts from the Business Process Meta-model are mapped to the usable constructs of the BPMN and related issues are analysed. Finally the basic conclusions are made and the general context is discussed.

Keywords: business process modelling, business system modelling, Business Process Modelling Notation.

1 Introduction - Business Process Management and Standards

Standards play very important role in the process of the technological, economic, as well as social development. Existence and quality of standards are the critical factors for the progress in any field. Process oriented management is the leading idea of last two decades. It's importance is even emphasized in the context of the economic crisis nowadays when the ability to change become the vital condition for the prosperity. Process oriented management lies on the border of the technology and management fields which requires the standards to absorb the substance of both fields. These new requirements are challenging especially for the standards for modelling business processes which traditionally follow from the IS/ICT field. This paper evaluates the current version of the Business Process Modelling Notation (BPMN) in the light of above mentioned facts.

The first complete explanation of the idea of process management as a style of managing an organization has already been published in [4]. The authors excellently explain the historical roots, as well as the necessity, of focusing on business processes in the management of the organization. The major reason for the process-orientation in management is the vital need for the dynamics in the organization's behaviour. It has to be able to reflect all substantial changes in the technology as well as in the market as soon as possible. The only way to link the behaviour of the organization to the changes in the market and technology possibilities is to manage the organization as a set of processes principally focused on customer needs. As customer needs, as

M. Cezon and Y. Wolfsthal (Eds.): ServiceWave 2010 Workshops, LNCS 6569, pp. 160–171, 2011.

well as requirements driven with the technology possibilities, are constantly changing the processes in the organization should change as well. That means that any process in the organization should be linked to the customer needs as directly as possible. Thus, the general classification of processes in the organization distinguishes mainly between:

- Key processes, i.e. those processes in the organization which are linked directly to the customer, covering the whole business cycle from expression of the customer need to its satisfaction with the product / service.
- Supporting processes, which are linked to the customer indirectly - by means of key processes which they are supporting with particular products or services.

Whilst the term "key process" typically covers whole business cycle with the customer - it is focused on the particular business case; the supporting process is typically specialized just to the particular service / product, which means that its product is more universal - usable in a number of business cases. This approach allows the organization to focus on the customers and their needs (by means of the key processes), and to use all the traditional advantages of the specialization of activities (by means of the supporting processes) at the same time. Key processes play the crucial role - by means of these processes the whole system of mutually interconnected processes is tied together with the customers' needs. Supporting processes are organized around the key ones, so that the internal behaviour, specialization, and even the effectiveness of the organizations' activities are subordinated to the customers and their needs.

Concluding from previous paragraph we can summarise the key principles of the process-oriented management of the organization:

Change as a principle - the concept of change changes its nature. If the organization should fulfil the need for dynamics stated above the change has to become an integral part of its life instead of something exceptional.

Critical need for modelling business processes is the direct consequence of the previous principle. Processes have to be modelled in order to allow:

- permanent following the nature of the business to ensure the correctness of changes according to general business rules;
- permanent seeking for possibilities of changes in the business with use of new possibilities.

Changing business means changing processes exploiting new possibilities which are not just in the field of technology but also in people minds, social system etc. All these possibilities for the change should be taken into the account while modelling business processes. In order to fully and meaningfully exploit the possibilities of change it is necessary to have the notion of the substance of business - what is necessary and what is not, what is changeable and what is not. It means that the business process modelling methodology should be able to find this substance of business by means of it's methods and techniques.

These principles express the essence of the requirements for the business process modelling methodology as well as for the incidental techniques, languages, and standards.

Standards are critically important because they allow the progress. In the field of modelling languages standards allow production of supporting systems - CASE tools. Producers of such systems need to believe that the number of possible customers will allow covering of their development costs; standards are allowing such accumulation of customers. If there are not standards the investment power of particular producers is to low to allow creation of the significant market with tools which forces the competitors to increase the quality of their products permanently. Without such permanent growth of quality the feedback to the theory (background of standards) is either missing or is not strong enough to allow the adequate growth of the theory. So the theory and the tools are mutually dependent. Theory needs tools to be evaluated and corrected in praxis which is the main condition of its qualitative growth. Tools need theory to produce good and usable standards which allow sufficient market possibilities as a vital condition for their development. Theory needs good tools and vice versa: tools need good theory. In the intersection of this mutually dependent factors lay standards.

Business Process Modelling Notation1 (BPMN) as a language for modelling business processes [1] is a most important standard fulfilling the above stated requirements for the standardisation. Among other popular standards ([5], [17]) only the BPMN became widely accepted by users as well as by CASE tools producers, and is developed concerning other related significant technology standards [11], [12], [15] which is the basic condition for fulfilling the full meaning of standardisation. This fact qualifies the BPMN for being a leading professional standard in the field of business process modelling. The other side of such a position is the responsibility for the progress in the field. Therefore this paper evaluates some characteristics of the BPMN from the perspective of the business system modelling methodology. For the wider context of this approach as well as for more general argumentation see [13]

2   Modelling Business Processes

The main basis for the methodical requirements for the business process modelling presented in this paper is the Business System Modelling Methodology, a product of the OpenSoul project [7]. Although this paper is aimed on the topic of the business process modelling namely on the BPMN language the context of the Business System modelling Methodology is very important and cannot be omitted. Therefore we pay some attention to the modelling of business systems before we focus on the business process modelling only.

Modelling the Business System

The methodology for the modelling of the business system is based on the idea of the two basic dimensions of the business system model (see Figure 1):

1. structure of the Real World (the view on the Real World as a set of objects and their relationships),
2. behaviour of the Real World (the view on the Real World as a set of mutually connected business processes).

Both dimensions have common intersection which contains, besides the static object aspects as attributes and data structures, also typical dynamic aspects as events, methods, and object states. Thus the description of dynamics is not just the matter of the behavioural model. It is the matter of the conceptual model as well.

Business process is a process of achievement the human will. It has the goal, and the product(s). It typically combines different business objects giving them the specific meaning (roles of actors, products, etc.). Business objects may be specified in detail by the description of their life cycles. Object life cycle is a description of business rules connected with the object in terms of states and transitions. Objects are typically taking different roles in different processes giving them the context (Real World rules) while business process, following the process goal, typically connects lives of several objects. For detailed discussion of the main differences between object life cycles and business processes see [8], [9], and [10].

Besides the two-dimensional approach to the business system modelling there are also two basic complementary views on the system (see Figure 1):

1.   global view on the whole system abstracting from details,
2.   detailed view on just a part of the system abstracting from the whole.

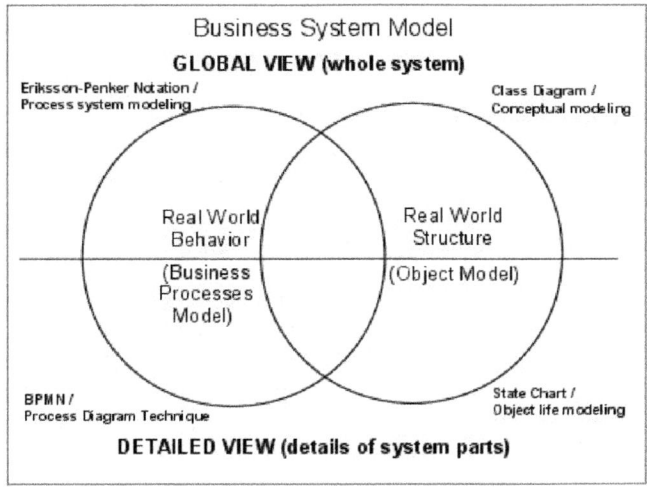

Fig. 1. Two Views on two dimensions of a Business System

Each global model describes the structure (objects in general) of the system while each detailed model is oriented on the dynamics (processes in general). Nevertheless it does not null previous principle of two basic dimensions of the Real World Model. If we combine these two basic dimensions with two basic views we get four basic kinds of model of the business system:

• global model of objects - conceptual model (Class Diagram)
• detailed model of one object - object life cycle (State Chart)

- global model of processes - model of the system of processes (Eriksson-Penker Diagram)
- detailed model of one process - model of the process run (BPMN diagram)

So we can speak about the process view on an object (detailed description of object's life cycle) as well as about the object view on business processes (global process model). In other words the world of objects has also its dynamics (behaviour) as well as the world of processes has also its structure (objects).

Table 1. Two basic views on two basic subjects of interest in a Business System

view / subject	Business Objects	Business Processes
Global view	conceptual model (Class Diagram)	process system model (Eriksson-Penker Diagram)
Detailed view	object life cycle (State Chart)	model of the process run (BPMN diagram)

Table 1 shows how the BPMN language as a process-oriented description of the business process covers only one part of the behavioural dimension of the Business System Model. BPMN does not cover the problem of global modelling of the process system. Mostly accepted modelling standard suitable for this purpose is the Eriksson-Penker Notation [3] created as an extension of the UML [16] what well corresponds with the fact that the global view on processes is object-oriented - it is the conceptual model of business processes in fact.

In accordance with the topic of this paper the following text is focused just on the detailed business process model, and BPMN language.

Modelling Business Processes as a Part of a Business System

Process Diagram Technique aims to offer the set of concepts, symbols and rules, using which the modeller is able to describe all substantial characteristics of the real world behaviour in as simple way as possible.

The OpenSoul project [8] provides the process meta-model" (Figure 3) which describes the key concepts of the technique together with their relationships. In the centre of interest there are two main concepts:

- Stimulus, and
- activity

Stimuli are of two main types:

- external (Event) and
- internal (State)

Activities are of two main types too:

- Processing Activity. The purpose of this activity is processing inputs to outputs) and

- Control Activity (Decision or Logical Connector). The purpose of this activity is to ensure right control of the process – succession of the right activities according to the internal process state(s) and/or external stimuli and information.

For simplification of the model there is also special kind of control activity defined – Logical Connector. It is the very simple (primitive) decision where does not need any information at the input (conjunction and disjunction).

Description of the process expresses the way how the inputs are transformed to the outputs by the activities in their defined succession. Input/Output Sets are defined in three types:

- Information Set
- Material Set, and
- Mixed Set

The main purpose of such an approach is to distinguish between the object of the processing ("material and the information for the processing control ("information").
In addition the technique allows modelling of the external aspects of the process: Actors (attendees or "victims" of the process activities), Organization units, Problems connected to the process, and any other external aspect whose relation to the process is important.

For exact description of the basic concepts and their relationships of the Technique, see the meta-model [8] also described in the following section.

Events, states, and activities of the process play a crucial role in the process model. The model describes two different but mutually interconnected matters:

- basic logic of the process (flow of activities);
- possible external impacts on the process (events).

States of the process are the consequence of the integration of these two matters. They represent waiting for the event (or combination of events) in particular place of the process. This way every process state expresses the need for synchronization of the external happening, manifesting itself by events, with the essential process logic. As the external happening is principally asynchronous with the process logic it is necessary to synchronize them - process must wait for every event (see figure 2).

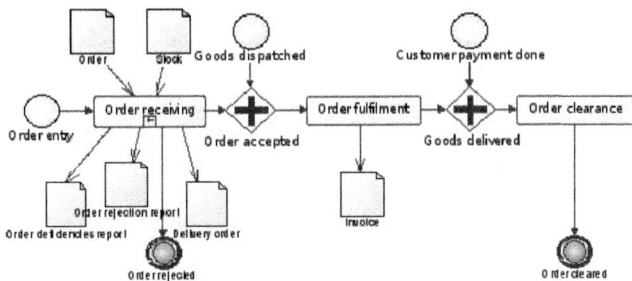

Fig. 2. Business Process Model (BPMN notation)

Figure 2 illustrates the use of above stated technique. It shows how the process description emphasizes the most important aspects of the process:

- events and their consequences – process activities and states (i.e. points of waiting for the event),
- inputs and outputs processed by the process including the main process product (i.e. the main reason for the process run).

Business Modelling Specification and Business Process Meta-model

Business Modelling Specification [8] consists of three associated packages:

- Business Substance Meta-Model package
- Business Process Meta-Model package
- Business Models Consistency package

Business substance and business processes represent two basic dimensions of the real world model mentioned in previous text. Each of both packages specifies basic concepts required for a model of given dimension together with basic rules expressing the business logic given by the dimension. As each of both models provides general basis of all possible models in given dimension, they both are Meta-Models. Business Models Consistency package provides general basis for modelling mutual interconnections and dependencies of both Meta-Models. The Business substance model is based on the UML Class Model with minimal extensions. Business process model has its own rules that are not present in current version of the UML. The inter-models consistency rules are not present in current version of the UML as well.

Business Process Meta-Model package (see Figure 3) specifies the basic concepts required for a model of a business process and defines basic needs/possibilities of their mutual interconnections (i.e. business process modelling logic - "how to model behaviour of the real world").

- Control Activity as a Stimulus inherits the stimulation competence. Together with that fact, from the multiplicity 1 (i.e. monopoly) of the stimulation association follows that Processing Activity can be stimulated either by Event or by Control Activity exclusively.
- Each Stimulus has to have at least one input state except the first one (Terminal Event). Terminal Event has no input state. This exception is expressed by the specific zero-multiplicity association with Terminal Event which overwrites the inherited general association between Stimulus and Non-Terminal State.
- Each State has to be the input for at least one Stimulus except the last one (Terminal State), which has no succeeding activity.
- Characteristics of terminal event as well as of terminal state are relative to the specified model. Usage of the model as a part (sub-process) of another model will change all terminal events of sub-process to regular ones and all terminal states to internal ones from the super-process point of view.
- Processing Activity and Decision are both composite aggregates of Input/Output Sets. As it follows from that fact, one particular Input/Output Set can input either to Decision or to Processing Activity exclusively.

For more detail as well as the wider context see the OpenSoul Portal [7].

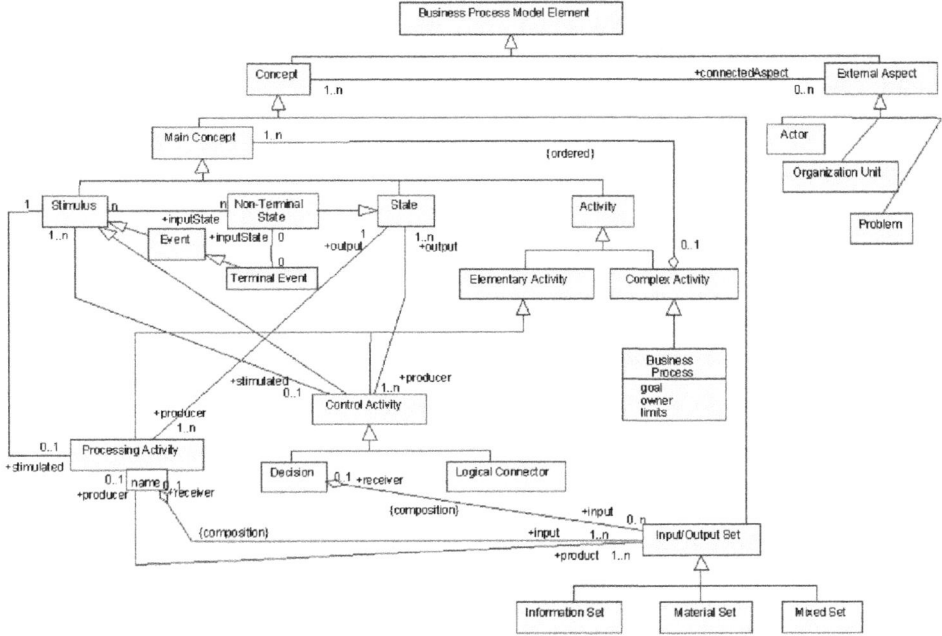

Fig. 3. Business Process Meta-Model package[8]

3   Evaluation of the BPMN towards the Methodology Requirements

In this section we deal with the question how to use the BPMN in accordance with the methodology. In the following text particular basic concepts from the Business Process Meta-model are mapped to the usable constructs of the BPMN.

Event is external stimulus for the activity, information about the event outside of the process and independent on it.

From the BPMN constructs it is possible to use the "Start" symbol with the name of the event for ad-hoc events, or the "Timer" symbol with the name of the event for timed events. Despite its name the Start symbol should be used several times – for each ad-hoc event. As the very start event of the process is always recognizable from the process logic there is no need to use specific symbol to identify it. BPMN offers a lot of other specific types of the event. From the Methodology point of view there is no need to classify events in more detail. Moreover, some of specific types of the event offered by BPMN may be implemented in various CASE tools contradictory to their origin defined in the meta-model.

Internal State of the process is a result of the preceding activity, waiting for the external stimulus, synchronisation of the process with the external event.

From the BPMN constructs we recommend to use the "Parallel (AND)" gate symbol which in the mode 1:n (merge) naturally means synchronization.

Terminal State - end state of the process.

BPMN offers specific constructs - the "End" symbol.

Activity is a basic element of the process - input(s) to output(s) processing. Activity is decomposable on principle, i.e. it can be always regarded as the process (on the deeper level of detail).
BPMN distinguishes between elementary and complex (compound) types of activity. Compound activity can be regarded as a standalone process and it is labelled with the + sign.

Decision - decision on the particular follow-up of the process. Decision is always an elementary (i.e. non decomposable) activity.
BPMN also offers the "complex decision" which in fact represents general decision. Nevertheless it is explained as a specific type of "gate" which consequently means any combination of primitive (i.e. predefined) decisions. This construction does not make a sense in general because such arbitrary combination of predefined meanings (and/or/xor) never can be unambiguous. Therefore this construct is unusable for exact specifications.

Logical Connector is a primitive decision without any information at the input (pre-defined decision).
From the BPMN constructs it is possible to use the standard gates AND, XOR, OR (inclusive). BPMN recognizes two basic sub-types of XOR (Data XOR and Event XOR). BPMN does not explain what the natural meaning of decision is. Therefore in some implementations some specific sub-types may contradict with the Meta-model which stated that decision is a kind of activity. It is because sometimes they use to be be implemented (and thus interpreted) as some different concept than activity. This is one of typical effects of the lack of semantic meta-model of the BPMN exactly defining the relation between the language and the methodology for business process modelling.

Input / Output Set - input into /output of the process.
BPMN offers two elements with this general meaning: Data Object and Message. For the mapping of the process run the difference between these two types of input/output is not important. It might become important if the global view (business processes system model - Eriksson-Penker Notation for instance) is added.

External Aspect means any external aspect connected to the process in the particular point.
BPMN uses the „swim lanes" style for expressing organizational units. Unfortunately it reduces possibilities of organization structure independent description of the process (what is the basic principle of process management, by the way). Fortunately, many CASE systems allow switching to the traditional description (using the "Actor" symbol for instance). From the BPMN constructs it is also possible to use the „Note" symbol. Another general possibility is to describe the aspect as an attribute of the process or its particular part.

4   Summary and Conclusions

In the previous section some aspects and problems connected with the BPMN are discussed. The following summary of most important facts shows some requirements for the future BPMN development.

Meta-model of the language: from the new proposed version 2.0 [2] BPMN will be based on the formal meta-model in style of the UML [16]. The meta-model follows the global principle of the OMG language specifications: principal independence of any methodology. The consequence of this attempt to separate the language from the expressed content is the fact that the meta-model is reduced mainly to the classifications of concepts with minimal information on their relationships, and consequently with minimal space for expressing the semantic constraints of the language. Philosophy of Language (see [6] for instance) undoubtedly shows that semantic aspects of the language always follow from the style of thinking; different languages represent different styles of thinking as it is visible on the principal difference between the European and Asian languages in comparison with the difference between related philosophy systems for example. The same rule is valid also in the field of formal languages. As the language aims to be technically "methodology independent" it is loosing the main characteristics of the language: the competence to express the content.

So we propose to develop the <u>semantic meta-model of the BPMN which exactly defines the relation between the language and the methodology for business process modelling</u>. The core package of such meta-model should express the main methodology principles of modelling business processes like it is in [8] for example.

Global business processes model: the Business System Modelling Methodology [7], []defines two basic complementary views on the business system - the global versus detailed one (see Figure 2). Current version of the BPMN represents just the detailed view (description of one particular business process). However the global perspective of business processes (view of all business processes as a system) is not substitutable with the detailed one (details of one single process run) in principle. Therefore we recommend <u>completing the BPMN also with the global view</u>. The <u>Eriksson-Penker Notation</u> [3] which is based on the UML [16] and widely accepted is the best candidate for such complement.

Needed changes in the current BPMN: based on the evaluation of the BPMN from the methodology point of view (see the previous section) we summarize following required changes of the BPMN:

- <u>including the concept of State</u>. State is completely missing as a concept in the BPMN meta-model. As a temporary solution of this problem the "Parallel AND" gate can be used (see the argumentation in the previous section). Nevertheless it causes consequential problems. The internal process state is not the synchronization only. It is just it's technical meaning. Semantically it represents the important cross-point in the process where the internal process logic meets possible external influence. Thus the importance of this concept overcomes the process itself as it represents the basic point of inter-process communication. Of course, it is necessary to watch the language not only from the technical perspective for taking this fact into the account. So the state should be a regular, and very important, concept of the BPMN meta-model.
- <u>restructuring Events</u>: BPMN contains a number of kinds of events of variois origins. Some of them use to be interpreted as production activities, some of them as decisions, data, flows or other "physical" substances. Consequently the

exact semantic meaning of this concept remains undefined. The Methodology defines the event as external influence on the process. It means:

o   event has no duration (it's main attribute is the time of occurrence),
o   event always represents some typical content according to its basic type.

There are two basic types of event:

- Ad hoc event always requires the additional information (i.e. it is always related to some data in technical sense);
- predefined event (Timer) does not require an additional information. It's only variable attribute is the time of occurrence because the content (meaning of the event) is predefined.

For detailed information about the Methodology contents see the Business System Specification [8].

The above mentioned requirements to the BPMN are mutually closely interconnected. The root of all problems can be found in the first paragraph where the need for semantic oriented meta-model is discussed. It is <u>the lack of the exactly defined relation between the language and the methodology for business process modelling</u>. This problem seems to be typical as it occurs also in other UML related standards for modelling. By the task of modelling the systems are overcoming the border between technology and other real world phenomena which are bringing completely new requirements for the content of languages. The conception of language is changing; languages have to adopt the ontology of related areas as it is clearly expressed in the S-GAIA model [14] for instance.

Acknowledgements. The work presented in this paper has been supported by Czech Science Foundation (GAČR) in the project 402/08/0529 Business Process Modelling.

References

1. Business Process Modeling Notation Specification, OMG Final Adopted Specification, dtc/06-02-01 (February 2006),
    http://www.bpmn.org/Documents/OMGFinalAdoptedBPMN1-0Spec06-02-01.pdf
2. Business Process Model and Notation version 2.0, OMG Adopted Beta Specification, OMG Document Number: dtc/2010-06-05 (June 21, 2010)
3. Eriksson, H.E., Penker, M.: Business Modeling with UML: Business Patterns at Work. Wiley, Chichester (2000) ISBN 978-0-471-29551-8
4. Hammer, M., Champy, J.: Reengineering the Corporation: A Manifesto for Business Revolution. Nicholas Brealey Publishing, London (1993)
5. Mayer, R.J., Menzel, C.P., Painter, M.K.: deWitte, P.S., Blinn, T., Perakath, B.: IDEF3 Process Description Capture Method Report. Knowledge Based Systems, Inc. (1997)
6. Miller, A.: Philosophy of Language. Routledge - Taylor & Francis, ISBN: 0–415–34981–8 (2007)
7. Repa, V.: OpenSoul Project, http://opensoul.panrepa.org
8. Repa, V.: BSM Specification,
    http://opensoul.panrepa.org/metamodel.html

9. Repa, V.: Modeling Objects Dynamics in Conceptual Models. Budapest August 31-September 2. In: Advances in Information Systems Development, pp. 139–152. Springer, New York (2007) ISBN 978-0-387-70801-0
10. Řepa, V.: Process Dimension of Concepts. In: Jaakkola, H., Kiyoki, Y., Tokuda, T. (eds.) Information Modelling and Knowledge Bases XIX, pp. 322–329. IOS Press, Amsterdam (2008)
11. Reference Model for Service Oriented Architecture 1.0, OASIS Standard (October 12, 2006), http://docs.oasis-open.org/soa-rm/v1.0/
12. Service Science Management and Engineering, http://www.ibm.com
13. Simeonov, P.L., Ehresmann, A.C., Smith, L.S., Ramirez, J.G., Repa, V.: A New Biology: A Modern Perspective on the Challenge of Closing the Gap between the Islands of Knowledge. In: Cezon, M., Wolfsthal, Y. (eds.) ServiceWave 2011 Workshops. LNCS, vol. 6569, pp. 188–195. Springer, Heidelberg (2011)
14. John Sutcliffe-Braithwaite, J., Badii, A.: Socio-technic systems: computational socio-geonomics & Enterprise Systems (in this issue)
15. UML Specification, v. 1.5. document ad/03-03-01, OMG (2003)
16. UML Superstructure Specification, v2.0 document 05-07-04, OMG (2004)
17. Workflow Management Coalition Standards Framework: http://www.wfmc.org

A Transformation from SBVR Business Rules into Event Coordinated Rules by Means of SBVR Patterns

Willem De Roover and Jan Vanthienen

Department of Decision Sciences & Information Management,
Katholieke Universiteit Leuven, Belgium
{willem.deroover,jan.vanthienen}@econ.kuleuven.be

Abstract. SBVR is becoming more and more popular as the meta-model for defining vocabulary based business rules. In an extended form SBVR can be used to declare a whole spectrum of business rules including control-flow and organizational rules. Enforcing the rules of the business in information systems is however not straightforward. SBVR leaves open the gap between defining business rules and actually enforcing them. In this paper, we examine if and how business rules can be expressed in SBVR and translated using patterns into a more uniform event mechanism, such that the event handling could provide an integrated enforcement of the defined business rules.

Keywords: business rules, event coordination, business processes, SBVR, declarative process modeling.

1 Introduction

A business rule is a statement that defines or constrains some aspect of the business. It is intended to assert business structure or to control or influence the behavior of the business[1]. In 2008 the Object Management Group(OMG) released the Semantics of Business Vocabulary and Business Rules (SBVR)[2]. SBVR makes it possible to write business rules in natural language such that business rules can easely be written by the business. Briefly summarized this allows business rules to be written by the business and for the business independent of IT. However SBVR doesn't mention how these business rules can be enforced. Simple and durable rules can easily be converted into a database model and OCL constraints. But more complex and volatile rules can not be hard coded and thus need another approach.

In this paper, we examine if and how complex and volatile business rules can be translated into a uniform event mechanism, such that the event handling could provide an integrated enforcement of business rules. To this end, we provide a pattern mechanism to transform SBVR rules into event-driven enforcement rules.

This approach is similar to what happens in business process modeling. A process modeling language like BPMN is used to design a process model which

M. Cezon and Y. Wolfsthal (Eds.): ServiceWave 2010 Workshops, LNCS 6569, pp. 172–179, 2011.

will then be translated into an event mechanism. However in this design and transformation proces, there is a lack of integration with most business rules.

The paper is structured as follows. In section 2 we give an overview of current practices. The different types of business rules are identified in section 3. Section 4 describes the use of SBVR for vocabulary constraints and process constraints. In section 5 and 6 we explain the SBVR transformation templates. To finalize we give an example in section 7.

2   Related Work

Model Driven architecture(MDA) [3,4] is a software development approach in which three architectural models are used that are build on top of each other like layers. SBVR is situated at the top layer which is the Computational Independent Model(CIM). This layer constructs business solutions for business problems. This is exactly where SBVR needs to be as it is a meta model for defining business vocabularies and rules. The middle, "Platform Independent Model", layer builds implementation models that are not tied to a particular execution environment. The bottom Layer is the Platform Specific model and considers implementations that are tied to a specific execution platform.

The notion of model transformation plays an important role in MDA as each model needs to be transformed into the corresponding lower level model. Our approach is situated in the first and second layer. SBVR rules, located at the CIM layer, are transformed into event-driven enforcement rules which are situated at the PIM layer.

In [5] Linehan extends IBM's Model Driven Business Transformation (MDBT) with SBVR rules to support restricted permission rules. MDBT is an implementation of the MDA framework. The extension extracts an SBVR vocabulary from the business operation model. This vocabulary can be used to create rules using a Rule Creation Wizard. These rules are translated into OCL constraints so that they eventually can be translated into implementation code.

Kleiner et al. [6] translates an SBVR model into an UML model. The mapping between SBVR and UML uses several non straightforward transformation rules that require several conditions and target elements from other rules. The transformation rules are implemented in the ATLAS Transformation Language (ATL) [7]. ATL is a transformation language developed for the transformation of a source language into another language.

ATL is also used by Kamada et al.[8]. SBVR compliant rules are transformed into Formal Contract Logic(FCL) Executable rules. However this approach ignores definitional business rules like some vocabulary rules.

[9] by Marinos et al. describes the implementation of a compiler of SBVR Structured English to SQL data models and queries. This is done in three steps. The first step converts SBVR into SBVR logical Formulation. In a second step this conversion is optimized to suit SQL. The last step finally transforms the logical formulation into SQL statements. It however remains unclear how certain rules, like derivation rules, are checked and how the derived values can be used in other rules.

Condec [10] is a language that allows to declaratively specify constraints on the activities of a process. For each constraint a template is defined that has a name, an LTL formula and a graphical representation. Business users define their processes by means of the constraints graphical representation. Using the templates the constraints are translated to their corresponding LTL formulas.

3   Business Rules Types

A distinction can be made between several business rules. In [11] a total of sixteen business rule types are identified that can constrain vocabularies and activities. Each business rule refers to one of the three aspects of business modeling that are generally considered [12]: control-flow, vocabulary and organizational aspects.

Control-flow Aspects. Business policy and regulations contain a lot of constraints (partial order, timing, exists, activity pre- and postconditions). In a trade community, for instance, different business protocols lay down the obligations of business partners and can be expressed in the form of temporal deontic rules [13].

Vocabulary aspects. The performer of an activity can perform particular manipulations (addition, removal or update) of business facts. These state transitions can be constrained by integrity constraints and derivation rules.

Organizational aspects. Organizational aspects relate to the visibility of business concepts and events and the authorization to perform particular activities.

4   Syntax and Semantics of Business Rules

The Semantics of Business Vocabulary and Business Rules (SBVR) [2] is a new standard for business modeling within the Object Management Group (OMG). SBVR provides several vocabularies that allow to describe business vocabularies and business rules which are supported by a First-Order logic.

In SBVR meaning and representation are separated, which makes it possible for a certain meaning to have several representation in the forms of words, sounds, figures, etc. Communities play a major part in separating meaning from representations. A community has a set of concepts for which there is a shared understanding. These concepts can be found in the community's body of shared meaning which contains noun concepts, fact types and Business rules. Noun concepts represent the meaning of business objects such as Order. In the same manner fact types represent the meaning of a relation between concepts, i.e. Order *contains* OrderLine. Business rules build on top of fact types and allow to constraint these fact types: Order *contains* at least one OrderLine.

Different language or speech communities can then assign a representation to these concepts making it possible to talk about the same concepts in different languages. One way of representing the concepts in SBVR is by means of a structured, English vocabulary for expressing vocabularies and rules, called SBVR Structured English [2]. A technique used by SBVR structured English is the use of font styles to designate statements with formal meaning. In particular,

- the term font (green) is used to designate a noun concept.
- the name font (green) designates an individual concept.
- the *verb* font (blue) is used for designation for a verb concept.
- the keyword font (red) is used for linguistic particles that are used to construct statements.

The definitions and examples in the remainder of the text use these SBVR Structured English font styles.

If SBVR would provide a vocabulary for defining process related concepts it would even be suitable for defining process-aware rules. However it does not provide such vocabulary and thus lacks support for concepts as agents, activities, process states and events. In [11,14] concepts like activities, agents and events are introduced by the EM-BrA^{2}CE Vocabulary. These concepts make it possible to define control-flow and organizational rules in SBVR.

5 Patterns for Transforming Business Rules into Event Rules

By using SBVR businesses are able to define their business rules on top of their business vocabulary. As previously stated SBVR makes it possible to cover a very wide variety of business rules. However SBVR itself does not make clear when business rules need to be triggered or how rules can be executed. Simple vocabularys rules like integrity constraints, which constrain the domain over which concepts can range, can be implemented by means of a database model. OCL constraints can be used to implement durable rules that stay consistent over time. However complex rules and rules that change frequently can not be hardcoded. They will need a mechanism that allows an easy interchangeability of rules.

To this end we provide a pattern mechanism to transform SBVR rules into event-driven enforcement rules. Each SBVR rule is transformed into one or more Event-Condition-Action (ECA) rules. This will happen by means of general templates which translate SBVR business rules into ECA-rules.

A derivation rule is a rule that specifies a certain value by means of the calculation described by the rule. One of the templates that can be used for the derivation rule is the following:

<Concept1>can be calculated as
    <Concept2>{plus/minus/multiplied by/divided by} <Concept3>
    {{plus/minus/multiplied by/divided by} <Concept(3+i)> }^{i}

The use of templates limits the possibilities in which rules can be formulated, but it allows for an easy extraction of the neccesary information from the chosen business rule. This information includes the type of the business rule, the concepts used in the rule and other information like possible cardinalities. Whenever a user selects the derivation template, the system knows that he is talking about a derivation rule and extracts the necessary concepts and information.

> Lineprice *of* each Orderline is calculated as the
> Productprice *of* the Product *of* the Orderline multiplied by the Amount
> *of* the Orderline

This information is used to transform the SBVR rules into Event-Condition-Action rules. Each template is connected with one or more defined ECA-Rules. The template serves as a transformation function from the SBVR rules to ECA-Rules. The set of ECA-rules is equivalent to the business rules that it represents. However ECA rules have the advantage that they make clear when they have to be checked. The condition of an ECA rule checks whether the business rule is violated and in case of a violation the system will be notified of this violation. The integrity constraint needs to hold during the lifespan of the assigned concepts. This means that the derivation rule needs to be checked on the creation of the derived concept and when one of the concepts used in the calculation is modified. In our running example this results in the following ECA-rules:

- On IsCreated(<Concept1>): compute(<concept1 >)
- On IsModified(<Concept2>): compute(<concept1 >)
- On IsModified(<Concept3>): compute(<concept1 >)
- {On is Modified(<Concept3+i>): compute(<concept1 >)}^{i}

There may be other rules that rely on concept1 within their computations or need to be checked when concept1 is recomputed. This means that whenever concept1 is modified the system will need to be notified of this event. This results in one more ECA rule:

> On compute (<Concept1>) : signal IsModified (<Concept1>)

The extracted concepts from the business rule can then be filled into the generated ECA rules. This results in the following instantiated ECA rules:

- On IsCreated(<LinePrice>): compute(<LinePrice >)
- On IsModified(<ProductPrice>): compute(<LinePrice >)
- On IsModified(<Amount>): compute(<LinePrice >)
- On compute (<LinePrice>) : signal IsModified (<LinePrice>)

6   Overview of Some Templates

Business rules can be used to constrain some part of our or vocabulary like integrity constraints, but they can also be used for other purposes like the constraining of process flow, etc. Control-flow rules can constrain the flow of a process. A precedence rule states that in order for an activity to be performed some other activity needs to be completed first.

<Activity1>must precede <Activity2>

This however does not mean that whenever Activity1 is performed Activity2 needs to be performed too. Whenever Activity2 is started, the system needs to check whether Activity1 is completed. This can be checked by means of the following ECA rule:

On start (<Activity2>) : if not completed (<Activity1>) then notify ()

The following template defines a rule that requires that if Activity1 is performed then Activity2 must be performed. This requirement does not determine when Activity2 needs to be performed, just that it needs to be performed such that the process can reach completion.

<Activity2>must happen in response to <Activity1>

To be conform with this requirement we keep track of a list of events that need to occur for a process to complete. If activity 1 is performed then the completion of Activity 2 has to be added to this event list. The following ECA takes care of this responsibility:

On complete(<Activity1>): add complete(<Activity2>) to TODO list

7   Example

In this section we will illustrate our approach with an example. This example is only a small segment of a much larger process in which a pilot prepares his plane for take off. The small segment requires that the pilot calculates the start up based on the weather condition before entering it into the system. To make the calculations as accurate as possible they are based on the most recent information. The pilot can receive a last weather report in the cockpit after boarding the plane. Based on this weather report the start up speed is calculated and entered into the system. This process is resembled by the following rules.

- Boarding Plane must precede receive latest weather report
  - On start(Receive latest weather report):
    if not complete(boarding plane) then notify()
- Calculate startup speed must happen in response to receive latest weather report
  - On complete(Receive latest weather report):
    add complete(calculate start up speed) to TODO list.
- Enter startup speed must happen in response to calculate startup speed
  - On complete(Calculate start up speed):
    add(complete(Enter startup speed)) to TODO list.
- calculate startup speed must precede Enter startup speed
  - On start(Enter startup speed):
    if not complete(calculate start up speed) then notify()

A pilot can only receive the latest weather report whenever he has boarded his plane. This means that whenever the activity receive latest weather report is performed that the pilot already has boarded the plane and thus that the boarding plane activity has been completed. When the receive latest weather report activity is completed the second business rule is triggered which requires that the start up speed is calculated based on the current weather conditions. This is enforced by adding the complete(calculate start up speed) event to a TODO list, which keeps track of all the events that still need to occur before the take off process can complete. In between these activities the pilot can do other activities as long as they comply to all business rules. By calculating the start up speed the complete(enter startup speed) event is added to the TODO list. This is required by the third business rule which states that after calculating the start up speed it needs to be entered into the airplanes' system. The fourth business rule states that the pilot can only enter the start up speed after it has been calculated it.

8   Conclusion

With the release of SBVR in 2008 the OMG offered us a set of vocabularies for defining business rules. SBVR allowed us to define a wide variety of business rules. It however remained unclear how these business rules needed to be enforced. Simple and durable business rules can be hardcoded but complex and more volatile rules will need another mechanism. We have examined if and how these business rules in SBVR can be translated such that the event handling could provide an integrated enforcement of business rules. In future work more attention will be given to the creation of templates, the development of a tool that uses these templates to transform SBVR rules into ECA rules and that creates an execution model that is compliant with these rules.

References

1. Group, T.B.R.: What are they really? (July 2000), www.businessrulesgroup.org
2. Object Management Group: Semantics of Business Vocabulary and Business Rules (SBVR), v1.0. OMG Document { dtc/08-01-02 (2008)
3. Miller, J., Mukerji, J., et al.: Mda guide version 1.0. OMG Document: omg/2003-05-01 (2003), http://www.omg.org/mda/mda_les/MDAGuideVersion1-0.pdf
4. Kleppe, A., Warmer, J., Bast, W.: MDA explained: the model driven architecture practice and promise. Addison-Wesley Longman Publishing Co., Inc., Boston (2003)
5. Linehan, M.: Ontologies and rules in business models. In: Eleventh International IEEE EDOC Conference Workshop, EDOC 2007, pp. 149–156. IEEE, Los Alamitos (2008)
6. Kleiner, M., Albert, P., Bézivin, J.: Parsing SBVR-based controlled languages. In: Schürr, A., Selic, B. (eds.) MODELS 2009. LNCS, vol. 5795, pp. 122–136. Springer, Heidelberg (2009)

7. Jouault, F., Allilaire, F., Bézivin, J., Kurtev, I., Valduriez, P.: ATL: a QVT-like transformation language. In: Companion to the 21st ACM SIGPLAN symposium on Object-oriented programming systems, languages, and applications, pp. 719–720. ACM, New York (2006)
8. Kamada, A., Governatori, G., Sadiq, S.: Transformation of SBVR Compliant Business Rules to Executable FCL Rules (2010)
9. Marinos, A., Moschoyiannis, S.P.K.: An sbvr to sql compiler. In: RuleML (2010)
10. Pesic, M., van der Aalst, W.M.P.: A declarative approach for exible business processes management. In: Business Process Management Workshops, pp. 169–180 (2006)
11. Goedertier, S., Haesen, R., Vanthienen, J.: EM-BrA2CE v0.1: A vocabulary and execution model for declarative business process modeling. FETEW Research Report KBI 0728, K.U.Leuven (2007)
12. Jablonski, S., Bussler, C.: Workow Management. Modeling Concepts, Architecture and Implementation. International Thomson Computer Press, London (1996)
13. Goedertier, S., Vanthienen, J.: Designing compliant business processes with obligations and permissions. In: Eder, J., Dustdar, S. (eds.) BPM Workshops 2006. LNCS, vol. 4103, pp. 5–14. Springer, Heidelberg (2006)
14. Goedertier, S., Mues, C., Vanthienen, J.: Specifying process-aware access control rules in SBVR. In: Paschke, A., Biletskiy, Y. (eds.) RuleML 2007. LNCS, vol. 4824, pp. 39–52. Springer, Heidelberg (2007)

About Adopting Event Processing in Manufacturing

Manfred Grauer[1], Bernhard Seeger[2], Daniel Metz[1],
Sachin Karadgi[1], and Marco Schneider[1]

[1] Information Systems Institute, University of Siegen, Germany
{grauer,metz,karadgi,schneider}@fb5.uni-siegen.de
[2] Department of Mathematics and Computer Science,
Philipps-University Marburg, Germany
seeger@informatik.uni-marburg.de

Abstract. Manufacturing enterprises strive for improvements in their monitoring and control of enterprise processes to sustain competitive advantages. In this context, enterprise integration (EI) across various enterprise levels and event processing are indispensable. However in reality, enabling EI and employing event processing for online monitoring and control of enterprise processes are elusive goals for many of the manufacturing enterprises. In the contribution, a framework for enabling EI is elaborated, which can be considered as a building block towards realizing the aforementioned goals. The framework encompasses various components: data collection engine, data aggregation engine, event processing engine, performance measurement, and offline analysis. This framework can be exploited in enhancing online monitoring and control of enterprise processes by employing event processing. The framework has been implemented and validated in an industrial scenario.

Keywords: Enterprise integration; event processing; event processing agent; event processing network; tracking; manufacturing processes.

1 Introduction

Today's manufacturing enterprises are facing increasing pressure due to globalization, uncertainties, and strict regulations, among others. To cope with aforesaid challenges, manufacturing enterprises are compelled to enhance their monitoring and control of enterprise processes (i.e., business processes and associated manufacturing processes) within and across different enterprise levels. VDI 5600 [1] classifies an enterprise into different manufacturing execution system (MES) levels as illustrated in Fig. 1: (i) enterprise control level, (ii) manufacturing control level, and (iii) manufacturing level. Similarly, IEC 62264 [2] categorizes an enterprise into several enterprise levels which can be mapped onto corresponding MES levels. Business processes are predominantly located at the enterprise control level, which are concerned with achieving enterprise's long term strategies essential to sustain competitive advantages. On contrary, manufacturing processes are employed at the manufacturing level to accomplish the objectives set at the enterprise control level.

MES levels can be described with numerous characteristics. Enterprise processes are associated with different time horizons resulting in a vertical integration gap or

M. Cezon and Y. Wolfsthal (Eds.): ServiceWave 2010 Workshops, LNCS 6569, pp. 180–187, 2011.

asynchronous flow of information. Attempts are being made to bridge the temporal integration gap based on ISO 15704 [3]. However, enterprise integration (EI) along the vertical direction is still an elusive goal and in most enterprises - it is not addressed or inefficiently realized [4]. In contrast to vertical integration, enterprise application integration (EAI) technologies can be utilized to realize a horizontal integration of an enterprise [5]. Additionally, events are simultaneously triggered during execution of enterprise processes at different MES levels. These events denote insufficient resource capacity, and breakdown of resources, among others. Nonetheless, events are not considered for online monitoring and control of enterprise processes. Overall due to the lack of an integrated enterprise and unhandled events, online monitoring and control of enterprise processes is hindered and perceived as a formidable challenge.

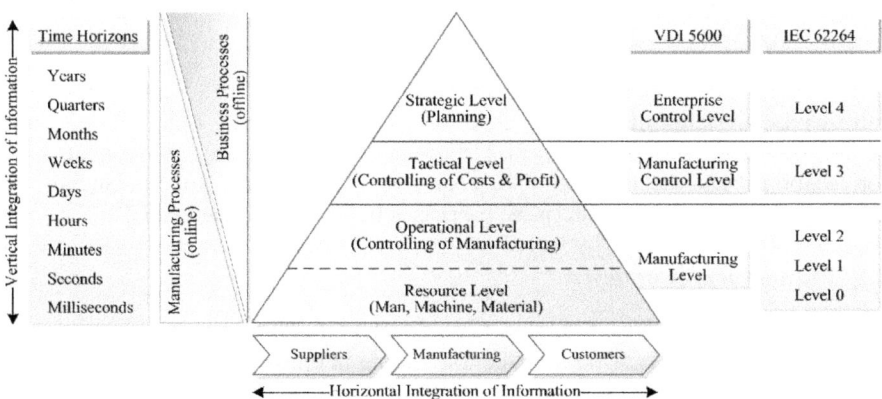

Fig. 1. Enterprise levels and their associated characteristics

In the current contribution, a framework based on an event-driven architecture (EDA) is envisaged to realize EI. An integrated enterprise is further exploited in attaining the vision of a real-time enterprise (RTE), which is based on the introduction of sense-and-respond and learn-and-adapt concepts into enterprise processes [6]. The remainder of the contribution is structured as follows. Section 2 presents a concise related work on event processing. The envisaged framework is elaborated in Section 3. Validation of the framework is described in Section 4. Finally, conclusion and future work are discussed in Section 5.

2 Related Work

Complex event processing (CEP) and event-driven architectures (EDA) are gaining more attention especially related to business processes to accomplish sense-and-respond [7]. For instance, fraud detection during a billing process [8], [9], fraud mobile calls detection [10] and monitoring of order delays [11]. Further, various software vendors are available to support (complex) event processing in business domains (e.g., RTM Analyzer [12], TIBCO BusinessEvents[TM] [13]). Similarly, research has been carried out in the area of business activity monitoring (BAM) based on event processing [14].

In contrast to financial enterprises, event processing is far away from adoption in manufacturing enterprises. However, it could be vital to incorporate manufacturing processes along with the corresponding business processes to reap the rich benefits of event processing. Therefore, attempts are being made to realize event processing in manufacturing. For example, a stream processing solution named public infrastructure for processing and exploring streams (PIPES) has been integrated with i-Plant®, a MES solution [15]. The solution exploits continuous query processing in factory automation. An open source framework for online monitoring and analysis of manufacturing processes has been presented [16].

3   Framework for Enabling Enterprise Integration, and Enhancing Online Monitoring and Control of Enterprise Processes

In the context of manufacturing enterprises, research has been carried out at Information Systems Institute for enabling EI, and enhancing online monitoring and control of enterprise processes [17], [18]. Section 3.1 elaborates components required for enabling EI. Section 3.2 presents event processing for enhancing online monitoring and control of enterprise processes based on the realized EI.

3.1   Framework Overview

A framework based on an EDA has been developed constituting various components as illustrated in Fig. 2. A data collection engine is employed for acquisition of real-time process data from physical resources available on shop floor. A level above, a data aggregation engine is in charge of integrating real-time process data with the corresponding transactional data from enterprise applications (e.g., ERP system). In addition, the integrated data is utilized to create and manage online tracking objects by an online tracking object manager for numerous enterprise entity types (e.g., product, resource, order) [19]. IEC 62265-3 regards tracking as an "activity of recording attributes of resources and products through all steps of instantiation, use, changes and disposition". Each tracking object is characterized by a set of tracking object items (e.g., pressure, temperature) and references to other tracking objects (e.g., product tracking object will have references to batch and order tracking objects).

Tracking objects are forwarded to all subscribed process visualization clients for displaying real-time information using gauges and charts. Further, process visualization clients provide interfaces for forward and backward traceability of enterprise processes managed by a request-reply manager. In addition, the integrated data is stored in a process database, which can be exploited for performing online analytical processing (OLAP) queries for detection of relevant situations (e.g., compliance violations), detecting new knowledge using data mining techniques, and so on. Apart from process visualization clients, tracking objects are utilized for online enterprise performance measurement and forwarded to an event processing engine for recognition of certain situations. On detection of a certain situation, the event processing engine dispatches online control objects to an online control object analyzer.

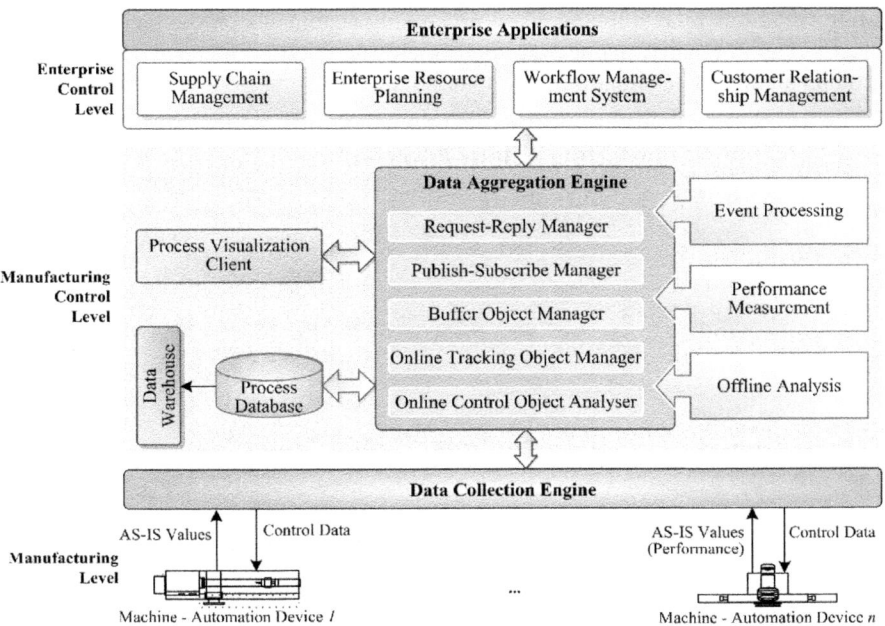

Fig. 2. Framework based on an EDA for enabling enterprise integration (EI), and enhancing monitoring and control of enterprise processes

3.2   Event Processing in Manufacturing

Event processing encompasses following components: (i) event producers, (ii) (complex) event processing, and (iii) event consumers [20]. In case of the aforementioned framework, the tracking object manager can be seen as a dedicated event producer publishing tracking objects to all subscribed clients (e.g., process visualization clients, event processing engine) as depicted in Fig. 3. Additionally, the context of the input event stream can be enhanced with the data from the process database. In contrast to simple events, tracking objects can be interpreted as complex events which are composed of numerous simple events (i.e., tracking object items). The event processing engine is responsible for detecting certain situations (i.e., situation awareness) occurred during execution of manufacturing processes from received streams of tracking objects and invoking appropriate (re-) actions. These (re-) actions are handled by the online control object analyzer. To accomplish these tasks, the event processing engine employs event processing agents (EPAs) to identify situations and deduce suitable (re-) actions.

An EPA manager deals with the definition and lifecycle of EPAs. Besides managerial properties (e.g., unique EPA name), an EPA is composed of an event processing statement as well as an abstract definition of an online control object. An EPA can be used for a combination of tasks. First, execute an operation (e.g., transformation, creation, aggregation, filtering and deletion) on the tracking object streams. Several EPAs can be interlinked to form an event processing network (EPN) using the aforesaid operations and managed by the EPN manager. Second, detect certain situations by employing event processing statements on the incoming tracking object streams. Finally, deduce an appropriate (re-) action intended to be performed based on an identified situation (e.g., manipulation of shop floor resources).

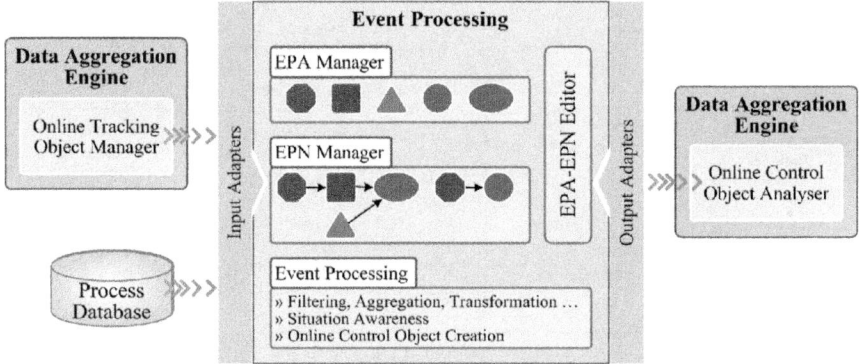

Fig. 3. Event processing in manufacturing

The EPA manager instantiates an online control object based on the abstract definition of an online control object associated with the appropriate EPA. In addition, the EPA manager also incorporates the event context while instantiating the online control object. This control object is forwarded to the online control object analyzer which can be seen as a certain event consumer as illustrated in Fig. 3. The online control object analyzer performs necessary actions by invoking services of the data aggregation engine. The EPAs can be defined dynamically by an enterprise member using an EPA-EPN editor and with the assistance of EPA templates. For simplified definition of event processing statements, an object model representing an event processing statement has been implemented. Enterprise members can define the (re-) actions within a certain EPA employing an abstraction mechanism.

4   An Industrial Case Study

The elaborated framework based on an EDA for enabling EI, and enhancing online monitoring and control of enterprise processes elaborated in Section 3 can be put into practice in different types of manufacturing, especially in batch manufacturing (e.g., casting processes) and discrete manufacturing (e.g., sheet metal forming processes). Here, an attempt is made to realize the framework for casting processes. The enterprise in consideration has special purpose machines with a high production rate (e.g., a molding machine can produce approximately 250 molds per hour). To efficiently utilize the capital intensive resources, online monitoring and control of enterprise processes is mandatory.

The casting process can be considered as a flow job shop model of scheduling where each job has to pass through a fixed sequence of resources. An overview of this sequence is illustrated in Fig. 4. Alongside the execution of this manufacturing process, real-time process data is acquired from various employed manufacturing and logistics resources. Therefore, numerous communication protocols (e.g., modbus, file parser) have been implemented. In addition, the gathered process data is equipped with transactional data taken from an ERP system.

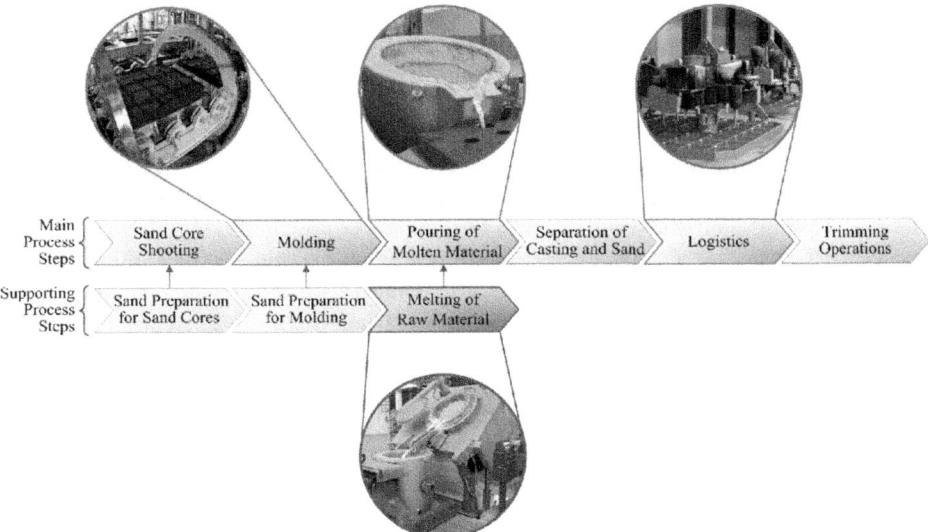

Fig. 4. Overview of main and supporting manufacturing steps of casting process

Based on the stream of process and transactional data, tracking objects are build for process entities like manufacturing orders, molds, castings, sand batches, and molten material batches. Streams of these tracking objects are analyzed using an event processing engine. On detection of certain situations, online control objects are created and send to the online control object analyzer. An online control object defines a certain (re-) action to achieve objectives set at enterprise control level concerning production, maintenance, quality, and inventory. The result can either be the visualization of an alarm message within a visualization client or the manipulation of a certain manufacturing resource (e.g., increase of applied pressure for molding).

5   Conclusion and Future Work

Manufacturing enterprises are coping with increasing pressure to maintain their competitive advantages. This necessitates enterprises to enhance their monitoring and control of enterprise processes. In this regard, a framework is envisaged with two-fold objectives. First as a prerequisite, the vertical integration of various enterprise levels to bridge the semantic and temporal integration gap. Second, the employment of event processing for enhancing online monitoring and control of enterprise processes based on an integrated enterprise.

Several components of the framework have been implemented. The data collection engine is capable to acquire real-time process data from different manufacturing and logistics resources on the shop floor. The data aggregation engine is in charge of enriching these process data with relevant context information (e.g., order information) from an ERP system. In addition, control-relevant process entities like orders, products and batches are represented by tracking objects, which are constantly analyzed by an event processing engine. As a (re-) action to the occurrence of certain situations, online control objects are either visualized within visualization clients as alarm messages or used to manipulate shop floor resources. Overall, the objective of the framework is the enhancement of production, maintenance, quality, and inventory of a manufacturing enterprise.

The implementation of the framework is based on Microsoft^{TM} .NET framework. Service-oriented and event-driven concepts are employed to achieve modularity, loose-coupling, and flexibility. In addition to aforementioned components, the framework can be enhanced by incorporation of online provisioning of key performance indicators (KPIs). Also apart from utilization in batch manufacturing, applying the framework in discrete manufacturing (e.g., sheet metal forming) is envisaged.

Acknowledgments. Parts of the work presented here have been supported by German Federal Ministry of Economics and Technology (BMWi) as part of "Central Innovation Programme SME" (ZIM) initiative (KF2111502LL0). Also, we are thankful to our industrial partner Ohm & Häner Metallwerk GmbH & Co. KG, Germany for the opportunity to implement the elaborated methodology and framework in a casting enterprise. Especially, we would like to acknowledge Dr.-Ing. Ludger Ohm, Dr.-Ing. Georg Dieckhues, and Jürgen Alfes for their valuable comments and support.

References

1. VDI 5600: Manufacturing Execution System (MES) - VDI 5600 Part 1 (2007)
2. IEC 62264: Enterprise-Control System Integration. All Parts
3. ISO 15704: Requirements for Enterprise Reference Architecture and Methodologies, ISO 15704:2000/Amd 1:2005 (2005)
4. Lasi, H., Koch, M., Kemper, H.G.: Process Transparency as a Critical Success Factor in the Industry (in German). Productivity Management (1), 29–31 (2010)
5. Linthicum, D.S.: Next Generation Application Integration: From Simple Information to Web Services. Addison-Wesley Professional, Amsterdam (2003)
6. Meyer, C.: Christopher Meyer on the Accelerating Enterprise. CIO Insight (2002), http://www.cioinsight.com/c/a/Expert-Voices/ Expert-Voice-Christopher-Meyer-on-the-Accelerating- Enterprise/ (Retrieved: January 20, 2011)
7. Chandy, K.M., Schulte, W.R.: Event Processing - Designing IT Systems for Agile Companies. McGraw Hill, London (2010)
8. Widder, A., Ammon, R.v., Schaeffer, P., Wolff, C.: Identification of Suspicious, Unknown Event Patterns in an Event Cloud. In: Proc. International Conference on Distributed Event-Based Systems (DEBS 2007), vol. 233, pp. 164–170 (2007)
9. Bass, T.: Fraud Detection and Event Processing for Predictive Business. Technical report, Tibco (2006)

10. Nguyen, T.M., Schiefer, J., Tjoa, A.M.: Sense & Response Service Architecture (SARESA): An Approach towards a Real-time Business Intelligence Solution and its use for a Fraud Detection Application. In: 8th International Workshop on Data Warehousing and OLAP (DOLAP 2005), pp. 77–86 (2005)
11. Schiefer, J., Rozsnyai, S., Rauscher, C., Saurer, G.: Event-Driven Rules for Sensing and Responding to Business Situations. In: Proc. International Conference on Distributed Event-Based Systems (DEBS 2007), pp. 198–205. ACM, New York (2007)
12. RTM Analyzer, http://www.realtime-monitoring.de/ (Retrieved: January 10, 2011)
13. TIBCO BusinessEvents, http://www.tibco.com/ (Retrieved: January 10, 2011)
14. Ammon, R.v., Silberbauer, C., Wolff, C.: Domain Specific Reference Models for Event Patterns - for Faster Developing of Business Activity Monitoring Applications. In: VIP Symposia on Internet related research with elements of M+I+T++, VIPSI 2007 (2007)
15. Cammert, M., Heinz, C., Krämer, J., Riemenschneider, T., Schwarzkopf, M., Seeger, B., Zeiss, A.: Stream Processing in Production-to-Business Software. In: 22nd International Conference on Data Engineering (2006)
16. Vijayaraghavan, A.: MTConnect for Realtime Monitoring and Analysis of Manufacturing Enterprises, http://www.systeminsights.com/ (Retrieved: January 10, 2011)
17. Karadgi, S., Metz, D., Grauer, M., Schäfer, W.: An Event Driven Software Framework for Enabling Enterprise integration and Control of Enterprise Processes. In: 10th International IEEE Conference on Intelligent System Design and Applications (ISDA 2010), Cairo, pp. 24–30 (2007)
18. Grauer, M., Karadgi, S., Metz, D., Schäfer, W.: Online Monitoring and Control of Enterprise Processes in Manufacturing based on an Event-Driven Architecture. In: Su, J., Muehlen, M. (eds.) BPM 2010. LNBIP, vol. 66, pp. 671–682. Springer, Heidelberg (2011)
19. Grauer, M., Metz, D., Karadgi, S.: Enhancement of Transparency and Adaptability by Online Tracking of Enterprise Processes. In: 10th International Conference on Information Systems (WI 2011), Zurich, Switzerland, pp. 282–291 (2011)
20. Etzion, O., Niblett, P.: Event Processing in Action. Manning, Greenwich (2011)

A New Biology: A Modern Perspective on the Challenge of Closing the Gap between the Islands of Knowledge

Plamen L. Simeonov[1], Andrée C. Ehresmann[2], Leslie S. Smith[3],
Jaime Gomez Ramirez[4], and Vaclav Repa[5]

[1] JSRC, Wilhelmstrasse 91, 10117 Berlin, Germany
plamen@simeio.org
[2] Université de Picardie Jules Verne, Faculté des Sciences, Mathématiques,
33 rue Saint-Leu, F-80039 Amiens. France
andree.ehresmann@u-picardie.fr
[3] Institute of Computing Science and Mathematics, School of Natural Sciences,
University of Stirling Stirling FK9 4LA, UK
l.s.smith@cs.stir.ac.uk
[4] Universidad Politécnica Madrid, ETSII-Dpto. Atomatica,
José Gutiérrez Abascal, 2 Madrid 28006, Spain
jd.gomez@upm.es
[5] The Department of Information Technology, University of Economics, Prague,
W.Churchill sqr. 4, 130 67 Prague 3, Czech Republic
vaclav@panrepa.com

Abstract. This paper discusses the rebirth of the old quest for the principles of biology along the discourse line of *machine-organism disanalogy* and within the context of biocomputation from a modern perspective. It reviews some new attempts to revise the existing body of research and enhance it with new developments in some promising fields of mathematics and computation. The major challenge is that the latter are expected to also answer the need for a new framework, a new language and a new methodology capable of closing the existing gap between the different levels of complex system organization.

Keywords: biological mathematics, biocomputation, interactions, events.

1 Introduction: The Quest

The domain of self-organization is common to physical and life sciences, to social sciences, economy and engineering. There has been a lot of research carried out in this field during the past 50 years and we have attained some progress. However, we still cannot pass a distinct boundary with our current state of science, methodology and technology. This is because we still cannot well understand complex natural systems and the processing of events within them.

The ultimate goal of modern science and engineering is to understand matters and to develop sustainable technologies emulating the building and organization principles of complex natural systems. However, before developing a technology we need to provide the basics, the formalisms, models and theories required to make this happen.

M. Cezon and Y. Wolfsthal (Eds.): ServiceWave 2010 Workshops, LNCS 6569, pp. 188–195, 2011.
© Springer-Verlag Berlin Heidelberg 2011

Basically, we have three questions to answer in this discussion round. First, what is the quest we are going for, second what needs to be done, i.e. our ambition and mission, and third, what are the next steps, i.e. our approach.

For the first question, we set out in the direction of reviving the final quest for discovering the principles of biology known from the works of Rashevsky [1,2] and Rosen [3,4] as topological biology, relational biology or complex systems biology along the focused discourse line of Michael Conrad's *machine-organism disanalogy* [5,6] within the technological context of biocomputation [7,8]. Despite these efforts to re-think theoretical biology by means of mathematics failing in practice, because the experimentalists simply did not understand and hence did not know how to implement the mathematical abstractions and the biological generalizations [9], these early attempts provide a good base to start from by revising and enhancing them with new methods and approaches from a modern perspective.

2   The Miss(ion)

Now, let us turn to the second question: what is being missed? When doing research in these areas we can easily observe a certain gap between big and small, a gap between machinery and cells, a gap between individuals and society from many perspectives. One of the major questions here is the complexity of interactions in living systems which are organized at multiple levels and at multiple timescales. These interactions are fairly well known at each single level.

However, what we do not know well is the view of the system and its operation as a whole. The top level and the lower levels of a complex natural system have been well studied in the past. For instance, in macro economy we have such models as fiscal and monetary policies involving a few basic parameters such as taxation or interest rates, whereas in micro economy we have economic models of individuals or classes of individuals, studied as individual decision-making units in a rather idealistic way. In neuroscience and psychology we have behaviors of the overall system and neurons, groups of neurons and their biochemical activity at the micro level correspondingly.

Yet, the big gap remains between these two dimensions: at the *mesoscopic* level. We still do not know how structures, processes and events trigger and organize (themselves) in between. An analogy for this gap could be found in the difference between the impact and interpretation of decision making processes using current models in psychology and sociology associated to the micro and macro levels organization, i.e. individuals vs. communities, societies, nations, etc.

Therefore, we need *a universal and extensible formal approach to explain the dynamics of hierarchical organization of biosocial phenomena at multiple levels and timescales along with the interactions between them.*

In summary, we are missing something very fundamental at the junction between the micro, macro and mesoscopic levels. We need to tackle what is missed in order to explain this gap between the levels of complex system organization. Whether it is a new framework, a new tool, a new language or maybe a new methodology, this needs to be explored.

Paradoxically, a similar phenomenon can be observed within the historical and epistemological framework of scientific development. This interdependence between the different disciplines in science has been shown as a series of the illustrations in a survey about Integral Biomathics [10] where the relationship between the natural sciences and formal models and theories was represented as a set of interdependent hierarchies within the spiral development of science. This model was recently formally represented using Memory Evolutive Systems (MES), a technique based on dynamic category theory to model evolutionary multi-scale adaptive self-organized systems [11,12]. The latter promises to be a well suited technique we can use to start our quest.

3   The Approach

What kind of *language* could be used to achieve the goals defined in the previous section? What kind of theory and what kind of models are suitable for our mission?

An emphasis on events [13], and in particular on *extreme events* (a term that is being explored in complex themes such as climate change and financial markets), may lead us to establish principles that may guide our research, such as the multiplicity principle [11] or the four Wandering Network principles [14].

As soon as we accept both *dynamics* and the *multiplicity principle*, we can move forward towards devising this new model framework and language for expressing the evolutionary dynamics of complex biosocial systems. Whereas expressing dynamics leads towards the integration of various temporal parameters into the model, the multiplicity principle allows us to account for the emergence of more and more complex individual levels of interaction and organization.

Another issue to solve on the way is the controversy between internal and external viewpoint of system description. Scientific models in natural sciences, such as physics and biology are usually external, done from a third person perspective which is not involved in the system processes and is not part of the model, the Observer. We need, however, also the so-called protobiological [15] and endophysical models [16] in our approach, which while being based on complex systems hierarchies [17], development and evolution [18] are capable to integrate the internal view at the system as part of it beyond synthesis [19] and "beyond the flat earth perspective in systems biology" [20].

Thus, the *coregulator* (CR) hierarchical organization construct of the MES theory [11] is a completely *internal* representation of e.g. neuro-cognitive system. It is real, i.e. related to the parts of the system, evolutionary and non-artificial formation, for instance explaining that we may observe some kind of virtualization and regenerative post-traumatic functional substitution of damaged brain segments by other ones, such as those in the visual or motor cortex [21]. This conclusion comes from the different links which arrive to the CRs allocated by observation. In this way, the individual CRs represent internal (hence partial) views of the system itself according to MES.

Nevertheless, category theory alone cannot take account of supplementary mathematical structures. In addition to hierarchy and dynamics using the CR construct, the MES formalism could be with additional capabilities from other domains in mathematics and computer science by replacing the categories by categories *enriched* in topology, higher order categories, stochastic maps or Bayesian networks, this in a similar way that Petri Nets developed diverse offsprings associated with such properties and functionalities as color, priority/weight, time, vector addition with states, stochastic states, degrees of liveness, etc. Thus, MES evolve to an 'enriched' MES integrating another kind of structure.

We can also describe a "Science" MES, in which each single CR can represent a whole formal theory. This MES provides the base for the integration of multiple domains of knowledge with their interactions In this way, we are able to express the development of science at successive moments of time within an evolving model of science [22], the emergence of a new theory, model or language based on two different domains of knowledge being expressed in this MES by a higher level CR And the links/interfaces between two different knowledge domains can be studied, possibly ensuring the correct transformation of data from the one domain into the other. Furthermore, a good practical approach to implement categories is the object-oriented paradigm in computer languages. Another complementary aspect of this implementation is the usage of functional (process-oriented) programming.

4   The Protomodel

In particular, we identify the following central question when modeling an evolving complex system: how many dimensions has the quality vector of a non-monolitic complex system? In our current view they are at least seven:

1. objects/components
2. functions/procedures
3. behaviours
4. relations/topology
5. patterns/categories
6. subsumption and composition hierarchy
7. hierarchy of the structural, temporal and procedural organization

However, in order to develop a new mathematical construction we need to identify first the problem at hand. What are we going to solve? Which examples can be used to develop and test the new approach? The *multiplicity principle* which generalizes the degeneracy property of the neural code is exactly what explains the possibility of multiple causes for the emergence and development of a natural phenomenon, such as the formation of more and more complex mental objects based on the neural activity. Another interesting approach is to use the capabilities of *fractals* in shaping and modulating the activity of biosocial systems.

Basically, there are two criteria for evaluating such approaches and principles: i) the level of complexity with its multiple temporalities leading to cascades of events backfiring between levels, and ii) the level of modeling uncertainty (where the multiplicity principle plays a role). They can be used as base for investigating the applicability of the novel mathematical formalisms to real world problems such as tumor development, theory of aging, global climate change, pandemic developments and stock market crashes.

The above domains have in common the emergence of *extreme events* in self-organizing systems characterized by nonlinear dynamics. Linear systems analysis is arguably one the major achievements of 20th century mathematics. However, it is questionable that linear analysis is a suitable strategy in the domains mentioned above. For example, complex phenomena such as the self-sustaining activity of the brain cannot be entirely explained in linear analysis basis.

5 The Challenges

We meet many challenges on the way towards discovering the principles of biomathematics and biocomputation. For the moment, we have identified the need of developing specialized mathematical theories and models and computational toolsets/solutions in the following areas:

- Mathematical models such as MES [11] of multi-scale systems and of their self-organization through the 'interplay' between their different regulatory processes accounting for their different complexities and rhythms.
- Computer simulation of MES or bridging Theoretical Neuroscience and Computational neuroscience.
  - o MES does not explain how the patterns of neurons are formed, or how the categories of neurons of higher complexity are created, but it does provide fresh theoretical insights that deserve to be explored by either empirical tests or computational simulations.
  - o Another issue is to reconcile the different aspects of CR modeling.
- Mathematics of non-linear processes (Are Platonic forms non-linear?)
  - o Complexity science aims to investigate nonlinear systems where the relevant features are both local and global in a way that is intrinsically not reducible. Thus nonlinearity is the chief factor in complexity science.
- 3D VR/AR (virtual/augmented reality) and 3D TV from molecular and system biology to computational medicine.
- Dynamic computer graphics for compositions of 3D curves: development of mathematical algorithms and software for computer graphics imaging of rotated 3D curves and fractals.
  - o Fractals of 2D curves show interesting geometry. Fractals or compositions of 3D curves show much more complex 3D geometry exhibiting interesting features. Their properties, however, could not be demonstrated with static views only. They need to be rotated. The preferable mathematical expression of a 3D curve is by parametric equations with 3 variables and a few parameters.

Herewith the development of precise standard languages to support the theory deserves a special attention. The expressive capabilities e.g. of BPMN, a language for business processes management is currently very purely for use in its own domain [23], not to mention biology.

Hence, we need

1. to pay attention to the grounding problem when using a particular language and a methodology capable to fuse or at least interconnect the different languages and models.
2. to develop dynamically extensible semantic meta-models of both object-oriented and functional languages and their combinations completing the models with the holistic view of the system.
3. to extend and redesign the available languages for system biology and to construct new ones that precisely define the concepts of *state* and *event* including their taxonomy (origin, occurrence, duration, frequency, etc.), [23].

In summary, we need to devise a playful environment for mathematics where one theory can be substituted with another in order to achieve creative discovery. It is time to develop new alternatives to those short-term strategies and conceptions of the past and present. One way to be pursued aims to track down the underlying principles, written in formal-mathematical terms that explain the organization of complex biological systems such as the cortex and other major areas in the brain. Anticipation and autonomy are other two issues that need to be addressed within this context.

6 The Outlook: On Interactions and Events

Everything that happens in (living) Nature is based on entropically driven interactions and self-assembly reactions. Their common characteristics are events. Interactions are continuous and everywhere; they are ubiquitous. An important aspect of interactions is their organization on a multiplicity of scales/viewpoints within the same context/location with different complexity levels and rhythms.

Yet, continuity itself depends on the timescale where it is observed. Generally, matters which appear discrete at small timescales can appear continuous at larger timescales. Hence, we have to do with scales and relativity here or perhaps even with scale relativity [24,25]. Another aspect of such complex irregular systems is the event-triggered emergence and development of abstract heterarchies (i.e. dynamical hierarchical systems inheriting logical inconsistencies between levels) in terms of time/state-scale re-entrant forms which are very difficult to formalize as dynamical systems because of their intrinsic inconsistencies [26]. Finally, there are interactions between heterogeneous viewpoints (models), modes or development stages of such systems (in a timeline that extrapolates to evolution), while their self-organization depends on the cooperation/competition between a net of internal regulatory processes executed by physical entities (organs) or CoRegulators (CR's) each operating in an internalistic, endophysical manner [16] at its own complexity level and with its own temporality [11]. Thus, events can result from the interactions between CoRegulators [13]. This interdependence can be observed at all scales in (living) Nature. Ultimately, multiscale interactions and their nonlocal characteristics at the deepest quantum level lead to the question and hypotheses about the emergence and evolution of consciousness [27].

In summary, human beings, being large lumps of matter (made up of large numbers of cells, each made up of large numbers of complex molecules, atoms, etc.)

comprehend the world as interactions. Given the scale at which they see things and processes, these events are made up of very large numbers of superposed interactions between entities at lower levels of organization.

Can the new software engineering paradigm of event-driven architectures and complex event processing for large enterprise systems [28] and a projected vision of computational socio-genomics [29] gain ground as model and technology bridging and automating research in the life science disciplines? This is a question we hope to answer in the course of our quest. Each time human thought has crossed a tenet's border allowing a new assumption, new tools were developed to prove the new hypothesis and advanced our understanding of the world. Real events, however, such as those we perceive, single or in the structures we perceive (companies, families, nation-states, flocks of birds, etc.) are more complex, and are made up of lower-level structures which are not indefinitely characterisable, and which probably do not need to be [30].

References

1. Rashevsky, N.: Topology and life: in search of general mathematical principles in biology and sociology. In: Bull. Math. Biophys, vol. 16, pp. 317–348. Springer, Heidelberg (1954) ISSN: 0092-8240 (Print) 1522-9602 (Online)
2. Rashevsky, N.: Life, information theory, and topology. In: Bull. Math. Biophys, vol. 17, pp. 229–235. Springer, Heidelberg (1955) ISSN: 0092-8240 (Print) 1522-9602 (Online)
3. Rosen, R.: A relational theory of biological systems. In: Bull. Math. Biophys, vol. 20, pp. 245–260. Springer, Heidelberg (1958) ISSN: 0092-8240 (Print) 1522-9602 (Online)
4. Rosen, R.: A relational theory of biological systems II. In: Bull. Math. Biophys, pp. 109–128. Springer, Heidelberg (1959) ISSN: 0092-8240 (Print) 1522-9602 (Online)
5. Conrad, M.: The brain-machine disanalogy. BioSystems 22(3), 197–213 (1989), doi:10.1016/0303-2647(89)90061-0
6. Smith, L.S.: Neuronal computing or computational neuroscience: brains vs. computers. Computational Thinking Seminars. University of Edinburgh, School of Informatics (October 17, 2007), http://www.inf.ed.ac.uk/research/programmes/comp-think/previous.html
7. Hong, F.T.: A multi-disciplinary survey of biocomputing: Part 1: molecular and cellular aspects. In: Bajić, V.B., Tan, T.W. (eds.) Information Processing and Living Systems, pp. 1–139. Imperial College Press, London (2005a)
8. Hong, F.T.: A multi-disciplinary survey of biocomputing: Part 2: systems and evolutionary aspects, and technological applications. In: Bajić, V.B., Tan, T.W. (eds.) Information Processing and Living Systems, pp. 141–573. Imperial College Press, London (2005b)
9. Cull, P.: The mathematical biophysics of Nicolas Rashevsky. Biosystems 88(3), 178–184 (2005); BIOCOMP 2005: Selected papers presented at the International Conference - Diffusion Processes in Neurobiology and Subcellular Biology
10. Simeonov, P.L.: Integral Biomathics: A Post-Newtonian View into the Logos of Bios. arXiv.org. (February 28, 2007), http://arxiv.org/abs/cs.NE/0703002 (also: in J. Prog. Biophys. Mol. Biol., vol. 102, 2/3, 85–121 June/July 2010)
11. Ehresmann, A.C., Vanbremeersch, J.-P.: Memory Evolutive Systems: Hierarchy, Emergence, Cognition. Elsevier Science. ISBN-10: 0444522441; ISBN-13: 978-0444522443
12. Ehresmann, A.C., Vanbremeersch, J.-P.: MENS a mathematical model for cognitive systems. Journal of Mind Theory 0(2), 129–180 (2009)

13. Ehresmann, A.C., Vanbremeersch, J.-P.: Analysis of complex events in Memory Evolutive Systems. In: Cezon, M., Wolfsthal, Y. (eds.) ServiceWave 2011 Workshops. LNCS, vol. 6569, pp. 153–159. Springer, Heidelberg (2011)

14. Simeonov, P.L.: The Wandering Logic Intelligence, A Hyperactive Approach to Network Evolution and Its Application to Adaptive Mobile Multimedia Communications. Dissertation, Technische Universität Ilmenau, Faculty for Computer Science and Automation (December 2002), Die Deutsche Bibliothek, urn:nbn:de:gbv:ilm1-2002000030

15. Matsuno, K.: Protobiology: Physical Basis of Biology. CRC, Boca Raton (1989) ISBN-10: 0849364035; ISBN-13: 978-0849364037

16. Rössler, O.E.: Endophysics: the World as an Interface. World Scientific, Singapore (1998) ISBN 981-02-2752-3

17. Pattee, H.H.: Hierarchy Theory. The Challenge of Complex Systems. George Braziller. ISBN-10: 080760674X; ISBN-13: 978-0807606742 (1973)

18. Salthe, S.N.: Development and Evolution: Complexity and Change in Biology. MIT Press, Cambridge (1993) ISBN-10: 0262193353; ISBN-13: 978-0262193351

19. Rose, M. R., Oakley, T. H.: The new biology: beyond the modern synthesis. Biology Direct, 2(30) (2007) doi:10.1186/1745-6150-2-30,
    http://www.biology-direct.com/content/2/1/30

20. Mesarovic, M.D., Sreenath, S.N.: Beyond the flat earth perspective in systems biology. Biol. Theory 1(1), 33–34 (2006)

21. Ramachandran, V.S., Blakeslee, S.: Phantoms in the Brain: Probing the Mysteries of the Human Mind. Harper Perennial (1999) ISBN-10: 068817217ö ISBN-13: 978-0688172176

22. Simeonov, P.L.: Integral Biomathics: A New Era of Biological Computation. In: Simeonov, P.L. (ed.) Science and Policy Forum on FET Flagships Workshop, Brussels, June 9-10 (2010), http://cordis.europa.eu/fp7/ict/fet-proactive/docs/flagship-ws-june10-30-plamen-simeonov_en.pdf

23. Repa, V.: Business Process Modelling Notation from the Methodical Perspective. In: Cezon, M., Wolfsthal, Y. (eds.) ServiceWave 2011 Workshops. LNCS, vol. 6569, pp. 160–171. Springer, Heidelberg (2011)

24. Auffray, C., Nottale, L.: Scale relativity and integrative systems biology. 1. Founding principles and scale laws. Prog. Biophys. Mol. Biol. 97, 79–114 (2008)

25. Nottale, L., Auffray, C.: Scale relativity and integrative systems biology 2. Macroscopic quantum-type mechanics. Prog. Biophys. Mol. Biol. 97, 115–157 (2008)

26. Gunji, Y.-P., Sasai, K., Wakisaka, S.: Abstract heterarchy: Time/state-scale re-entrant form. Biosystems 91, 13–33 (2008)

27. Hameroff, S., Penrose, R.: Orchestrated reduction of quantum coherence in brain microtubules: A model for consciousness. Mathematics and Computers in Simulation 40, 453–480 (1996), doi:10.1016/0378-4754(96)80476-9

28. Luckham, D.: The Power of Events: An Introduction to Complex Event Processing in Distributed Enterprise Systems. Addison-Wesley Professional, London (2002) ISBN-10: 0201727897; ISBN-13: 978-0201727890

29. Sutcliffe-Braithwaite, J.: Socio-technic systems: computational socio-geonomics & enterprise systems. In: Cezon, M., Wolfsthal, Y. (eds.) ServiceWave 2011 Workshops. LNCS, vol. 6569, Springer, Heidelberg (2011)

30. Bard, J.: A systems biology view of evolutionary genetics: network-driven processes incorporate much more variation than evolutionary genetics can handle. This variation is hard to formalise but allows fast change. Bioessay 32(7), 559–563 (2010),
    http://www.ncbi.nlm.nih.gov/pubmed/20544731,
    doi:10.1002/bies.200900166.

Events, Neural Systems and Time Series

Leslie S. Smith[1], Daniel Metz[2], Jungpen Bao[3], and Pedro Bizarro[4]

[1] Computing Science and Mathematics, School of Natural Sciences,
University of Stirling, Stirling FK9 4LA, UK
[2] Information Systems Institute, University of Siegen,
Hölderlinstraße 3, 57076 Siegen, Germany
[3] Department of Computer Science and Technology,
Xi'an Jiaotong University, Xi'an 710049, China
[4] Informatics Engineering Department, University of Coimbra,
3030-290 Coimbra, Portugal

Abstract. Different types of events occurring in computer, neural, business, and environmental systems are discussed. Though events in these different domains do differ, there are also important commonalities. We discuss the issues arising from automating complex event handling systems.

Keywords: complex events, autonomous robotics, computing events, cognitive events.

1 Introduction: Events in Different Contexts

Events can be considered as a unifying paradigm crossing disciplinary boundaries. Events happen[1]: events are considered to occur at a particular time and place, and to involve a number of participant entities. Generally, events have (a non-null set of) causes, and also (a non-null set of) effects[2]. Events happen both inside a system and in its environment. Events occur in all types of area: here we discuss events in computer systems and networks, neural systems, business, and the environment, but this represents only four example areas. What we consider to be an event often depends on our standpoint, and what we are currently interested in: events that are not of interest still occur, but we ignore them.

In terms of computer systems and networks, events range from the change of state of a signal line inside a CPU chip or the failure to find a datum in a CPU cache, to the pressing of a button on a mouse, to receipt of a protocol packet, to failure of a link, or, at a higher level, the placing of an order or the receipt of a shipment, or at a still higher level the introduction of a new device to the market or the release of a new web portal. There are a number of different theoretical bases that can and have been used for events primarily in this context. These range from Petri nets [12] to calculus of communicating systems [9] to communicating sequential processes [6] to communicating agents [10]. Each

---

[1] "Events dear boy, events": ascribed to Harold Macmillan, ex Prime Minister of the UK, when asked by a reporter what was most likely to blow a government off course.
[2] Events with no effects can safely be ignored.

M. Cezon and Y. Wolfsthal (Eds.): ServiceWave 2010 Workshops, LNCS 6569, pp. 196–202, 2011.
© Springer-Verlag Berlin Heidelberg 2011

of these has been taken up in some areas of computer systems and networks, but they have not yet found application outside of this domain. Here, we are concerned with what the events are, rather than with analysing or organising them. Clearly these different levels of events are inter-related: each higher-level event actually is made up of a large number of lower level events.

In terms of neural systems, one needs to start by considering what the events might be[3]. Events could range from arrival of an action potential at a synapse (one might start at a lower level, for example with the release of a vesicle from the presynaptic terminal, or the arrival of molecules of neurotransmitter from such a vesicle at a single post-synaptic ion channel), or with the detection of some percept in the auditory or visual cortex, or the execution of a motor command. There is little agreement about the nature of information transfer inside the brain (beyond that it is mediated by action potentials), which makes the issue of what is an event controversial (particularly at the level above single spikes: is an event the reception of a stream of spikes from one other neuron? Or a volley of spikes from a number of neurons? Or the collection of spikes that make up a synfire chain?)

In terms of businesses, events may take many forms, ranging from the initiation of the development of a new product, the release of a new product (by that particular business, or one of its competitors), to changes in prices of raw materials, or the opening of a new factory or office. There is a standardised notation for these events developed by the Object Management Group/Business Process Management Initiative (http://www.bpmn.org/): see [13]: this is oriented towards orchestration of these events in a computational context. As with computer events, many of these can be decomposed: for example the opening of a new factory is the culmination of a long sequence of events which presumably started with a decision being taken to open a new factory (or rather, before that, with the events that led to the requirement for a new factory). The relevant events may be internal to the business, or may be within the business's operating environment.

In terms of events in the (natural) environment, these may be associated with a particular occurrence, for example a tree falling over in a forest. As for both computer events and neural events, this event is made up from many other events: in this case it can be considered as the culmination of a set of less visible events that started, perhaps, with the seed from which the tree grew sprouting. We note also that the environment may refer to the environment of some other entity (such as a computer, or a business) in which case the events of interest will be those affecting the that entity.

The primary difference between computer events[4] and the neural and environmental events is that for the computer events, we know how lower level events lead to higher level events, and how higher level events are orchestrated by lower

---

[3] It may be that events are not the best way of describing what is happening in such systems, but they are nonetheless useful, and give us a means of comparing different system types.

[4] In complex event processing (CEP) an event is an object that can be subjected to computer processing [8]: but this is a somewhat circular definition here.

level events, whereas for both the environmental and neural systems this knowledge is a great deal patchier. In systems which have been designed, the event hierarchy is part of that design. Unlike built systems, natural systems do not need to keep to a careful hierarchy of events - they can (and surely do) cross putative levels: indeed, one could argue that the association of levels with events is a human way of organising these otherwise unorganised events. Events in the business area lie somewhere between these poles: they often will have a clear set of constituent (sub-)events. However, there will also be events with a much less clearly defined hierarchy of (sub-)events (for example, a key employee leaving).

The issue then is whether this event-based view of business, environmental and neural systems is useful. It clearly is useful for computer systems and networks. For business systems, there can be a direct connection to events in computer systems, although this does not capture all the events in a business context. For neural systems, we currently always need to ask about the level of the events in which we are interested: further and most critically, we do not understand how synaptic/action potential events lead to higher level events. (We have some understanding of how such events lead to further synaptic/action potential events, but these further events are essentially the same level. Are there higher level events in neural systems? We clearly do have (first-person) mental events, and we believe that these are mediated by action potential/synaptic events: but the relationship between these two is not yet anything like fully elucidated. There are higher-level theories of mental function (such as those of [5] or [3]), but these are largely narrative models[5] rather than precise simulations. For natural environmental systems, the issues are perhaps easier, since we already have a large volume of physics, much of which is about the inter-relationship between events in the physical world. The events that we are interested in can only be those that we can detect or infer, and these are then the inputs to our computational systems (and, indeed, our own neural systems as well).

2   Contexts 1: Events and Robotics

Robots interact with their environment and this interaction can be considered to be mediated by events. These may be generated by the environment, and sensed by way of the robots sensors (whether visual, auditory, tactile, or whatever), or they may be generated by the robot, in which case we would more usually call them actions. These output events are not sensed as such by the environment, but result in the generation of new and perhaps different events by the environment as detected by the robots sensors. There may also be events generated by the robot which are internal: what we might describe as cognitive events, resulting from sensory events, and perhaps actions as well.

Real (natural) environments are not well defined[6]. Environments are inherently changeable, and largely unpredictable. Even simple actions, such as

---

[5] That is, stories of how a system might work.

[6] This might, of course, be different for an artificial environment, such as that in a game or other simulation.

turning a robots driving wheel will not always have the same effect - wheels slip, for example. Further, the sensor data received from the environment is always uncertain: this may be due to noise, or deficiencies in the sensors themselves, but may also be due to variation in the environment, for example variations in the lighting affecting the visual sensor, or extraneous sounds and reflections affecting an auditory sensor.

The aim in much of robotics is effective autonomous operation, in spite of these difficulties. Unpredictability and variation in operation are just some of the problems in this area: there are others as well, such as goal setting, and adjudging performance.

3   Contexts 2: Time Series

Time series are sequences of data, often measurements, over a period of time. Each value can be considered to be an event. Often the values are recorded at regular intervals, but this need not always be the case. Analysis of time series may have several aims: classification of the time series, prediction of future events (such as the next few values of the time series), or error or novelty detection (that is: has something generating the time series changed in some way).

Time series arise in many domains (certainly including all those discussed above). One particular area of commercial interest is in demand forecasting. Utilities (gas, electricity, water etc.), automated teller machine networks, telephone companies, internet service providers, call centres and many other businesses all have multiple levels of seasonal variation in demand. The operators of these industries want to know (for example) likely immediate and short-term requirements, as well as if some particular form of error condition (for example large scale leaks in the water industry, or system failures in an ATM network) holds. Further, the environment in which these time series values are being recorded is not constant: external events can have a major effect on the time series. For example, major sporting events, of sudden changes in weather, or even television programming may influence user behaviour in a non-random way, and thus result in major changes in demand.

The operators have good reasons for needing this information: altering their capacity to respond to alterations in demand may require time. For utilities, generators may need to be started up, power grid lines or pipelines reassigned, or (for ISPs) new servers assigned, or low-bandwidth pages set up. These operators have had coped with these problems for many years: they have staff whose job it is to predict demand, and their experience is a major asset to these companies.

4   Automating Complex Event Handling Systems

In both the above contexts, there are existing solutions. But these solutions are incomplete. Robotic behaviour is generally brittle, automated time series prediction is known to be a difficult problem, and understanding the ways in which human predictors of demand operate (or eliciting their knowledge) can be difficult. Static rule based systems work only in static known environments. This suggests that adaptive systems will be necessary to cope with altering environments. But how should such adaptation be implemented? When should a system learn? What should a system learn? How should what is learned be applied to the problem at hand?

In the relatively restricted case of time series prediction, at first sight, these questions appear to boil down to issues of selection of mechanisms for prediction (of which there are many). However, in reality, there is extraneous information available as well as the actual numbers in the time series. Then one needs to consider which aspects of this additional available information should be used or even if one should be seeking out further information not currently available. In the relatively less restricted domain of autonomous robotics, these two aspects of what might be learned become issues of altering the decision system, and seeking out appropriate perceptual input (that is, issues of active perception). The robot can move and/or alter its sensors to alter what might be detected by its sensors. Further, by appropriate movement, it can learn more about what it is sensing, because it knows what it has altered in order to alter the sensation received. Animals do this all the time, moving their whole bodies or their heads to alter visual, auditory and olfactory perceptions. In a business context, finding appropriate extraneous information, and bringing it to the locations at which decisions are made is a difficult task: one can argue that neural decision making shares many of the same problems, particularly relating to the range of possibly relevant information that might be available. The amount of data that might be processed is generally huge: as we attempt to process more, the problem becomes harder, but if we restrict what is processed, the lack of data may mean that important information is lost. Knowing or learning what matters, and what may safely be ignored is is challenging: a related problem exists in statistics where it is called feature selection [2][7], and remains the subject of current research.

Non-static situations require non-static responses: we cannot expect to predetermine all responses or predictions. Such learning needs to be underpinned by some form of change or adaptation. Widder et al. present an approach to identify suspicious, unknown events in an event cloud [15]. Discriminant analysis is applied to detect unknown or suspicious combinations of events which havent be seen in the past. This approach can be used for fraud detection (see the ATM example above). We believe it is possible to make a learning system more robust than a non-learning system, but such an outcome is not necessarily the case. Simple neurally inspired learning systems (such as back-propagating neural networks or radial basis function networks) essentially learn statistical information about their environments [1]. For such learning systems, the larger the volume of training data available, the better: although even here, the data needs to be appropriate and clean: feature selection is again important. There are other types of learning as well, for example reinforcement learning [14], where what is required is a signal to show when the behaviour is appropriate (reward) or inappropriate (punishment). In the case of event streams, similarity search techniques are applied to react to recurrent situations and to predict (business) processes (e.g.,[11]). Similarly, historical data (events) can be analyzed to establish a proactive control of manufacturing processes (e.g., [4]). The similarity search techniques are better, if the volume of available data (events) increases. Nevertheless, a risk might be the solidification of what has been learned in the past (that is, innovation can be hindered). But even for animals, learning can go wrong, as appears to be the case in, for example, autism.

One advantage that modern computer systems have in this area is the availability of large amounts of processing power and memory. Parallelism means that, for example, all the sensors in a robotic system can be processed at the same time, and cross-modal percepts can be computed, continuously. Thus even if certain types of processed sensor information are not always required, they can be made instantaneously available. Further, memory can be used to look back on actions taken and predictions made in the light of more recent events, and these can, for example, be re-run using different learning techniques to adjust what might be applied to future events, enabling more sophisticated learning techniques. The issue is determining which particular current and historical events are most relevant. Similarity search techniques may also prove useful in this context.

5 Conclusions

Events do provide a useful unifying paradigm across a wide range of domains, including the four that we have discussed here. We can interpret events both in terms of the input (from outside) to a system, and the output (to outside) from a system, as well as being internal to either the system itself, or the environment of the system. This is useful in the making the system/environment concept applicable in areas outside of the robot/environment system area, for example, in the business/business environment domain. A similar approach can be taken to the application of event-based approaches to prediction/error-detection in utilities, and these can use the same types of learning based approaches, and event selection techniques.

There are some differences: e.g. the nature of active sensing is different in utilities, (where it is about the search for appropriate extraneous information) from in robotics (where it is about the way in which the robot itself can alter its own input), and business events come in many diverse forms, not all of which can easily be placed in formal contexts such as those in [13]. However, events can be used in quite different domains, and similar techniques and technologies used across those domains. There remains, however, a need to work on the best way of organising and theorising about these events, and in selecting a technology for this which can be used by those designing and analysing these systems across different domains.

References

1. Bishop, C.: Neural Networks for Pattern Recognition. Oxford University Press, Oxford (1995)
2. Blum, A., Langley, P.: Selection of relevant features and examples in machine learning. Artificial intelligence 97(102), 245–271 (1997)
3. Garforth, J., McHale, S.L., Meehan, A.: Executive attention, task selection and attention-based learning in a neurally controlled simulated robot. Neurocomputing 69(16-18), 1923–1945 (2006)
4. Grauer, M., Karadgi, S., Müller, U., Metz, D., Schäfer, W.: Proactive control of manufacturing processes using historical data. In: Setchi, R., Jordanov, I., Howlett, R.J., Jain, L.C. (eds.) KES 2010. LNCS, vol. 6277, pp. 399–408. Springer, Heidelberg (2010)
5. Hawkins, J., Blakeslee, S.: On Intelligence. Times Books (2004)
6. Hoare, C.: Communicating Sequential Processes. Prentice-Hall, Englewood Cliffs (1986)
7. Liu, H., Motoda, H., Setiono, R., Zhao, Z., Chawla, S., Salehi, E., Nyayachavadi, J., Gras, R., Zagoruiko, N., Borisova, I.: Feature selection in data mining. In: JMLR Workshop and Conference Proceedings, vol. 10 (2010)
8. Luckham, D.: The Power of Events. Addison-Wesley, Reading (2007)
9. Milner, R.: A Calculus of Communicating Systems, vol. 92. Springer, Heidelberg (1980)
10. Milner, R.: The Space and Motion of Communicating Agents. Cambridge (2009)
11. Obweger, H., Suntinger, M., Schiefer, J., Raidl, G.: Similarity searching in sequences of complex events. In: Proc. of Int. Conf. On Research Challenges in Information Science (RCIS), pp. 631–639 (2010)
12. Petri, C.: Communication with automata. Tech. Rep. AD0630125, DTIC (1966)
13. Shapiro, R., White, S., Palmer, N., zur Muehlen, M., Allweyer, T., Gagne, D., Silver, B., Fischer, L.: BPMN 2.0 Handbook. Future Strategies Inc. (2010)
14. Sutton, R., Barto, A.: Reinforcement Learning: An introduction. MIT Press, Cambridge (1998)
15. Widder, A., von Ammon, R., Schaeffer, R., Wolff, C.: Identification of suspicious, unknown event patterns in an event cloud. In: Jacobsen, H.A., Mühl, G., Jaeger, M.A. (eds.) Proceedings of the 2007 Inaugural International Conference on Distributed Event-Based Systems, DEBS 2007, pp. 164–170 (2007)

A Text Copy Detection System Based on Complex Event Processing Architecture

JungPen Bao, Yong Qi, Di Hou, and Hui He

Department of Computer Science & Technology, Xi'an Jiaotong University,
Shaanxi Province, 710049, P.R. China
{baojp,qiy,houdi,huihe}@mail.xjtu.edu.cn

Abstract. The Text Copy Detection plays an important role in the Intellectual Property Protection. It is a typical resource consuming system. The traditional software architecture, in which a single detection process fulfills the whole detection flow, does not release the power of Cloud Computing. The paper introduces a Complex Event Processing based text copy detection system, which will be developed to an open web service. The new architecture is suitable for Cloud Computing, and the other advantages are discussed.

Keywords: Text Copy Detection, Complex Event Processing, Cloud Computing.

1 Introduction

There are billions of documents in the world wide web, and the amount is increasing in a huge number every day. However, a lot of documents have overlapped contents, even if the same. The overlapped contents may be copied, plagiarized, or quoted from others, be legal or not. It is Text Copy Detection or Plagiarism Detection to automatically find out those overlapped text from a collection of millions documents aided by a computer. Obviously, this is an important application in terms of Intellectual Property Protection, Digital Library and Information Retrieval. The task is hard for human detectives because the amount of documents is too huge to complete. In spite of the amount, it is also hard for computers because a computer does not understand the meaning of a sentence so that it is very easy to cheat a computer by changing some words.

Since 1995, Brin[1] etc. introduced the first Copy Detection System by means of matching sentences based on a hash map function. Later they improved their method by means of words bag. A plenty of text copy detection algorithms adopt these 2 basic ideas and other text features, such as n-gram in Ferret[2], semantic sequences[3] and word concepts[4].

The text copy detection algorithms are diverse but the infrastructure of all these detection systems are less difference. The detection core runs a process on a high performance computer or a cluster because that task will consume a quantity of resources including CPU time, memories and hard disks. The detection process is inputted by a new arrival document, and output detection results at last. This is a

M. Cezon and Y. Wolfsthal (Eds.): ServiceWave 2010 Workshops, LNCS 6569, pp. 203–207, 2011.
© Springer-Verlag Berlin Heidelberg 2011

traditional computing architecture, which is fit for a single computing node but not for cloud computing. The whole detection flow is tightly enclosed in the same processing space so that all materials have to squeeze into the limited physical memory no matter how large they are in a single server or cluster. The cloud computing could supply huge resources but they are not guaranteed in the same space. Indeed, most resources are loosely connected together. If we chop the detection flow into pieces and drop them in computing Clouds, then the huge resources power will explode. Hence, we introduce a novel text copy detection system based on Complex Event Processing architecture.

2   Architecture of the Text Copy Detection

The basic parts of a TCD system includes: text submission and collection, text clean and feature selection, plagiarism detection, result exhibition. Normally, there is a text warehouse to store all of protected text, and a text features collection is maintained in memory in some data structure, such as Inverted Index. Text clean, feature selection and plagiarism detection are a flow of detection operations. In traditional architecture, a process runs through the flow, issues detection result at the end. When we have a new algorithm about one of the detection operations, either a new program is built or the process reloads a new module dynamically. This is a tightly coupled way. Nowadays loosely coupled way is more preferred.

The Complex Event Processing model becomes a popular software architecture[5], which is an inherent distributed network software. The basic input is considered as a primary event, which means something happens. The source of an event could be an object in the real world or an virtual one, such as a train stops at or passes by a platform, money is withdrawn from an ATM, a stock price is rising. Widder and Ammon[6] etc. presented a CEP system to detect insurance fraud. Bizarro[7] etc. introduced a CEP benchmark project in order to compare different CEP systems.

Events that is organized in a stream or a cloud can be spread out in the network and provoke several event processing engines. That is a straight way in the cloud computing environment. In order to develop a text copy detection web service in light of cloud computing, we present a novel architecture of TCD which is based on Complex Event Processing model and composed of loosely connected bundles not DLL(dynamic link library). The whole CEP based TCD runs on an OSGi platform. The detection operations are implemented by a combination of bundles. Namely, there are at least a bundle for text clean, a bundle for feature selection and a bundle for plagiarism detection. Each bundle pursues only a limited object.

- Text Clean Bundle

Text clean means to convert variable raw text materials into a uniform format and remove irrelative tokens. The uniform format usually is plain text encoded in ASCII or UTF-8. The irrelative tokens depend on detection strategy, such as redundant white space characters, unreadable characters, meaningless symbols, and stop words. Some detection algorithm performs word stemming on this stage, i.e. different morphological words are stemmed to the same word or token. Whatsoever, the input of the text clean bundle is a raw text, and the output is the clean tokens. Each character in the raw text is a primary event. Based on a syntax parser and a dictionary, primary events are combined into a valid word and invalid combinations are filtered. For text clean bundle, an event in the output stream is a valid token/word.

- Feature Selection Bundle

The feature selection bundle extracts features from a clean text. Features are organized into a vector, called feature vector. In this bundle, the input primary event is a token and the output events are feature vectors. There are 2 kinds of popular text features. One is based on statistic information, such as TF-IDF, mutual information and information gain. The other is based on string map by some type of hash function, in which a feature string is mapped into a hash code.

- Plagiarism Detection Bundle

The input primary events of plagiarism detection bundle are text feature vectors. In this bundle, a feature vector that is made from a user submitted text is compared with a feature vector that is made from a stored protected text. If the two vectors are matched according to some feature similarity metric, then a doubtable plagiarism event is reported. Namely, a submitted text is so similar to a protected text in the text warehouse that it may be an intelligence property conflict. If no vector is matched, then no event happens. In other words, the function of the plagiarism detection bundle is to filter and report those doubtable input texts. At last user will get a final report to show the details of the doubtable plagiarism texts.

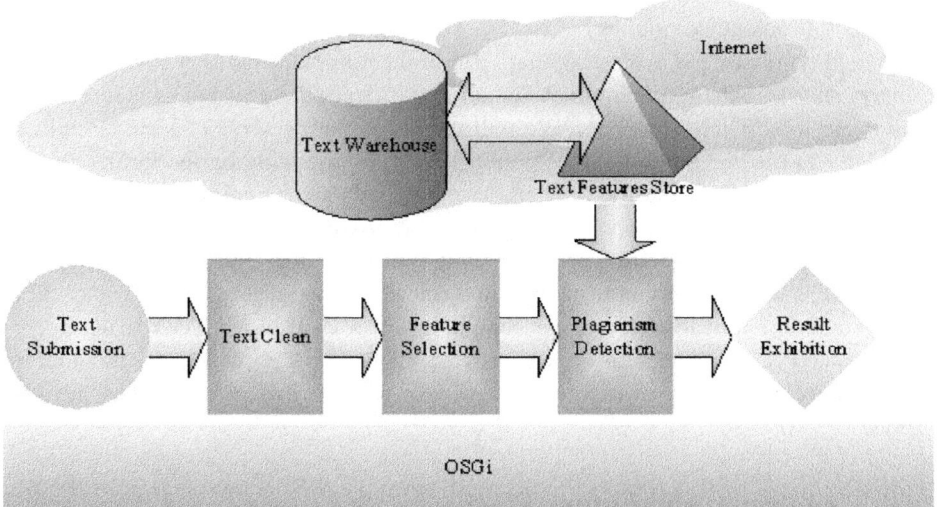

Fig. 1. The basic architecture of the Text Copy Detection system based on Complex Event Processing model

3   Discussion

Comparing to the stand alone TCD process, the CEP based TCD has the following features:

- A bundle runs an algorithm.

No matter text clean, feature selection or text detection, there are plenty of algorithms. Each of them accepts almost the same input, normally plain text encoded in ASCII or UTF-8, outputs a user defined formatted text or vector. Hence, the OSGi system can load and activate those different bundles at the same time. That means we can use different methods to detection the plagiarism texts at the same time so as to plagiarism proof and the detection confidence are more sufficient. Another virtue is that different bundle that represents different algorithm can run at different machine or computing node. It is very important to divide jobs into pieces and distribute tasks in a balance way. Users are easy to control each bundle's life in order to configure the whole system's efficiency.

- Loosely coupled operation flow.

Bundles are connected through internet protocol or SOAP (Simple Object Access Protocol). A bundle may send its results to one or many receivers, which are defined in the bundle's destination property. A bundle can redirect its output when it is reactivated. Therefore, the streamline of the detection operation is not fixed, but flexible and configurable at running time. Users can subscribe to their own personal detection combination. That is to say, our CEP based TCD supports individuation service well.

- Ready for cloud computing.

Cloud computing is a very popular term in the computer industry and will play an important role in the future Internet. An attractive idea is that everything is service from hardware to software resources. We will use a computing service as easy as electric service. On the one hand, huge computing ability is available on the virtual cloud so that high space complex processes and large scale data consuming processes can find necessary facilities easily and cheaply. On the other hand, users will pay for essential services not for a whole software. TCD will consume a large amount of memory and hard disk, since the amount of texts in the Internet is increasing day after day. It is a very suitable application for cloud computing. The CEP based TCD is designed to supply text copy detection service as a WEB service, which is flexible and configurable. It is easy to deploy the detection service over one or many pieces of cloud.

4   Conclusion and Future Works

The text copy detection system needs huge computing resources to keep its performance. There is no serial relationship between documents so that it is suitable for deploying multi-engines in the cloud computing environment. Considering a new arrival document as an event, the CEP based TCD system will take the advantages of cloud computing.

Our TCD system will contain several plagiarism detection bundles, each of them runs a different detection algorithm. The biggest challenge is the cross languages bundle, in which text in different languages will be converted into concept sequences according to a bilingual ontology, such as English-Chinese wordnet. The CEP based TCD system is a web service prototype system in the cloud computing. We believe this system architecture can be applied in many information service systems.

Acknowledgements. This research is supported by the National Natural Science Foundation of China (Grant No. 60903123).

References

1. Brin, S., Davis, J., Molina, H.G.: Copy detection mechanisms for digital documents. In: Proceedings of the 1995 ACM SIGMOD International Conference on Management of Data, San Jose, California, pp. 398–409 (1995)
2. Bao, J., Lyon, C., Lane, P.: Copy detection in Chinese documents using Ferret. Language Resources And Evaluation. 40(3-4), 357–365 (2006)
3. Bao, J., et al.: A fast document copy detection model. Soft Computing - A Fusion of Foundations. Methodologies and Applications 10(1), 41–46 (2006)
4. Lukashenko, R., Graudina, V., Grundspenkis, J.: Computer-Based Plagiarism Detection Methods and Tools: An Overview. In: Proceedings of International Conference on Computer Systems and Technologies, CompSysTech 2007 (2007)
5. Fülöp, L.J., et al.: Survey on Complex Event Processing and Predictive Analytics. Technical Report, University of Szeged, Department of Software Engineering (2010)
6. Widder, A., Ammon, R.v., et al.: An Approach for Automatic Fraud Detection in the Insurance Domain. In: AAAI 2009 Spring Symposia/Intelligent Event Processing, Stanford, March 23-25 (2009)
7. Mendes, M.R.N., Bizarro, P., Marques, P.: A Performance Study of Event Processing Systems. In: Proceedings of the First TPC Technology Conference on Performance Evaluation & Benchmarking (TPC TC) 2009, Lyon, France, August 24 (2009)

Author Index

GPSR Compliance

The European Union's (EU) General Product Safety Regulation (GPSR)
is a set of rules that requires consumer products to be safe and our
obligations to ensure this.

If you have any concerns about our products, you can contact us on
ProductSafety@springernature.com

In case Publisher is established outside the EU, the EU authorized
representative is:

Springer Nature Customer Service Center GmbH
Europaplatz 3
69115 Heidelberg, Germany

Batch number: 09490872

Printed by Printforce, the Netherlands